659.2
H397m

DETROIT PUBLIC LIBRARY

DETROIT PUBLIC LIBRARY
BUSINESS, SCIENCE
AND TECHNOLOGY

DATE DUE

MAR 05 1998

MAR 19 1998

BC-3

BST

HOW
HOW
HOW
HOW
HOW
HOW

MARKETING PUBLIC RELATIONS

HOW
HOW
HOW
HOW
HOW
HOW
HOW
HOW
HOW
HOW
HOW
HOW
HOW
HOW

THE HOWS

Marketing Public Relations

THAT MAKE IT WORK

Rene A. Henry Jr.

IOWA STATE UNIVERSITY PRESS / **AMES**

659.2 H397m

FEB 12 1996

TO ALL MY CHILDREN

Rene A. Henry Jr., Fellow, Public Relations Society of America, is the executive director of University Relations at Texas A&M University.

© 1995 Iowa State University Press, Ames, Iowa 50014
All rights reserved

Authorization to photocopy items for internal or personal use, or the internal or personal use of specific clients, is granted by Iowa State University Press, provided that the base fee of $.10 per copy is paid directly to the Copyright Clearance Center, 27 Congress Street, Salem, MA 01970. For those organizations that have been granted a photocopy license by CCC, a separate system of payments has been arranged. The fee code for users of the Transactional Reporting Service is 0-8138-2208-4/95 $.10.

♾ Printed on acid-free paper in the United States of America

First edition, 1995

Library of Congress Cataloging-in-Publication Data

Henry, Rene A.
Marketing public relations: the hows that make it work / Rene A. Henry Jr.—1st ed.
p. cm.
Includes bibliographical references and index.
ISBN 0-8138-2208-4
1. Public relations. 2. Industrial publicity—Marketing.
I. Title.
HD59.H44 1995
659.2—dc20 95-1077

Deborah, Catherine, Bruce and Paige

CONTENTS

FOREWORD

Considering the number of recent books on marketing public relations and the coverage given to the subject in the public relations, advertising and marketing press—not to overlook the new college level courses in schools of communications—one would be led to believe that marketing public relations is a late 20th century phenomenon brought about by the "doing things smarter" aftermath of corporate downsizing and restructuring.

No way!

Marketing communications has been around a long time. The fact is Burson-Marsteller began life as a marketing public relations firm more than four decades ago. And we would never dare claim to be the originator of the concept that public relations can be an important element of the marketing mix. Dan Edelman, at about the same time, believed just as strongly in the concept as he put together the first media tour ever for his client "Toni," the bottled permanent wave ("Which twin has the Toni?").

But there has been a change. The big one is that brand marketers are increasingly coming to realize that public relations techniques merit a segment of the marketing budget and they're now backing their hunches with budgets. This is not new in business-to-business product categories, where marketing public relations has long had an active role in the marketing mix. It is, however, a relatively recent happening in the consumer product, especially package goods, categories.

The stumbling block, in my experience, has and continues to be that public relations efforts cannot be measured as precisely as media advertising or other forms of marketing communications. Brand managers want to know what they get for their budget dollars with quantitative mathematical precision (not a totally unreasonable position). Our handicap, as public relations practitioners, has been in measurement of results—in accountability. Counting clippings and time-on-air and assessing a value based on advertising rates is simply not good enough.

Nor is the problem that we don't know how to do the research to measure the effectiveness of what we do under the rubric of public relations. The problem is that the cost of really valid research often exceeds the cost of the program. The dollars for doing the research that would demonstrate the effectiveness of the marketing public relations program simply have not been available on a continuing basis.

While that has not changed, the brand marketer's view of the consumer has undergone change. The quantitative approach to the relationship between the brand and the consumer is giving way to qualitative considerations that involve an ongoing relationship. Creating and maintaining a relationship is proving to be a factor in building and maintaining market share. And that's a job that marketing public relations can be called on not only to do but even to take the lead. After all, what is public relations really all about? It's building relationships.

One care we in public relations must take is not to overclaim the merits of marketing public relations. For certain, marketing public relations is no substitute or replacement for advertising in reaching the mass consumer market with product messages on an ongoing basis. But for sure, marketing public relations can add value to the much larger dollars spent for paid advertising media if used strategically and effectively.

Marketing public relations can, at certain periods in the product life cycle, create interest and excitement. It can make a product timely and topical. By so doing, it reinforces both the credibility and the effectiveness of the advertising. Marketing public relations can also extend the reach of advertising, especially to niche markets where it may be uneconomical to advertise. And, most of all, marketing public relations can build long-term ongoing relationships with the customer. Marketing public relations can provide that linkage with the customer that retains the loyalty that assures continued usage.

Rene Henry has subtitled his book "The Hows That Make It Work." That's what makes it different from the score or more recent works on marketing public relations. A 60-second glance at the table of contents demonstrates the scope of today's marketing public relations. It covers a broad front that's backed up by information useful to both the senior professional and the entry levels.

The amount of detail provided is overwhelming—in a sense, a directory-of-directories for many categories of activity that fall under the marketing public relations umbrella, down to and including telephone numbers and ZIP codes. All in all, a refreshing and useful work that will bring about the benefits we know marketing public relations can produce.

HAROLD BURSON
Founder and Chair
Burson-Marsteller, New York

PREFACE

I was fortunate early in my career to work with some good teachers and professional colleagues who took time to help me get the right start in the public relations business. I never took a course in journalism or one in public relations, but I learned from experienced professionals the fundamentals that lead to a successful career in public relations. I appreciate the encouragement, support and advice they and other mentors have given me throughout my career.

As I have been given good advice, I also have taken time to work with and mentor young people. I have always looked for opportunities to give them a chance to work as an intern, a student worker or in getting that first entry-level job.

Unfortunately, so many people I have hired for entry-level positions do not have the necessary basic skills. They not only do not know how to put together a simple mailing list, but they have never heard of most of the publications needed to do this task. Chapter 3 serves as a resource in this area. Many others still think that the only way to deliver a story to the media is by mail. Chapter 4 talks about the various special distribution services that will give the practitioner a variety of opportunities. I have worked with some respected colleagues who don't even understand basic planning and budgeting. Chapter 19 provides an overview of one of the most important of all business practices.

What seems to be missing is a solid foundation in fundamentals. Just as a building is only as strong as its foundation, I believe professionals in any field are only as good as their knowledge of the basics.

This book is about the basics and the fundamentals of public relations. It is intended as a resource and reference for the experienced professional, a valuable reference book for the young professional, an instructional tool for the teacher of public relations and a guidebook for the future practitioner. This book also can be a valuable primer to anyone in management, from a CEO to an executive with marketing or public relations responsibility, who does not possess experience in this area. The checklists and dos and don'ts provide them with another management tool.

Entire books could be written on the subjects of sports marketing (Chapter 13), special events (Chapters 11 and 12), market research (Chapter 2) and ethnic and special markets (Chapter 14). These chapters will give the reader insight into these specific areas of marketing public relations.

There also are many corporate, association and government executives who have positions or titles associated with public relations, but who never attained the fundamental, basic skills. For them, this book is a must read.

I am a strong believer in knowing the basic and fundamental skills. Perhaps this is because sports have always been an important part of my life and my career. The most successful coaches I know, at any level of competition—recreational, college or professional—stress fundamentals. Athletic ability alone will never produce a championship team.

I don't believe you can ever place enough emphasis on fundamentals. Without the basics, everything else is moot. This book contains the building blocks that can serve as the foundation for anyone choosing a career in public relations or marketing.

ACKNOWLEDGMENTS

The author wishes to thank the following people, whose contributions helped make this book possible:

Harold Burson, founder and chair, Burson-Marsteller, New York
Sherylon Carroll, associate director, Office of University Relations, Texas A&M University, College Station
Bob Condron, associate director of media relations, U.S. Olympic Committee, Colorado Springs
Mitchell P. Davis, Broadcast Interview Source, Washington, D.C.
John DeFrancesco, DeFrancesco Goodfriend Public Relations, Chicago
Cliff Dektar, APR, Fellow PRSA, senior vice president, The Lippin Group, Los Angeles
Anthony G. Dempster, former executive director of Strategic Planning, Texas A&M University, College Station
Lillian Fickey, administrative assistant to the executive director, Office of University Relations, Texas A&M University, College Station
Fay Fleming, vice president of marketing, Provident Counseling, St. Louis, Mo.
Lori A. George, account supervisor, Porter/Novelli Public Relations, Washington, D.C.
Francis D. Gomez, director of public programs, Philip Morris Companies, New York
Michael Harrigan, president, Trigon Sports, Falls Church, Va.
Wendy Hayes, account executive, Edelman Public Relations Worldwide, New York
Chris Kater, account executive, Modern Talking Picture Service, Inc., Washington, D.C.
Lloyd Kirban, former senior vice president and director of research, Burson-Marsteller, New York
Walter K. Lindenmann, senior vice president and director of research, Ketchum Public Relations, New York
Mark Manoff, vice president, Medialink, Washington, D.C.
Craig Miller, assistant executive director for media and public relations, USA Basketball, Colorado Springs
John Mosher, principal, Ibex, Washington, D.C.
Steve H. Murdock, professor of sociology and professor and head of the Department of Rural Sociology, Texas A&M University, College Station, and chief demographer for the State of Texas
Margaret Nathan, principal, Stern, Nathan & Perryman, Dallas

Sharon Neelley, manager of special events, Office of University Relations, Texas A&M University, College Station

Lou Nieto, director of ethnic marketing, Kraft USA, Glenview, Ill.

Octavio E. Nuiry, manager, public relations, AD Rendón, Irvine, Calif. and president of the Hispanic Public Relations Association

Fernando Oaxaca, president, Coronado Communications, Los Angeles

Harvey P. Posert, vice president for communications and industry affairs, Robert Mondavi Winery, Oakville, Calif.

Hank Rieger, publisher, *Emmy* magazine, Academy of Television Arts & Sciences, North Hollywood, Calif.

H. Zane Robbins, principal, Arthur Andersen & Co., Chicago

Marsha Robertson, motion picture and entertainment industry executive, Playa del Rey, Calif., and former vice president of national publicity for MGM/UA Film Company

Jay Rockey, founder and chair, The Rockey Company, Seattle

Don Smith, president, Don Smith Consultants, New York, and president New York City Sports Commission

Barbara Smith, administrative assistant, Burrelle's Information Services, Livingston, N.J.

Andrew Stern, chairman, The Sunwest Group, Dallas

Lane B. Stephenson, deputy director, Office of University Relations, Texas A&M University, College Station, Texas

Fred Thompson, principal, Kerr Kelly Thompson, Greenwich, Conn.

Lesa Ukman, executive editor, and **Jon Ukman,** publisher, International Events Group, Chicago

Hal Uplinger, president, Uplinger Enterprises, Larkspur, Calif.

Lynne Choy Uyeda, president, Lynne Choy Uyeda and Associates, Los Angeles, and president of the Asian American Advertising and Public Relations Association

Susan Colvin White, assistant professor of business, Division of Business, Northwestern State University, Natchitoches, La.

Gary Zabel, Hollis Directories, Middlesex, England

MARKETING PUBLIC RELATIONS

1

HOW TO MAKE MARKETING PUBLIC RELATIONS WORK FOR YOU

Marketing public relations is a comprehensive, all-encompassing, public awareness and information program or campaign directed to mass or specialty audiences to influence increased sales or use of an organization's product or service. Marketing public relations is the successful combination of a variety of communications techniques, which, when skillfully and professionally used, will help a company achieve its sales and marketing objectives.

What once was considered product publicity, as part of a public relations effort, has slowly evolved into a sophisticated package that can directly impact bottom-line profitability. For too many years, those responsible for advertising and those responsible for publicity operated separately and independently, even though both had the same goal: to increase a company's sales of its products or services.

Until 1984, the Public Relations Society of America gave only one Silver Anvil award for marketing. The Silver Anvil is the highest honor given in the profession and is PR's equivalent of an Oscar, Emmy or Tony. Today, there are 16 different marketing communications categories in the annual Silver Anvil awards competition. Public relations' highest honors are given for marketing communications in diversified business services; financial services and professional business firms; government; association and non-profit organizations for both new services and established services; as well as for new products and established products marketed to consumers and those marketed to business customers.

Even when those responsible for advertising and those responsible for publicity were working with the same product manager or brand manager, there was almost no coordination, mutual planning or cooperation. In fact, all too frequently, many advertising executives looked upon money spent on public relations or publicity as being money that could be spent on advertising and commissionable to the advertising agency. On copy themes and creative ideas there also was the ever present, competitive not-invented-here syndrome.

A nationwide study of marketers by the Strategic Directions Group in Minnesota reported that marketers "tend to be reluctant about trying new and innovative ideas and methodologies" and the majority apply the not-invented-here rule. The study illustrated that most marketing people don't want anything to do with fresh ideas if they or their firm didn't create them. The study also pointed out that mass-function marketing can be very impersonal compared to public relations, which has to be personal and targeted.

At one time some of those responsible for product publicity reported to advertising, both in-house and at agencies, and pressure would be brought to bear on some media to use a publicity release about a company or product because of the money being spent on advertising. This worked with some trade magazines and even some consumer media.

However, this practice virtually disappeared as marketing communications became more sophisticated and integrated; those responsible for public relations were given more authority with their responsibility, and media learned they could say "no." There are still instances, however, where a company, for any number of reasons, will exert pressure on media based on its advertising dollars spent on that media.

COORDINATION AND COOPERATION ARE CRITICAL TO SUCCESS

Only when a company brought its advertising people together with its public relations people and directed all involved—whether company employees or agencies serving the company—to work together as a team was there any appearance of a coordinated marketing or communications effort.

Throughout the years the definitive lines of various communications techniques that included publicity, public relations, promotion, special events and advertising began to blur and meld together. Marketing public relations has emerged as the single, descriptive and all-inclusive vehicle.

While there still may be competition for budgets between those responsible for advertising and those for public relations, today there generally is a cohesive, coordinated effort for a program or campaign. There are a number of reasons for this change:

• Corporate marketing executives look at the total package and what is needed to reach an established sales or marketing goal. A marketing executive then will dictate the mix and responsibility for various techniques used in the package.

• Public relations firms have expanded and broadened their scope of services to include many marketing functions once provided only by advertising agencies.

• Advertising agencies likewise have expanded and broadened their scope of services to include public relations, publicity and other services once provided only by public relations firms.

• Major international advertising agencies have acquired public relations firms, and the two organizations work closely with one another for business development and to best serve existing clients.

• Some public relations firms have bought or merged with advertising agencies to form all-service, turnkey communications agencies.

MARKETING PUBLIC RELATIONS SELLS MANY THINGS

Whether it is a product, a service or a concept, marketing public relations is the preferred strategic communications vehicle. Marketing public relations motivates a person to prefer and buy one brand of a product—such as a soft drink, compact disc player, VCR, toothpaste or automobile—over that of a competitor. Lawyers, accountants and architects use marketing communications to create a demand for their services. It sells seats in movie theaters for a first-run feature film. It gets vacation dollars spent in a particular resort area or on one airline or hotel instead of another.

Marketing public relations influences a viewer to watch a certain television program as compared to one on another channel or to use the pay television channel to watch a sports or entertainment special. Hospitals, museums and performing arts groups use marketing communications to meet their goals. It has been used to launch new home appliances, fashions and other consumer products and to sell new homes or resort condominiums.

Here are just a few examples of how marketing public relations worked for different types of companies:

• When Whirlpool Corporation became the last major home appliance manufacturer to enter the microwave oven market, it developed a comprehensive campaign that included major *sell to* (selling product to the trade or distribution market) and *sell through* (to the consumer) segments. Simultaneous efforts were directed to the trade and to the consuming public to create an awareness of the value and quality of the new Whirlpool microwave ovens. Publicity releases were carefully timed, taking into consideration different lead times for publications directed at the various targeted audiences so that consumer publicity would not appear and create a demand before dealer showrooms had the product available for sale. The distributor-dealer campaign included a unique and award-winning series of direct mail items, trade magazine advertising and publicity, and convention exhibit participation. Feature stories presenting new kitchen concepts and product publicity in family service and shelter magazines and newspapers, combined with appearances by company representatives on local television programs, embraced the consumer effort.

• The motion picture campaigns by Disney's Touchstone Pictures for *Dick Tracy* and Carolco Pictures for *Terminator 2: Judgment Day* filled the seats of theaters throughout the country with moviegoers presold on wanting to see the movies. These campaigns involved publicity releases during production of the movie, prior to the movie's national distribution, merchandise tie-ins, personal appearances and media interviews by the respective stars (Warren Beatty, Madonna and Arnold Schwarzenegger), and special events. Carolco targeted its *Terminator 2* film to young men with support from the Subway sandwich chain, which featured "T2" lunch specials and gimmicky cups, further increasing rating points, impressions and public attention to the film.

• The tourist development campaign by Charleston, S.C., and other regions devastated in 1990 by Hurricane Hugo quickly revitalized the area's tourist industry. Campaigns included advertising, stories in newspaper and magazine travel sections, and tourism representatives making appearances on radio and television. Following the conclusion of the 1991 Persian Gulf War, the airline industry conducted a similar effort to allay the fears of many former fliers who had stopped traveling by air.

• The publicity effort to newspaper and magazine television editors and general interest magazines maximized audience viewership of the PBS miniseries *The Civil War,* setting all-time ratings records. Almost anyone who read the television section of a newspaper was aware of the program well in advance of the series being aired.

• For years professionals in law, accounting and architecture shied away from publicity or any effort that could be regarded as sales or business development. An increasingly competitive environment has seen almost all professional organizations seek exposure to increase sales.

This can be accomplished in many ways by having leading executives of the firm speak at important industry conferences and conventions and have prepared remarks available for the media. If a firm specializes in a practice involving the housing industry, for example, then a feature story or interview with an executive on a subject of industry importance can create an awareness of the firm's services and capabilities. Newspaper and magazine editors and television assignment editors should be aware of a special expertise an articulate executive may have so that person is called and quoted on breaking issues.

With a carefully strategized plan, Simon & Schuster skyrocketed Kitty Kelly's unauthorized biography of Nancy Reagan on the best-seller lists.

For a number of years McGraw-Hill ran a full-page ad in a number of publications stressing the importance of advertising. Today that effort would be integrated into a total marketing communications effort. However, the message of McGraw-Hill is one to consider when undertaking any program. The ad shows a dour faced, balding executive with glasses and a bow tie sitting in an arm chair on rollers with his hands in his lap. The copy reads:

> I don't know who you are.
> I don't know your company.
> I don't know your company's product.
> I don't know what your company stands for.
> I don't know your company's customers.
> I don't know your company's record.
> I don't know your company's reputation.
> Now—what was it you wanted to sell me?

McGraw-Hill says the moral is to start sales before the sales rep calls and do it with McGraw-Hill business publication advertising. Marketing public relations can help presell a product or service in the same way.

THE ELEMENTS OF MARKETING PUBLIC RELATIONS

There are many techniques that can be used in marketing public relations. In a comprehensive campaign, all the techniques or elements are focused on the same primary objective. There must be interaction and coordination among all the elements. There must be a central, uniform copy theme or platform that each element projects or reinforces, so that throughout the campaign, the same story is being told over and over again.

All the following elements of marketing public relations are described in more detail in subsequent chapters in this book.

Publicity is the written news release or feature story that creates a greater public awareness of the product, service or concept. It also can be an electronic video release or news or feature clip for television. Publicity can be a single story, a photo and caption release, or a press kit. It also can begin as a story concept to be developed further by an editor, writer or radio or television reporter. Publicity should have continuity, and for an ongoing campaign, frequency and persistency.

Advertising is a paid message completely controlled by the advertiser and scheduled in print, on radio or television, or for outdoor or transit advertising. By purchasing the time on radio or television or buying the space in a newspaper or magazine or on a billboard, the company can determine exactly what it wants to say, when it wants to say it and how it wants to say what it wants to say.

Special Events can be as selective as having a simple golf or tennis outing to one that involves entertainer or athlete celebrities with customers. A special event can focus attention on the product or service the company is selling. Non-profit organizations use special events as fund-raisers, which can include art exhibits, fashion shows, dances, fairs, tours, marathons and bazaars.

Sponsorship can range from Roger Penske's Marlboro Championship Auto Racing Team to the Mobil Cotton Bowl or the AT&T Pebble Beach National Pro-Am Golf Tournament. Southland Corporation built the 7-Eleven Cycling Velodrome and McDonald's the swim stadium for the 1984 Olympic Games in Los Angeles. Since Kool held its first jazz festival, live entertainment has been a popular means of marketing for scores of companies including the Trident and Freshfruit Candies sponsorship of the NBC Comedy Tour starring Jerry Seinfeld and Miller Genuine Draft's involvement in live music concerts. All these sponsored efforts resulted in name and visual identification for the company or its brand product in print media and television.

Printed Materials can include newsletters, pamphlets and brochures on various subjects which further create identity for a product. Armour-Dial gave away a flyer on tennis tips from Vic Braden to promote Tone soap. A consumer's guide to roofing was published by 3M to promote the sale of asphalt roofing, to support product manufacturers to whom the 3M sold mineral granules for asphalt roofing. Sunkist published a series of giveaway flyers on basketball tips to support a marketing effort for its retail customers.

Speakers' Bureaus are an excellent way to reach out at the grass-roots level. Company spokespersons should be selected and trained and provided with supporting materials including prepared speeches and materials. These spokespersons can be from headquarters or regional offices. Carefully planned, a speaker's bureau can effectively extend an organization's resources by using surrogates or paid experts or celebrities. Participation in any of the nearly 6,000 trade conventions and conferences each year affords another medium of exposure for a company or organization. A leading ballpoint pen manufacturer once retained handwriting experts to appear on radio and television talk shows and, during the course of the interview, mention the brand name of the product. To launch what became a best-selling cookbook called *Crockery Cookery,* the publisher had the author tour major U.S. cities making television appearances and meeting with newspaper and magazine editors. There are hundreds of similar stories in which companies or organizations have retained individuals to act as company, product or issue spokespersons.

Electronic Media are the most dynamic media today and there are countless opportunities for exposure on local radio and television talk and news shows, network and syndicated talk shows, television cable systems—even sound bites on the evening network television news programs. Products and concepts also can be written into story lines of prime-time network shows, movies made for television and feature films that eventually will be shown on television.

Audiovisual Materials can include films, video, slide programs and audio tapes and CDs. Programs can be used to support company representatives for use on commercial or cable television, for distribution to programs and clubs to use as a focal point of a program, or for a self-liquidating premium.

Coalition Support is effective when third-party support is needed. This is especially important in political campaigns and in building a grass-roots base of support to address a controversial national issue such as pro-choice or pro-life, pro-or-anti-nuclear energy, or gun control.

Government Relations is a discipline that is not generally associated with marketing communications. However, in a fully integrated campaign or program it is a key element. It is smart business for a company or organization to keep elected, appointed and career people in the administrative, regulatory and legislative branches of government well informed of its activities and developments. A toy manufacturer would want to have an established relationship with the Consumer Product Safety Commission. A manufacturer of mobile homes would be in regular contact with officials at the U.S. Department of Housing and Urban Development as well as with the appropriate housing subcommittees in the U.S. Senate and U.S. House of Representatives that authorize legislation and appropriate program funding. Likewise, a computer hardware manufacturer that recognizes opportunities with the new democracies in central and eastern Europe would be in contact with both the Department of Commerce and the Agency for International Development.

Seeking recognition and honor by a federal department or agency is an important validation for a company and its products or services. Companies that have been recipients of the U.S. Department of Commerce's annual Malcolm Baldridge award have widely advertised and publicized their recognition. The same is true for companies that have been honored for their outstanding efforts in equal employment opportunity and affirmative action by the U.S. Department of Labor and companies and individuals so honored with a Presidential End Hunger award from the Agency for International Development.

Others recognize the importance of having testimony read into the *Congressional Record,* having a special event either honoring members of Congress or hosted by one or more members of Congress, and especially one which will provide a photo opportunity involving the president of the United States in a setting such as the Rose Garden or Oval Office.

Regulatory decisions or legislative action could dramatically impact the sale of a product or service and thereby the bottom-line profit or loss of a company. It is critical that government relations then be an integral part of the overall planning, strategy and execution of marketing communications. This relationship is even more important in many countries throughout the world where there can be overnight changes in leadership or where, by the stroke of a pen, a company can find it no longer can do business in a country and the opportunity has been turned over to its competitor. Here it is important to develop programs that provide open doors and access to a country's leadership and where special events and activities support both the policy aims of the country and the company's marketing objectives.

Some companies may encourage government regulation and legislation to give their product a unique or proprietary advantage over competitors. Volvo, one of the first automobile manufacturers to install seat belts, led the campaign to have them required for all automobiles, while at the same time stressing the safety features of its line of cars. A company manufacturing protective headgear with a major share of the market would find it advantageous to gain support from organizations such as the National Head Injury Foundation and bicycling organizations to encourage legislation requiring bicyclists to use helmets. While all manufacturers would benefit, the one with the greatest market share would see gross sales and gross profit increase significantly. Altruism may be one motivation, but increased sales and profits would be the driving force.

Sports Marketing, while certainly not new as a public relations technique, became the buzzword of the 1980s for many companies and agencies. Few companies have used sports marketing as effectively on an international basis as has Coca-Cola, which has found it can open doors to and establish a relationship with heads of state. In the 1990s there are a multitude of opportunities for a company in this area, which will be described in detail in Chapter 13.

Ethnic Markets may be a part of the target market for the campaign. In addition to understanding the language, customs and other particulars needed to reach any such special audience, a totally constructed subcampaign may be necessary.

WHATEVER YOU CALL IT—IT INCREASES SALES

Just as marketing public relations evolved as the lines blurred between product publicity, public relations, promotion and advertising, its definition can be expanded to include other concepts of public relations communications.

Regardless of what anyone may call a particular endeavor, if the communications activity relates to selling a product, a service, or even a concept, then it should most appropriately be called marketing communications.

For example, some call the following activities public affairs, but indeed the effort is that defined as marketing communications:

- The American Red Cross and other non-profit, charitable organizations' appeals on television for public donations of money during relief efforts following the San Francisco earthquake in 1989 and the devastating floods in Bangladesh in 1991.
- A major endowment campaign by a college or university, which may include special events, receptions or dinners for targeted donors, timed placement of feature stories and articles in general-interest magazines to create a greater heightened public awareness, and any other technique that results in a financial contribution to the institution.
- The National Rifle Association's comprehensive campaign to defeat the Brady Bill, which it feared could reduce the sale of firearms for its corporate members. Elements of this campaign certainly include government relations and a forceful lobbying effort.
- Any effort by the Tobacco Institute or the Smokeless Tobacco Council to gain public support against any regulatory or legislative activity that would impact on sales of cigarettes or smokeless tobacco products, ranging from increased taxes on the products to sponsorship of a racecar or events such as the Virginia Slims Tennis Championships.
- The Roman Catholic Church's use of a leading public relations firm to launch an anti-abortion advertising campaign. The Church of Scientology also hired a public relations agency to advance its cause.

Marketing Communications by Non-Profit Organizations

Any non-profit organization seeking to raise money must first increase its awareness and need to the audience being targeted for the giving. The public awareness campaign, which is essentially marketing communications, should be launched before the request is made for money and should continue during the thrust of the funding program. If someone is being asked to give money, it not only is easier to obtain a gift, but to obtain a larger gift, if that person already is convinced of the importance of the need by the recipient. Marketing public relations should be an integral part of any funding and development campaign.

The SEC Frowns on Marketing Public Stocks

While regulated by the Securities and Exchange Commission, there have been instances in which companies whose stocks are publicly traded have considered their stock to be a product and completely ignored financial and investor relations programs to undertake a marketing communications program designed solely to increase the trading activity and price of that stock. The SEC has strict financial public relations guidelines regarding what can and cannot be done by a publicly held company. Many such efforts have been illegal, and the SEC has found both the company and its officers and the public relations agency and its employees guilty.

There is a fine line between what is legal and acceptable and what is considered hype to tout a stock. Years ago the author was the luncheon guest in the residence of a chair and CEO of a prominent electronics industry company whose stock was listed on the New York Stock Exchange. During the course of the luncheon the host made it clear that he was not interested in having a program created and implemented that would increase the sale of his manufactured products, but only in selling more stock. "If you want to represent my company," he said, "consider that the next room is filled with stock certificates and that is the product—the only product—I want to sell!" That, however, is illegal.

Selling the Candidates to America

In the broadest sense, a political campaign uses marketing communications. "Selling" an individual to the American voting public to be president of the United States is essentially a marketing communications program. The same is true for congressional candidates and those at state and local levels. However, neither the Democrats nor the Republicans have yet effectively coordinated all the campaign elements to achieve maximum benefits. While both parties use every known technique, including paid space advertising, direct mail, publicity, coalition support, surrogate speakers, special events, and printed and audiovisual materials, there is almost no coordination.

As with most political organizations, a political campaign is a group of fragmented offices and departments, each of which is zealously and jealously guarded by the individual responsible. Teamwork is needed so everyone has the same ultimate goal—get the candidate elected—but they may be doing it in different ways, telling different stories and having no uniform concept.

Where a private sector corporation would mold the diverse elements into one dynamic and cohesive team, the political strategists generally go to great lengths to divide the entire organization into a number of fiefdoms and turfs for no logical or explainable reason. For the most part, one team will be involved with the primary campaign, another for the national convention, a third for the general campaign, and a fourth for the successful candidate, the inaugural festivities. This management philosophy not only impedes the potential effectiveness of the campaign, but also destroys any possible continuity.

IN-HOUSE STAFF VS. OUTSIDE AGENCY

The most important consideration should be "Who will do the best job?" If budget is a major consideration, doing the campaign in-house is not necessarily the most economical approach. Here are a few things to consider:

1. What are the in-house resources, experience and capabilities for this effort?
2. Will this effort detract from ongoing assignments for the in-house staff?
3. What creative input is needed to make the campaign work? Has the theme been developed?
4. Can new thinking and creativity be expected from an outside party?
5. What elements of the overall campaign already are supported by in-house staff?
6. What elements of the overall campaign can be provided by agencies with which the company has an ongoing relationship?
7. Are there specialty considerations, such as use of a celebrity? Creating an event? Sponsoring an event? Sports marketing?
8. Should a consultant be retained for specific counseling on a specific element of the program, whether or not that consultant is hired to undertake the program or direct the in-house staff?
9. What are the marketing communications capabilities and experience of the advertising agency?
10. What are the marketing communications capabilities and experience of the public relations agency?
11. Because of the scope of the program, should a new agency be retained?
12. Should that agency be retained on an ongoing basis for this specific campaign?
13. What is the budget allocation for the agency?
14. To what degree do you want the agency to supplement in-house staff resources?

15. Are the company's established goals and objectives reasonably achievable?

16. Should additional staff be hired for in-house staff?

17. If an agency is to be retained, who will work on the account? (A company is only as good as the individual responsible for doing the job.)

18. If this is a national effort, can the program be handled by people in one office? How important is it to have offices in major U.S. cities?

19. Can goals be better achieved by hiring the firm with the best single individual, regardless of size and offices, and then using affiliates in various cities?

20. If the campaign is international in scope, should one firm handle the entire program and use affiliates in foreign countries or should another firm be hired internationally? Can the firm selected for the United States handle the overseas assignments?

When interviewing and considering an outside agency, ask for the following:

1. A capabilities statement of the firm.
2. Specific qualifications for this particular assignment.
3. Biographies including the disciplines, experience and qualifications of the principals who will create and oversee the campaign.
4. The disciplines, qualifications and experience of the account people who will be involved on a daily basis with the campaign.
5. A statement regarding an understanding of the goals and objectives.
6. How the agency is compensated, fees and expenses.

Many companies will ask agencies competing for the business to develop speculative presentations filled with ideas that cannot be copyrighted or protected by the agencies. Some companies today will compensate a firm for the time spent in developing a speculative presentation and even pay for some transportation costs during the presentation process.

Ethically, a company should not use any idea presented to it on speculation by an agency or firm unless that agency is compensated for its idea and gives the company permission to make use of its concept. The company also should not share these ideas with the firm it selects to do its work unless all presentation ideas are shared with all the competing companies and, again, permission is so granted. Unfortunately, few people in business today have this level of integrity.

2

HOW TO MAKE USE OF RESEARCH

Research should be the first step of any campaign. Research helps you develop your campaign strategy, your timeline and your copy theme. It even gives you a benchmark by which to measure results.

Before undertaking research, know the answers you want or you hope to get. Sometimes research will just reinforce or reaffirm a gut instinct, but documented information is always superior to guessing. If you are introducing a new product, wouldn't it help if you knew what the customer wanted? Sizes, specifications? Price range? Convenience features? Appearance? Available colors? And if you are ready to launch a comprehensive marketing public relations campaign, it would help to know what the public is expecting, its attitudes on issues or products, why it behaves the way it behaves, and key words that significantly help a message to be received, heard and understood.

Through the years, the author has used research extensively for a number of campaigns. The author also has used different types of research depending on the anticipated results. There are many ways to gather information for research, ranging from telephone surveys to mailed questionnaires to personal interviews and focus groups. Knowledge of available data bases and industry trade publications can provide excellent research for product comparisons or getting background information on a competitor. Often research will start with a focus group that produces qualitative information that could lead to a public opinion poll.

THE FOCUS GROUP

The predecessor of the focus group that we know today was first chronicled by academicians and researchers during World War II. The U.S. Army produced a number of films for enlisted men to justify America's entry into the war. The films were shown to small groups of soldiers who then discussed in detail specific parts of the films. It was necessary to have a sophisticated interviewing technique to determine audience reactions to the films. In the early 1940s Dr. Robert K. Merton, a Columbia University sociologist, published a monograph about this new technique which he called "the focused interview" (1987). The focus group technique of research further was popularized by 1960s group therapy methods used by psychoanalysts and psychologists (Merton and Kendall 1946). It is based on the idea that individuals who share common problems will reveal them in the security of a group session. The researcher selects, screens and recruits the participants for a focus group. A group of from as few as eight to as many as 12 people are then brought together in a room with a professional discussion leader who gets the people involved in conversation regarding the issues being researched. This process results in qualitative information regarding attitudes, feelings and human reaction. Almost all focus groups are tape recorded and many are televised through a one-way glass mirror with a videocamera located in an adjacent room (Gornall 1966).

The discussion leader or moderator will take the group through a series of prepared questions during a two- to three-hour period. The participants usually are compensated for their time ($50 to $100) and served simple refreshments. Generally a focus group will have similar demographics, such as being all golfers or tennis players, or all community leaders, or involved in women's issues or even of an ethnic group.

Following the meeting of the focus group, a transcript of the conversations will be typed and reviewed by all concerned. Videotapes will be reviewed. The transcripts of the focus groups are carefully reviewed and questions are developed for a public opinion poll questionnaire. Different questions may be asked of special demographic groups. Sometimes just one focus group is sufficient to obtain the information needed.

QUANTITATIVE RESEARCH

The opinion poll can be a questionnaire mailed to a targeted audience with a request that it be completed and returned, or the poll can be conducted by personal interview or telephone interview. This poll results in information related to numbers, percentages and statistics. There is little opportunity for an interviewer taking an opinion poll to get into detail regarding how someone really feels about a product or issue. The questions asked generally provide forced-choice answers.

DEMOGRAPHIC AND PSYCHOGRAPHIC RESEARCH

Demographic research is just that. Groups are divided by age, race or ethnicity, education, geographic location, income level, political party preference or some other statistical and quantitative determination. Psychographic research, on the other hand, occurs when groups are divided according to attitudinal behavior, how people think and what they believe, emotional attitudes such as a preference for being physically fit or caring about one's appearance, or how they will be motivated on particular issues. Demographic and psychographic research can be used in conjunction with one another, depending on the objective of the research.

STATISTICS

Disraeli once noted that there are three kinds of lies—lies, damned lies and statistics. While it is not quite necessary to group all of statistics in with lies, Susan Colvin White, assistant professor of business at Northwestern State University in Natchitoches, Louisiana, says you should consider carefully the statistics you are given. She says there are two key areas to examine in a given set of data: the "central tendency" of the data and the associated spread or dispersion (White 1994).

There are three fairly common measures of central tendency: (1) mean, (2) median, and (3) mode. Likewise there are three typical measures of dispersion: (1) range, (2) variance, and (3) standard deviation. Measures of dispersion are used to summarize the shape of the distribution of the data in the data set. The most commonly used shape is the bell-shaped curve.

Measures of Central Tendency

Dr. White (1994) says that the mean is the most commonly used measure of central tendency. It is the simple average of all the observations in the data set. The median is the middle observation in the data set after it has been sorted in numerical order. The mode is the most frequently occurring observation.

The term *average* can refer to any of these three measures; for data that follow a bell-shaped curve, the mean, the median and the mode are all equal. She notes, however, that when the data are skewed in one direction, the mean can be greatly affected. The median is not affected by outliers, and the mode provides a measure of the most common observation or range of observations. It usually is best to report all three measures of central tendency.

Measures of Dispersion

A measure of central tendency alone does not give the whole picture, Dr. White warns. She cites, for example, when given an opportunity to invest in Stock A, which has a mean return of 14 percent, or Stock B, which has a mean return of 12 percent, a person most likely would chose Stock A. If you knew that the return on Stock A varied from a high of 26 percent to a low of -12 percent and the return on Stock B varied from a high of 20 percent to a low of 4 percent, you might change your mind about investing in Stock A (White 1994).

She says it is important to discuss dispersion as well as central tendency. In this example, you were given the highest and lowest possible returns. From these you could find the range for the two stocks; the range is simply the difference between the maximum and the minimum observations. The variance is the "average" squared distance from an observation to the mean, and the standard deviation is the square root of the variance. The standard deviation usually is preferred to the variance because it is measured in the same units as the data.

Mean: $\bar{x} = \dfrac{\sum_{i=1}^{n} x_i}{n}$

Variance: $s^2 = \dfrac{\sum_{i=1}^{n}(x_i \;\; x)^2}{n-1}$

Standard Deviation: $s = \sqrt{s^2}$

Bell Curve:

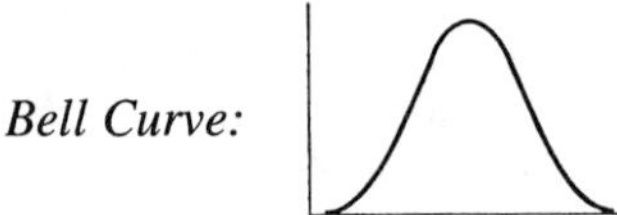

The Bell-Shaped Curve. The "bell curve," or bell-shaped curve, is called the *normal distribution* by statisticians and it is widely used. The bell curve is symmetric about the mean, and the mean, median and mode are all equal. Approximately 68 percent of all observations will fall within one standard deviation of the mean (x ± s), approximately 95 percent of all observations will fall within two standard deviations of the mean (x ± 2s), and almost all the observations (99.9 percent) will fall within three standard deviations of the mean (x ± 3s).

Dr. White says many types of data follow the bell curve. She says a quick test is to see if the mean, median and mode are roughly equal and if the data follow the 68 percent, 95 percent and 99.9 percent rules. If your data do follow the bell curve, then you are telling the whole story by reporting the mean and standard deviation. However, if your data do not follow the bell curve, then you should report all the measures of the central tendency and some measure of dispersion.

She says you do not need to test your data for the 68 percent, 95 percent and 99.9 percent containment if the mean and median are radically different. However, if the mean, the median and the mode are all equal, the data do not necessarily follow the bell curve. Then you need to check the ranges (x ± s), (x ± 2s) and (x ± 3s) to verify that your data are shaped approximately like a bell curve.

Real Estate Prices. Dr. White offers real estate prices as an example of data that do not follow the bell curve. She notes that in fact, real estate prices in an area are typically skewed, in that the mean and the median will not be equal. Consider the following data which are selling prices for real estate in a mid-size city (White 1994):

Observation	*Sales Price* *$*
1	32,000
2	49,000
3	63,000
4	51,900
5	42,500
6	42,000
7	216,900

The mean for this data is $71,043. That seems a bit misleading because only one property in the set of seven sold for more than $63,000. The mean has been affected by the outlier of $216,900. The median for this data set would be $49,000. The $49,000 is a more representative measure of the "center" of this data set. The mode, in this case, would be in the $40,000 to $49,999 range. In this case you should report the mean, the median and the mode and at least one measure of dispersion.

SIX RESEARCH TECHNIQUES

Dr. Walter K. Lindenmann, senior vice president and director of research for Ketchum Public Relations, New York City, compares six different approaches or techniques, grouped three pairs, that can be used when carrying out research projects—qualitative vs. quantitative, secondary research vs. primary research and custom studies vs. omnibus studies (Lindenmann 1993).

Here is how he defines them:

Qualitative research vs. quantitative research

Qualitative	Quantitative
Soft data	Hard data
Usually open-ended, free response, unstructured	Usually closed-ended, forced choice, highly structured
Exploratory, probing, fishing expedition type of research	Descriptive or explanatory type of research
Usually valid but not reliable	Usually *both* valid and reliable
Rarely projectable to larger audiences	Usually very projectable to larger audiences
Generally uses non-random samples	Generally uses random samples
Examples	Examples
Focus groups	Telephone polls
One-on-one, in-depth interviews	Mail surveys
Observation, participation, role-playing studies	Mall intercept studies
Convenience polling	Face-to-face interview studies
	Shared cost or omnibus studies
	Panel studies

Secondary research vs. primary research

Secondary	Primary
Old	New
Second-hand data	Original data
You look for and try to utilize what's already available	You design and carry out research that's specific and directed to your needs
Sources	
Roper Center for Public Opinion Research at the University of Connecticut	
University of Chicago National Opinion Research Center	
U.S. Census Bureau	
Various on-line data bases	
American Demographics	
Census and You	
Gallup Poll Monthly	
PR Reporter	
Public Relations Review	
Research Alert	
Public Perspective	

Custom studies vs. omnibus studies

Custom	Omnibus
Not shared, private	Shared with others
You call the shots regarding timing, sample design, etc.	Others call the shots regarding timing, sample design, etc.
Usually more expensive	Relatively inexpensive

Generally substantive, in-depth, more evaluative in nature

Sources

The Green Book, International Directory of Marketing Research Companies and Services, published annually by the New York Chapter of the American Marketing Association, 310 Madison Avenue, New York, NY 10017

The Blue Book, A listing of more than 200 research agencies and organizations published annually by the American Association for Public Opinion Research P.O. Box 1248, Ann Arbor, MI 48106

Generally surface or superficial in nature

Sources

Cambridge Reports, Inc. (CRI Omnibus)
Gallup Organization
Market Facts (Telenation)
NFO Research
Opinion Research Corporation (Telephone Caravan)
R. H. Bruskin Associates
Roper Organization (LIMOBUS)
Simmons Market Research (ECHO)

Dr. Lindenmann defines public relations research as an essential tool for fact and opinion gathering; a systematic effort aimed at discovering, confirming and/or understanding, through objective appraisal, the facts or opinions pertaining to a specific problem or problems.

He notes that the use of public relations research, measurement and evaluation is increasing. The Ketchum Public Relations Research and Measurement Department conducted 80 major studies in 1993, up 25 percent from the previous year. Of these, 57 percent were efforts to measure and evaluate the impact of public relations while 43 percent of the studies were carried out for planning purposes and to support promotional and publicity activities of Ketchum clients.

RESEARCH WITH SCIENTIFIC AND EDUCATIONAL OPINION LEADERS

Genentech, Inc., a San Francisco-based biotechnology firm, asked Ketchum Public Relations for help in forming lasting alliances with biology teachers, scientists and other experts through an interactive electronic network it had built, called Access Excellence. In connection with that assignment, researchers at Ketchum initially were asked to carry out exploratory research—using focus groups and one-on-one in-depth interviews—with opinion leaders from the scientific and educational fields to obtain their reactions to this pioneering concept. Once that project was completed, Ketchum's research department then worked with the Roper Organization in designing and carrying out a full-scale, nationwide survey of 500 biology teachers to examine their interest in possibly using the new computer network as a link to the scientific community and as an aid in the classroom. The biology teachers survey findings were publicized by Genentech as part of a Washington, D.C., press conference that announced the Access Excellence concept (Lindenmann 1994).

NATURAL-SETTING, ETHNOGRAPHIC RESEARCH

According to Dr. Lindenmann, some client research questions are so complex that using traditional forms of research such as focus groups, telephone interviews or mall intercepts cannot obtain the full range of information that may be needed. He says that firms are relying now on techniques borrowed from the fields of anthropology and sociology to carry out studies. For a company that needed to obtain highly sensitive information pertaining to its products and services as those products and services are actually used in community settings, Ketchum designed and carried out a natural-setting, ethnographic research project that involved sending a team of professional staff members into selected community settings, using observation, participation, role playing and informal interviewing techniques to assess, as discreetly as possible, target audience segment use of and actual on-premises reactions to the particular products under study (Lindenmann 1994, 14).

ON-SITE, TASTE-TEST RESEARCH

As part of a nationwide promotional campaign for its non-alcoholic beverage, Sharp's, the Miller Brewing Company sponsored in numerous cities across the country what it called the Sharp's Great Taste Invitational, a series of events at which consumers were invited to taste samples of the product. In connection with the events, Miller executives asked Ketchum Public Relations to conduct on-site, taste-test research in nine markets, exploring not only consumers' taste preferences regarding Sharp's, but also their preferences in music, food and clothing. A total of 682 interviews were conducted. The research findings—including the fact that taste testers preferred rock music, Italian food and jeans to other types of music, food and clothing—were later publicized by Miller (Lindenmann 1994, 19).

IMAGE SURVEYS

Image surveys are another research tool that can be effective in some cases. For example, a major bank needed to assess how effectively it communicates with selected target audience groups in several counties in which the institution has branch offices. A multi-phased image survey of how the bank is perceived in comparison to its major competitors was designed and carried out. The project featured telephone interviews with 600 retail consumers, including 160 with representatives of small business establishments with annual sales below $5 million; 45 with representatives of companies with sales of $5 million or more; 25 each with institutional customers and elite private banking customers; and 50 with key area community influentials or opinion leaders. The research findings were used by Ketchum and its client for marketing communications and public relations program planning (Lindenmann 1994, 19).

USING RESEARCH TO DESIGN SPORTS MARKETING EFFORTS

SCOPE, an acronym for Sports Compatibility Profile, is a research program developed by Burson-Marsteller and used exclusively for its clients. SCOPE enables consumer goods companies to identify the sports most associated with their brands and those of their competitors. It provides a firm with a sports-related venue to reach consumers and also creates a "halo" effect for the firm's products or services by association with the sport. By the same token, SCOPE isolates the sports that appear to be important competitive-brand users. By designing marketing efforts geared to these sports, it can reach and influence competitive-brand users to switch brands.

According to Dr. Lloyd Kirban, former senior vice president and director of research for Burson-Marsteller, SCOPE is a segmentation approach based on the level of consumers' involvement in one or more of 51 different sports. Using Simmons Market Research Bureau's annual survey of about 20,000 households, the research program links specific sports involvement to consumers' product purchase behavior (Kirban 1994).

Involvement is measured in multidimensional terms by combining such behavior as watching or listening to broadcasts about a specific sport to attending the event to actively participating in the sport. According to Dr. Kirban, at one end of the involvement spectrum are the "fanatics," whose behavior reveals a strong commitment to the sport, while at the other end of the continuum are the "dilettantes" who infrequently watch or listen to specific sports events but do little else.

CHECKLIST FOR PUBLIC RELATIONS RESEARCH

Ketchum Public Relations's Dr. Lindenmann offers a checklist of some of the major factors he believes public relations practitioners should think about or watch as they consider research to make sure that they are getting exactly what they need.

Don't reinvent the wheel. Don't automatically assume a completely new study is needed. Do a literature search and secondary analysis to see if someone else has already done a similar study or gathered similar data.

Be flexible. Many public relations people think only of conducting telephone polls or of studying focus groups. Other techniques are available and depending on the circumstances may even be better:

- mall intercept studies
- a mail survey
- content analysis of what appears in the media
- conducting observation, participation or role-playing studies
- doing face-to-face or in-person interviewing
- undertaking a panel study in which the same individuals are interviewed more than once over a period of time to investigate the processes of response change regarding the same topic or issues, or in which a group of individuals deliberately recruited because of their special demographic characteristics are interviewed more than once over a period of time for various clients on a broad array of topics or subjects
- piggybacking some questions on a large market research company's nationwide omnibus poll

Define beforehand what you want the research to do for you and how the results are to be used. This will determine if a descriptive survey is good enough or if explanations also are needed as to why people have particular opinions and attitudes. Defining the results will be used to determine whom to survey.

Remember that for most public relations practitioners, "why" is far more important that "what" or "how." It is relatively easy in research to find what people's views toward given topics or issues are or how they feel about something. But the "what" and "how" are usually of only limited use because a public relations program or campaign cannot be built on this information. To get at the "why" may require more emphasis on qualitative than on quantitative research.

Give serious thought to the total population to be studied and then, once that has been decided, to the appropriate selection of the sample that will represent that population. Samples can be selected randomly, or by chance, or judgmentally. In measuring consumer attitudes, a random sample probably makes more sense. But in seeking, for example, to determine attitudes of the media toward a corporation and its industry, a judgmental sample might be most effective. The basic question to be asked when drawing a sample is, "How precise and unbiased should it be for the study to have any reliability and validity?"

Consider the eligibility of potential respondents. Consider screening criteria for potential respondents, because you may wish to interview only certain demographic segments of the population. Are the individuals being interviewed the appropriate individuals to be included in the sample frame of the survey?

Spend a good deal of time on the survey instrument to be used when collecting data. Is it better to have a closed or forced-choice questionnaire or an open, free-response questionnaire? The closed is less expensive and easier to tabulate but may suggest answers to the respondents that possibly bias the findings. The open is more expensive and allows the respondents to answer in their own words but is difficult to code and analyze. Consider conducting a pretest of the questionnaire before the actual field work is undertaken.

Find out as much as you can about those who will be doing the interviewing. Are they experienced? What are their qualifications? For focus groups, how familiar is the moderator with the subject?

When focusing on the fielding of a study, consider the "no-shows," the "refusals" and the "no answers." Obtaining a 100 percent response or completion rate is impossible for any research project. Set parameters beforehand regarding those respondents who cannot be researched, who refuse to cooperate or do not give answers to the questions.

Find out as much as you can about what form the analysis and final research report will take. Will the researchers provide only a set of statistical tables or a full analysis and interpretation of the findings? If there is an analysis and interpretation, on what will it be based? Who will do the analysis? What are their backgrounds? Who will code the questionnaire responses? What criteria will be followed for building codes? Be involved in the project every step of the way. Have a say in how the data are to be analyzed and become involved in the plan for data analysis and interpretation.

Protect the confidentiality of both respondents and survey results. There are many codes of ethics that research organizations rely on when they design and carry out research projects. Most of these codes protect the confidentiality and anonymity of the individuals who are interviewed or who are participating in the studies. Be sure to protect the confidentiality of the research project, and make sure that the research supplier never refers to or passes on the research findings to others without permission (Lindenmann 1993, 7).

REFERENCES

Broom, Glenn, and David M. Dozier. 1990. *Using Research in Public Relations.* Englewood Cliffs, N.J.: Prentice Hall.

Gornall, John M. 1966. *Monthly Marketing Ideas.* National Association of Home Builders, pp. 6-7.

Kirban, Loyd. 1994. Memorandum to the author. February 21.

Lindenmann, Walter K. 1993. *A Guide to Public Relations Research.* New York: Ketchum Public Relations, pp. 15-19.

____. 1994. *A Brief Look at Public Relations Research at Ketchum.* New York: Ketchum Public Relations. January, p. 13.

Merton, Robert K. 1987. "Focused Interview and Focus Groups: Continuities and Discontinuities." *Public Opinion Quarterly.* (Winter):550-66.

Merton, Robert K., and Patricia Kendall. 1946. "The Focused Interview." *American Journal of Sociology* 51: 546-57.

White, Susan Colvin. 1994. Memorandum to author. April 19.

3

HOW TO USE RESOURCES TO TARGET PUBLICS

Once the program objectives are defined, the target market must be identified. This can be one or more audiences depending on the objectives and the structure of the campaign.

Markets can be segmented into various publics according to the message being communicated. The way a message would be conveyed to a wholesaler or retailer would not necessarily be the way the message would be delivered to the consumer, for example. The campaign will spell out these targeted audiences or publics and the marketing communications tools selected to reach each public.

Media outlets are a cornerstone of most marketing communications and public relations programs; therefore, the next step is to identify the media needed to reach the targeted audience. A number of excellent publications can help you do this. Media directories and reference publications can be purchased that not only will identify various newspapers, magazines, newsletters and trade publications, but also describe the types of editorial materials published, list names of editors, and provide an address, telephone number, circulation and other pertinent information about the publication. Other media publications provide detailed information on radio and television and cable network programming, including the names, addresses and telephone numbers of individuals to contact regarding talk shows.

In any circumstance, the marketing communications professional should become familiar with a publication or program before contacting an editor or producer with an idea. Few publicity releases are ever sent to the editor in chief of a major metropolitan newspaper. Instead they are directed to an editor, columnist or writer by name or by department. A story intended for use by the business section of a newspaper could be addressed to the business editor by name, to Business Editor, or to the individual who is responsible for a specific industry.

Getting the story to the right editor is most important. Writers and editors, just like people in other fields, change jobs, get promoted, move on, retire or die. One editor noted that a public relations firm had been sending publicity releases to a person who had not been at that publication for 18 years!

The mailing list should be selective and constantly monitored to ensure its correctness. Determine the contact at each media outlet who will be most important. Purge the mailing list to make sure that there are not duplicate mailings of the same story to more than one person at a media outlet. Never "double plant" a story, by mailing the same story to more than one person, unless it is done solely for information purposes and this is noted on the mailing. By avoiding duplication and people who may not use the material sent, costs can be trimmed and the mailing budget used most effectively.

HOW TO CUSTOMIZE YOUR LISTS

Once the media for the targeted market have been identified and a list prepared, they should be segmented by audience. The publicity release intended for a trade magazine would not be the same one sent to a consumer magazine, for example, or for a radio talk show. Some lists may be used for mailing while others would be used for contact purposes. The print media probably will receive more publicity mailings than will the broadcast media.

Organize the mailing lists according to how they will be used and give each a name, letter or number. Then a cover sheet can be prepared and attached to each publicity release during the approval process so those responsible can immediately see who is scheduled to receive the mailing.

To be most effective, organize the list into sections, such as A, B or C. The A-list would be most selective and receive possibly everything that is mailed. The B-list might receive only certain mailings, the C-list even fewer. The list then should be organized into categories and alphabetized by organization or media category. Typical categories could be internal distribution, newspapers, radio, television, wire services, business magazines, trade magazines and papers, free-lance writers and miscellaneous.

The lists can be used several ways. They can be computerized or mechanized for quick retrieval and internal use. The directories can be used as a resource when needed. The list can be given to a mailing house to use when producing mailings. And there are sources that will handle distribution using their own lists.

It is important to keep any list current. This accomplishment will come through use. Some publishers of reference directories will provide periodic supplements with corrections, and these changes should be noted and entered.

HOW TO KNOW WHAT EDITORS WANT

There are newsletters and services available that will let you know what certain media may be planning for stories in order to take advantage of editorial opportunities. Following are some available subscription sources:

Bacon's Media Calendar Directory. This is a comprehensive media directory that provides complete editorial calendar information in one edition. The directory includes editorial profiles, audience information, editorial lead times for special issues and advertising and editorial contacts with rates and closing dates. The directory publishes a list of trade shows and conventions with dates, locations and contact information. Cost is $250 from Bacon's Media Directories, 332 S. Michigan Ave., Chicago, IL 60604, (312) 922-2400, (800) 621-0561, fax (312) 922-3127.

Partyline. This weekly, two-page newsletter is a roundup of media placement opportunities giving the reader information on what editors are looking for and how to contact them. The annual subscription cost is $150. Contact editor-publisher Morton Yarmon at 35 Sutton Place, New York, NY 10022, phone (212) 755-3487 or fax (212) 755-3488.

BUILDING YOUR REFERENCE LIBRARY

Many of the available directories are similar, and it is not essential to have all those recommended in this chapter. Because of changes, however, it is important to have a current edition of the publication being used. A year-old newspaper directory is just as outdated as one listing members of Congress after an election.

Leading reference libraries generally carry several of the following directories, and it may not be necessary to purchase as many as one might think to build the necessary media lists. Some of the directories outlined in this chapter also are available on computer disk. Many of the publishers will sell mailing list labels of listings from their directories.

Newspaper Directories

Bacon's Newspaper/Magazine Directory. The newspaper volume lists 1,700 U.S. and Canadian daily newspapers and 8,100 U.S. weekly newspapers. The listings for daily newspapers with circulations of 25,000 and more include the names of up to 31 department editors and four columnists. Other daily newspaper listings include 26 department editors. The volume is arranged alphabetically by state and then by cities within each state. Special lists include news services and syndicates, national newspapers, newspaper-distributed magazines and Sunday supplements, syndicated columnists, and African American presses. The magazine volume lists 9,500 business, trade, consumer and farm publications in the United States and Canada, organized into 211 market classifications. A cross-index of industry or market classifications allows custom lists to be created for specific campaigns. Listings include editorial profiles, publicity materials used and direct phone lines to editors. The subscription includes midyear updates and free phone-in updating. The two-volume set costs $270.00. Order from Bacon's Media Directories, 332 S. Michigan Ave., Chicago, IL 60604, phone (312) 922-2400, (800) 621-0561, fax (312) 922-3127.

Burrelle's Media Directory—Newspapers and Related Media. This two-volume set has nearly 1,800 pages of information about every daily newspaper and more than 9,100 weekly newspapers published in the United States. Listings include address, phone and fax numbers, circulation figures, advertising and press deadlines, wire service sources and key contacts and professional titles. The directory also includes listings of all Canadian daily newspapers. Frequency and circulation are included with a list of business, legal and religious newspapers, daily college and university newspapers, and daily and non-daily ethnic newspapers including those for Hispanic, African American, Jewish and Native American readers. Daily newspapers are listed by ADI code and circulation groups. They also are indexed by state capitals and key cities. Information is contained on newspaper-distributed magazines, newspaper-distributed supplements, and syndicate and news services. The information is offered in three formats: (1) a printed version, (2) CD-ROM format with its own search engine and electronic files in a number of software formats, and (3) a vertically integrated software package. Cost for each set is $125, printed or on computer disk. The price is less if ordered with other directories published by Burrelle's Media Directories, 75 East Northfield Ave., Livingston, NJ 07039-9873, phone (201) 992-6600 or (800) 631-1160.

Editor and Publisher Year Book. This 1,000-page newspaper encyclopedia is divided into eight sections with information on U.S. daily newspapers, U.S. weekly newspapers, Canadian newspapers, foreign newspapers, syndicates, news services, mechanical equipment and organizations. Daily newspaper information lists corporate officers, news executives, editors, department heads and columnists, circulation, advertising and mechanical information. Foreign newspapers include those of the United Kingdom and Ireland, Europe, the Caribbean, Mexico and Central America, South America, Africa, the Middle East, Asia and the Far East, Australia, New Zealand and the Pacific Ocean territories. The weekly newspaper section includes specialized publications such as African American, religious, foreign language, military, gay and lesbian and college and university newspapers. One section includes all syndicates based in the United States. The book is available for $100 from Editor and Publisher, 11 West 19th St., New York, NY 10011, phone (212) 675-4380, fax (212) 929-1259.

Working Press of the Nation Newspaper Directory. More than 7,000 daily, weekly and specialized newspapers are listed alphabetically by state, city and name. The directory has more than 60,000 contact names indexed by specific subject areas. The directory has an index of special interest newspapers including business, sports, college, agricultural, ethnic, religious, foreign language and others. It is available for $165 from National Register Publishing, P.O. Box 31, New Providence, NJ 07974-9903, phone (800) 521-8110, fax (908) 665-3560. Cost savings are available if the directory is ordered with other directories from this publisher. IBM-compatible magnetic tapes and/or diskettes can be obtained for permanent use in either a label program or for data base use.

Magazine Directories

Bacon's Newspaper/Magazine Directory. See previous listing under Newspaper Directories.

Burrelle's Media Directory—Magazines and Newsletters. This 1,310-page directory contains information on more than 12,000 trade, professional and consumer magazines and newsletters. The magazines and newsletters are separated into 290 subject classifications. Individual listings include circulation, coverage, ownership, description of editorial content and names of editors with address, phone and fax. For example, for *Country Living* the reader is told that the editors need to have a news release six months in advance of publication and that the editors are interested in "features on furnishings, interiors, cooking, antiques, home building, real estate, travel and gardening." The listing for *Hard Hat News* tells the practitioner that it is published twice a month, the editors want information related to the heavy construction equipment industry and the deadline for a news release is the Friday before publication. Special publication editions also are listed. There are indexes of cross-reference classifications and alphabetical listings by publication name. Cost for the single volume is $125, or less if purchased with other Burrelle's directories. The information also is available to purchasers on computer disk or various software formats. For information contact Burrelle's Media Directories, 75 East Northfield Ave., Livingston, NJ 07039-9873, phone (201) 992-6600 or (800) 631-1160.

National Directory of Magazines. Contains complete information on 20,000 large and small U.S. and Canadian magazines, including an extensive description of publication, staff, advertising and list rates, circulation size and production information. Cost is $395 from Oxbridge Communications, Inc., 150 Fifth Ave., Suite 636, New York, NY 10011, phone (212) 741-0231 or (800) 955-0231, fax (212) 633-2938. Computer disk called OXMODE is available for $1,500, and information and lists can be selected and sorted by advertising breakouts, printing data, direct marketing, job title, publication type and region.

Working Press of the Nation Magazines & Internal Publications Directory. More than 6,000 consumer, service, trade, professional, industrial, farm and agricultural publications are listed by subject group. An index cross-references magazines by titles and subject group. The directory has detailed information on more than 3,000 internal publications of U.S. companies, government agencies, clubs and other groups. It is available for $165 from National Register Publishing, P.O. Box 31, New Providence, NJ 07974-9903, phone (800) 521-8110, fax (908) 665-3560. IBM-compatible tapes and/or diskettes can be purchased to use for labels or a database. Cost savings are available if purchased with other directories from this publisher.

Radio and Television Directories

Bacon's Radio/TV/Cable Directory. Lists more than 9,000 radio and 1,800 television and cable stations with names of 70,000 staff contacts at thousands of news and interview shows. Separate sections for television and radio are organized geographically by state and then by city. Both sections include network affiliation, mailing and studio addresses and contacts for news, interview, and panel discussion programs. Feature sections are on networks, cable satellite systems, superstations, and radio and TV syndicators, plus an index of network and syndicated news and talk show programs with profiles and contacts as well as radio stations by format. College and public broadcasting stations are listed. Maps are included of the top 30 markets. The two-volume directory is available for $270 from Bacon's Media Directories, 332 S. Michigan Ave., Chicago, IL 60604, (312) 922-2400, (800) 621-0561, fax (312) 922-3127.

Broadcasting & Cable Yearbook. This publication lists television and radio networks; television and radio stations in the United States and Canada; cable systems and multiple system operations in the United States and Canada; public broadcasting networks and affiliates; radio and television news services; programming suppliers, producers and distributors; sports networks; and foreign language and special programming. It also contains a history of broadcasting, cable and new technologies, a guide to law and regulation, the FCC and its rules and regulations, and directories of government agencies, group ownership and media cross ownership. There also is a listing of satellite services used by North American operators and a directory of professional services such as broker and financial firms, law firms and talent agents. The 1,400-page yearbook costs $169.95. Contact Order Department, R. R. Bowker, P.O. Box 31, New Providence, NJ 07974, phone (908) 464-6800 or (800) 521-8110.

Burrelle's Media Directory—Broadcast Media. This is a two-volume set of more than 1,600 pages of information about radio, television and cable stations. The stations are listed alphabetically by state and then by the city in which each station is located. They are categorized as commercial stations, public stations, college stations and educational stations. Ownership, average audience, the station's public service announcement policy, public calendar programming and network affiliation information also are included. Part One, the first volume, lists more than 9,700 radio stations with information about types of programs and interviews the station broadcasts and names of key executive and programming personnel. Part Two lists more than 1,450 television stations and 550 cable systems with over 25,000 subscribers. Cost for the set is $250. As with other Burrelle's directories, information is available in a printed version, CD-ROM format with its own search engine and electronic files in a number of software formats, or a vertically integrated software package. Published by Burrelle's Media Directories, 75 East Northfield Ave., Livingston, NJ 07039-9873, phone (201) 992-6600 or (800) 631-1160.

Talk Show Selects. For anyone interested in placing a company representative on a radio or television talk show, this 300-page directory in a convenient three-ring binder profiles 780 of the most influential talk show hosts, producers and programming executives. The contacts listed are those who are responsible for deciding who does and does not get on the air. In addition to the show name, call letters, street address, phone and fax numbers, every listing has the name of the right person to contact, whether it is the host, producer, talent coordinator or program director. Only regularly scheduled programs with substantial audiences are chosen.

The directory gives detailed market reports of the top 25 markets in the country. A call letter index organizes the stations alphabetically. ADI information, network affiliation and station format also are included. Here is a listing, for example, for "Ron Seggi's Startalk" on the Universal Studios Radio Network: "Includes live interviews with four guests daily, airing M-F, 10:00 a.m.-12:00 p.m. (ET). All fields of entertainment with some health and politics. Also heard internationally in 86 countries." The producer is listed with phone, fax and address for this Universal Studios Radio Network program. For the Jim Whitmeyer "Talk of the Town" program at WAAV-AM in Wilmington, N.C., the listing is: "'Talk of the Town' is a M-F, 6-8 a.m. (ET) general interest magazine program. Co-hosted by Donn Ansell. Telephone guests cannot take calls from listeners, in-studio guests can. Show covers newsy topics like environment, nuclear energy, tobacco, education, sports. No fluff please. Potential guests should mail information first then call." Cost for the directory is $185.00 from Broadcast Interview Source, 2233 Wisconsin Ave. N.W., Suite 540, Washington, DC 20007, phone (202) 333-4904 or (800) 955-0311, fax (202) 342-5411. Computer disks are available on IBM or Macintosh, dBase IV, WordPerfect or ASCII.

Television & Cable Factbook. Three volumes provide detailed information on every television station in the United States, Canada and major foreign markets. Cable systems are listed alphabetically by state and city with information on equipment and key personnel. One volume is a buyer's guide that also lists regulatory agencies, program sources and pertinent congressional committees. Available for $405 from Warren Publishing Inc., 2115 Ward Court N.W., Washington, DC 20037, phone (202) 872-9200, fax (202) 293-3435.

The Top 200+ National TV, News, Talk and Magazine Shows. This report features the top 200 national television news, talk and magazine shows, who to contact, how to book the show, what subjects the show is interested in, names of the hosts and other details. It is directed at anyone wanting to book a guest appearance on a national television talk show. Cost is $30 from Ad-Lib Publications, P.O. Box 1102, Fairfield, Iowa 52556, phone (515) 472-6617 or (800) 669-0773, fax (515) 472-3186.

Working Press of the Nation TV and Radio Directory. Lists more than 13,000 radio and television stations and networks including key personnel names and titles. More than 25,000 local radio programs are listed by subject with names of radio directors and personnel by interest area, such as disc jockeys, farm directors and sports directors. Price is $165 for the individual volume or discounted if purchased with other directories from National Register Publishing, P.O. Box 31, New Providence, NJ 07974-9903, phone (800) 521-8110, fax (908) 665-3560. Also available with IBM-compatible magnetic tapes or diskettes for label or data base programs.

International Directories

Bacon's International Media Directory. This book lists more than 22,000 business, trade and consumer publications and more than 1,000 national and regional newspapers for 16 western European countries. It is organized alphabetically by country, and magazine listings are divided into 64 major market classifications. Magazine and newspaper listings include full mailing addresses, telephone and telex numbers, editors' names, publication frequency and circulation. A unique publicity coding indicates the types of releases accepted by each magazine. Available for $270 from Bacon's Media Directories,

332 S. Michigan Ave., Chicago, IL 60604, phone (312) 922-2400, (800) 621-0561, fax (312) 922-3127.

Editor and Publisher Year Book. See previous listing under Newspaper Directories.

Encyclopedia of Associations: International Organizations. This annual directory lists more than 13,500 multinational membership organizations from Afghanistan to Zimbabwe, including U.S.-based organizations with a binational or multinational membership. The two-volume, 2,800-page resource lists names of directors, executive officers and other personal contacts complete with a mailing address and English translations for organizations with foreign-language names. Entries are arranged in 15 general subjects including business, law and government, science and technology, education, culture, health and medicine, religion and sports. Indexes allow organizations to be checked geographically, by executive or by name or subject of organization. Cost is $490 from Gale Research Inc., P.O. Box 33477, Detroit, MI 48232-5477, phone (800) 877-4253, fax (313) 961-6083.

Guía de medios centroamericanos de communicación (Central America and Panama). This 287-page directory lists more than 4,000 individual news media, foreign correspondents, journalist associations, advertising agencies and public relations firms, embassy and government press representatives and journalism school faculties. Cost is $45 from Latin American Journalism Program, Florida International University, 3000 N.E. 145th St., North Miami, FL 33181, phone (305) 940-5672, fax (305) 956-5498.

Hollis Europe. While this is primarily a 700-page guide to 3,000 public relations agencies and the public relations contacts at more than 500 of the leading companies in 30 western, central and eastern European countries, it also lists research and information sources, public relations support companies and U.S. headquarters of international networks. Cost is 99 pounds for an annual subscription with updates. Contact Hollis Directories Ltd., Contact House, Sunbury-on-Thames, Middlesex, Great Britain, TW16 5BR, phone 0932 784781 (within UK) or 44 932 784781 (outside UK), fax 0932 787844 (within UK) or 44 932 787844 (outside UK).

Hollis Press & Public Relations Annual. This 1,000-page reference is a complete guide to doing business in the United Kingdom. In addition to listing media sources and news contacts, it lists contacts for official and government bodies, embassies, educational institutions and environmental and nonprofit organizations. Also included are in-house prolocutors in industry, the arts and trade associations as well as public relations firms and their clients. The guide can be ordered for a full subscription service including three updated supplements for 89.99 pounds or 69.99 pounds for the book only. Contact Hollis Directories Ltd., Contact House, Sunbury-on-Thames, Middlesex, Great Britain TW16 5 HG, 0932 784781 (within UK) or 44 932 784781 (outside the UK), fax 0932 787844 (within UK) or 44 932 787844 (outside UK).

Media People—The Media Guide (Australia). This directory lists all metropolitan, suburban and regional press, radio and television stations in Australia plus all public relations companies and accredited advertising agencies and media bodies such as the Australian Broadcasting Authority. The company also publishes a comprehensive monthly updated *Media People Guide,* which gives information and contacts as well as personnel and programming. Services also include contact lists and press release distribution. Cost is $A 58.50 from Media Monitors, P.O. Box 2110, Strawberry Hills, New South Wales 2012, Australia, phone (02) 310-3155, fax (02) 319-0616.

The Uplinker. This complete television reference source lists 416 television networks in 161 countries with names of more than 2,400 executives with name, title, address, telephone, fax and telex. Executives listed include managers, program people, department heads, heads of production, and those in charge of sports, news, engineering, and sales acquisitions. In many cases the private telephone and private fax numbers of the people are included. The directory lists the transmission system of each country (NTSC, PAL or SECAM), Greenwich Mean Time of each country, the number of television sets in use within a given country and satellite signatories and capabilities. The directory also lists 128 international distributors of television programming and 22 broadcast organizations and associations as well as the top 50 television markets according to television sets. Cost is $100 from Uplinker Enterprises, P.O. Box 1058, Larkspur, CA 94977, phone (415) 927-7878, fax (415) 924-0707.

World Radio TV Handbook. This 580-page guide lists the world's radio and television networks and stations and their frequencies with addresses and telephone, fax and telex numbers. The book lists important international broadcasting and intergovernmental organizations. User's guide is in English, French, German and Spanish. Cost is $19.95 from Watson-Guptill Publications, Inc., 1515 Broadway, New York, NY 10036, phone (212) 764-7300, fax (212) 536-5359.

The World's News Media. This comprehensive reference guide gives a country-by-country overview of press and broadcast media and media organizations around the world. It provides names and addresses, circulation data, political organization, editorial politics, historical background and the restrictions and regulations under which the organizations operate. Available for $198 from Gale Research Inc., P.O. Box 33477 Detroit, MI 48232-5477, phone (313) 961-2242, fax (313) 961-6241.

Multimedia Directories

All-In-One Directory. This 6 by 9-inch, 500-page, spiral-bound directory lists more than 21,000 outlets including all daily newspapers, all weekly newspapers, all television stations, and all radio stations as well as African American and Hispanic media, farm publications, trade press, general and consumer magazines and news syndicates. Cost is $80 from Gebbie Press, P.O. Box 1000, New Paltz, NY 12561-0017, phone (914) 255-7560. Available on IBM-compatible and Macintosh computer disks at $95 per set or three sets for $257.

Gale Directory of Publications and Broadcast Media. This guide has been expanded to 43,000 entries including listings for radio and television stations and cable companies. The entries are arranged geographically in two volumes. The third volume has a map reference section and a geographical listing of newspaper feature editors, 16 magazine and newspaper subject indexes, a radio station format index and a master name and keyword index. The set is available for $340 from Gale Research Inc., P.O. Box 33477, Detroit, MI 48232-5477, phone (800) 766-4253, fax (313) 961-6083.

National PR Pitch Book. This book indexes media by newspapers, magazines, wire services, television, radio and national and cable shows. Some 12,000 names are included as contacts with direct telephone lines, fax numbers and mail information. Included are 176 newspapers with more than 100,000 circulation and all 279 local news and talk radio stations in the top 20 ADI markets. All 216 top television stations and local programs are included in the top 20 ADI markets. The book has individual comments about the recommended contacts. For example, here is what is listed for Bob Magnuson, business editor of *The Los Angeles Times:* "Bob Magnuson says the section emphasizes personal finance, consumer news, technology—wants to make news 'necessary.' Prefers news releases. Will interview or attend press conferences anytime, if important. Please, no unsolicited faxes. If you must fax, address information to appropriate editor." Here is the listing for Jennifer Raemsch, the fashion and style producer for ABC News's "Good Morning America": "(Pron. 'ramsh.') There's no idea that isn't a good idea. Fashion segments cover all aspects of the industry. Designers are brought on air for demonstrations, explanations. Two stories per month, run when appropriate: e.g., when a major trend has emerged or at the start of a clothing season. Segments don't focus on one company's product, but on different products related by theme. Provide photos. Follow-ups unhelpful unless release is extremely timely; otherwise Raemsch will call you if interested. (212) 456-5920." Cost is $345.00 from Bulldog Reporter, 2115 Fourth St., Berkeley, CA 94710, phone (800) 959-1059 or fax (510) 549-4342.

News Media Yellow Book. Lists 20,000 journalists and opinion makers at more than 2,900 national media organizations. Includes news services, feature syndicates, syndicated columnists, newspapers, news bureaus, radio and television stations and networks, cable systems, trade and consumer magazines, newsletters and foreign media. Names of journalists covering 150 outlets range from art and aviation to the White House. Published semiannually, the cost is $170 for two editions from Monitor Leadership Directories, Inc., 104 Fifth Ave., 2nd Floor, New York, NY 10011, phone (212) 627-4140, fax (212) 645-0931.

Periodical Title Abbreviations. This two-volume directory translates 145,000 different abbreviations for magazine, journal and newspaper abbreviations into full titles by both periodical title and abbreviation. The reference includes both U.S. and foreign periodicals, lists major sources of abbreviations for future reference and identifies duplicated abbreviations. Each volume costs $200—by abbreviation or by title. Order from Gale Research Inc., P.O. Box 33477, Detroit, MI 48232-5477, phone (800) 766-4253, fax (313) 961-6083.

Power Media Selects. This 243-page loose-leaf directory comes in a three-ring binder and identifies 700 of the most influential print and broadcast media outlets. Listings are by media category and type of news covered, contact name and title, publication, column or program name, phone, street address and fax. Included are 2,312 journalists and 834 news organizations at news wire services (AP, UPI and Reuters); news and feature syndicates including Dow Jones News Service and King Features; syndicated columnists; national newspapers; Sunday supplements; top daily newspapers and magazines as well as topical and special interest magazines and newsletters; and network and top market radio and television talk shows. The editors have written comments with most of the listings. For example, for Dow Jones News Service in San Francisco: "Brief phone calls are accepted, but Dow Jones editors and reporters tend to pick up news off PR Newswire and BusinessWire first. Faxed news releases also receive attention. Include the name and phone of the chief financial officer of the company." To help its users, this is what the directory wrote about *Mother Jones* magazine: "Just slightly or more to the Environmental Right. MJ would be happy if we all rode bicycles and stopped using disposable diapers." Demographic information also is included, such as this listing for *Redbook:* "Description: nutrition, medical, beauty, fiction. Target audience: young mothers with family and job, ages 25 to 44 years. If Mom reads it, so does her daughter. Loyal following, well earned." Available for $166.50 from Broadcast Interview Source, 2233 Wisconsin Ave. N.W., Suite 540, Washington, DC 20007, phone (202) 333-4904 or (800) 955-0311, fax (202) 342-5411. The directory is available on computer disks in IBM or Macintosh on dBase IV, WordPerfect or ASCII.

Standard Periodical Directory. More than 85,000 U.S. and Canadian periodicals are contained in this comprehensive directory, arranged in alphabetical sequence by subject from accounting to zoology. Price is $495 for the directory or $695 for a CD-ROM computer disk that allows a quick search of facts and data ranging from publishing and circulation to production and advertising. There is a discount if both are purchased. For information contact Oxbridge Communications, 150 Fifth Ave., Suite 636, New York, NY 10011, phone (212) 741-0231 or (800) 955-0231, fax (212) 633-2938.

Regional Directories

Chicago Media Directory. Published by the Publicity Club of Chicago, this contains a media section and a listing of the club's members. The *Chicago Sun-Times* and *Chicago Tribune* listings are departmentalized with editors and reporters by beat. The community newspaper section lists each paper separately. Television audience figures are included with network newscast listings and radio summaries show the station and its location. There are sections listing professional organizations and resources. Cost is $95 for non-members from the Publicity Club of Chicago, 200 N. Michigan Ave., #300, Chicago, IL 60601, phone (312) 541-1272, fax (312) 541-1271.

Greater Philadelphia Publicity Guide. This 279-page directory lists media contacts in the eight-county Greater Philadelphia area including daily and non-daily newspapers, special interest and trade publications, ethnic and foreign-language publications, college and university student newspapers, wire services and news bureaus, cable television systems and radio and television stations with interview, news and public service personnel. Cost is $51.95 from Balset Company, Box 365, Ambler, PA 19002, phone (215) 628-8729.

Hudson's State Capitals News Media Directory. The only directory devoted exclusively to the press corps covering the 50 state capitals, this 316-page directory lists 2,448 news outlets, including wire services, local and suburban newspapers, out-of-town newspapers, radio and television stations, magazines and newsletters and radio and television guest interview and discussion programs. Available for $99 from Hudson's Media Directories, P.O. Box 311, Rhinebeck, NY 12572, phone (914) 876-2081.

Hudson's Washington News Media Contacts Directory. This 466-page guide to the media in the United States capital lists 4,671 contacts in news bureaus, newspapers, radio, television, news services, magazines, newsletters and syndicates along with 5,036 correspondents and editors. The directory is published quarterly and is divided into 27 sections, including state-by-state listings of radio and television stations and newspapers represented in Washington, D.C. Fax numbers are included. Cost is $155 from Hudson's Media Directories, P.O. Box 311, Rhinebeck, NY 12572, phone (914) 876-2081.

Metro California Media. Listings for 3,442 print and broadcast media and 9,537 contacts are included in this 500-page directory. It includes all daily and weekly newspapers, ethnic publications, consumer magazines and syndicated writers in California. Radio and television stations, cable systems and news service bureaus are included. Sources are listed alphabetically for 22 metropolitan areas. Cost is $139.50 from Public Relations Plus, Inc., P.O. Box 1197, New Milford, CT 06776, phone (800) 999-8448.

New Jersey Media Guide. This 254-page directory lists all 567 New Jersey towns with the daily and non-daily newspapers as well as radio, television and cable television stations. Media information includes address, phone, fax, ownership and key editors. The guide is available for $89.95 plus $5 postage and handling from Resource Communications Group, 3011 North Lamar Blvd., Austin, TX 78705, phone (800) 331-5076, fax (512) 458-2059.

New York Publicity Outlets. This 500-page directory has 10,387 contacts at 2,852 print and broadcast media in the metropolitan New York area complete with addresses, phone numbers and fax numbers. There are an average of 3,500 changes in listings each year. Included are names of editors, reporters, columnists, correspondents and bureau chiefs as well as contacts at radio and television stations and networks. The directory is available for $139.50 from Public Relations Plus, Inc., P.O. Box 1197, New Milford, CT 06776, phone (800) 999-8448.

Vermont Media Directory. This publication contains information on more than 200 Vermont and bordering states' newspapers, magazines, radio and television stations and college publications. The directory also includes practical how-to-get-publicity sections with media tips, placing feature stories and working with local media. Cost is $141.50 including shipping from Kelliher/Samets/Volk, 212 Battery St., Burlington, VT 05401, phone (802) 862-8261.

Virginia/DC Comprehensive Media Guide. This directory lists more than 2,000 contact names at 555 media organizations in Virginia and the District of Columbia, including bureaus, and is divided into six sections: (1) all media, (2) daily newspapers, (3) non-daily newspapers, (4) radio, (5) television and (6) wire services. Each entry lists mailing and street addresses as well as phone and fax numbers. Cost is $46.95. A companion directory, *The Media Market Guide,* which sorts the region's media into 19 distinctive markets, is available for $115.95. Mailing labels as well as computer disks also are available. For information contact Dominion Media Services Co., P.O. Box 29352, Richmond, VA 23242, phone and fax (804) 360-7000.

Newsletter Directories

Burrelle's Media Directory—Magazines and Newsletters. See previous listing under Magazine Directories.

Hudson's Subscription Newsletter Directory. This 12th-edition directory lists 4,200 business, professional and consumer newsletters worldwide by 46 major subject headings, which are further broken down into 157 categories. Each newsletter listing gives the name of the publication, the publishing company, address, telephone number and fax, names of editor and publisher, subscription price, frequency, founding date and press release information. It includes alphabetical and geographic indexes and lists of publishers who publish three or more newsletters. It is available for $140 from Hudson's Media Directories, P.O. Box 311, Rhinebeck, NY 12572, phone (914) 876-2081.

Newsletters in Print. More than 12,000 newsletters are listed on 1,500 pages and divided into seven broad categories and 33 specific subjects. Topics include business and industry; family and everyday living; information and communications; agriculture and life sciences; community and world affairs; science and technology; and liberal arts. Indexes and appendices by title, keyword, subject, publisher and other areas simplify tracking down specifics. Available for $185 from Gale Research Inc., P.O. Box 33477, Detroit, MI 48232-5477, phone (800) 877-4253, fax (313) 961-6083.

Oxbridge Directory of Newsletters. Some 20,000 North American newsletters are listed in 168 subject categories on 1,000 pages, indexed by title, with complete editorial and subscription information. Cost is $395 from Oxbridge Communications, Inc., 150 Fifth Ave., Suite 636, New York, NY 10011, phone (212) 741-0231 or (800) 955-0231, fax (212) 633-2938.

Specialized Media Publications

Associations Yellow Book. This volume is published semiannually and contains names, addresses, phone and fax numbers of officers and management for more than 1,150 trade and professional organizations in the United States. Budgets also are included. Price is $170 for two editions from Monitor Leadership Directories, Inc., 104 Fifth Ave., 2nd Floor, New York, NY 10011, phone (212) 627-4140, fax (212) 645-0931.

Business and Financial News Media. This specialized directory lists editors, reporters and columnists of major daily newspapers, magazines and radio and television outlets who specialize in covering business and financial news. Independent writers, nationally syndicated columnists, wire services, newspaper groups and news bureaus also are listed. If you wanted to promote a business news story in Ohio, the directory would enable you to find all major newspapers, local TV and radio shows and all their business contacts in that state. The computer disk could help prepare a report or labels. The directory is available printed at $155, in a computer disk version for either IBM or Macintosh (or compatible equipment) at $255 or a combination of both for $355 from Larriston Communications, P.O. Box 20229, New York, NY 10025-1518, phone (212) 864-0150, fax (212) 662-8103. The contacts also are available on labels for $140 or four sets of labels for $475.

Business Media Directory. More than 8,000 business editors, beat reporters, columnists, free-lancers and show producers at more than 1,000 top newspapers, magazines, and radio and television stations are listed in this 6 by 9-inch ring binder. The directory provides full address, phone/fax, profiles, station target audience, indexes of subject specialists, personnel and media. The $250 cost includes midyear printed updates. Contact Bacon's Media Directories, 332 S. Michigan Ave., Chicago, IL 60604, phone (312) 922-2400, (800) 621-0561, fax (312) 922-3127.

Caduceus 94* [or current year]*: The Health and Medical Media Directory. Contacts at national and local print, television and radio outlets and more than 200 medical publications are listed in this directory. It also includes the profiles of more than 500 reporters who were surveyed by the publisher. The 400-page directory comes in a three-ring binder, and the $339 cost includes three updates during the year. Contact Caduceus Communications, Inc., 1300 West Belmont, Suite 402, Chicago, IL 60657, phone (800) 229-1832.

College Media Directory. There is information in this directory on frequency, circulation, publication, advisor, budget, sources of financing, advertising and subscription rates of 6,000 student and alumni newspapers, humor magazines, art and literary journals, and yearbooks on 3,500 campuses. Lists also include names, addresses and phone numbers of presidents and student activities directors. Price is $145 from Oxbridge Communications, Inc., 150 Fifth Ave., Suite 636, New York, NY 10011, phone (212) 741-0231 or (800) 955-0231, fax (212) 633-2938.

Computer Media Directory. This professional reference source has information on more than 800 publications covering the general micro-, mini- and miniframe computer markets plus those dedicated to electronics engineering and design, specialized vertical markets, computer manufacturing and technology marketing and distribution. The information is in a three-ring binder and lists more than 2,800 editors, reporters and columnists who staff the publications that cover the computer, office automation and electronics technology fields in the United States and Canada. The listings include the individual's job title, area of interest, mailing address and phone numbers. Updated quarterly, the directory provides subscribers with a current summary of the editorial calendar schedules for the top 100 computer publications. Cost is $295 for the directory with quarterly updates; available for $100 in IBM-compatible and Macintosh diskettes. Contact Morrisey Standard, 724 Gilman St., Berkeley, CA 94701, phone (510) 525-4691, (800) WOW-BOOK (in U.S.) or (800) PR-MEDIA (in Canada), fax (510) 525-2501.

Directory of Women's Media. A 120-page edition listing media by, for and about women. Listed are national and international periodicals, publishers, news services, radio and TV outlets, cable TV stations, bookstores and special library collections. The 1989 edition is $25 from the Women's Institute for Freedom of the Press, 3306 Ross Place N.W., Washington, DC 20008, phone (202) 966-7783. A current edition is being published by the National Council for Research on Women, 530 Broadway, 10th Floor, New York, NY 10012, phone (212) 274-0730.

Encyclopedia of Associations. This three-volume, 3,500-page directory is a prime source for information on more than 22,500 organizations with national membership. Complete information is included on trade and professional associations, social welfare and public affairs organizations, labor unions, fraternal and patriotic organizations, and religious, sports and hobby groups with voluntary members. The 1994 edition includes 700 new organizations and over 100,000 revisions and updates from the previous year. Cost is $375 from Gale Research Inc., P.O. Box 33477, Detroit, MI 48232-5477, phone (800) 877-4253, fax (313) 961-6083. Also available on CD-ROM and on-line through DIALOG as well as on diskette and magnetic tape.

Jewish Press in America. This directory lists all Jewish newspapers and magazines in the United States and Canada. It is available for $15 from Joseph Jacobs Organization, Inc., 60 East 42nd St., New York, NY 10165, phone (212) 687-6234, fax (212) 687-9785.

Medical and Science News Media. Media that specialize in medical and science news are featured in this guide. More than 2,000 contacts are listed in radio, TV, cable outlets, networks, major daily newspapers, general and specialized medical and science magazines, on-line services, wire services, newspaper groups and news bureaus. Cost is $155 or $255 for an IBM- or Mac-compatible computer disk. The cost for both book and disk is $355. Labels are available for $140 or four sets at $475. Contact Larriston Communications, P.O. Box 20229, New York, NY 10026-1518, phone (212) 864-0150, fax (212) 662-8103.

National Directory of Corporate Public Affairs. This comprehensive guide lists 14,000 public relations and public affairs professionals from 2,000 corporations engaged in corporate public, community, investor, consumer, media, legislative and regulatory relations. Corporate foundations and contributions are published as well as political action committees and the major candidates they support. Also listed are in-house state and federal lobbyists and contract lobbyists at the state capitals. Available for $90 from Columbia Books, Inc., 1212 New York Ave. N.W., Washington, DC 20006, phone (202) 898-0662.

National Directory of Mailing Lists. There are 15,000 available responder mailing lists in this one-volume book available for $345 from Oxbridge Communications, Inc., 150 Fifth Ave., Suite 302, New York, NY 10011, phone (212) 741-0231 or (800) 955-0231, fax (212) 633-2938.

National Trade and Professional Associations of the U.S. This directory lists 7,500 trade associations, professional societies and labor organizations with national memberships. The primary index is arranged alphabetically by organization name. Five subsidiary indexes are organized by acronym, subject of interest, executive's name, budget and geographic location. Price is $75 from Columbia Books, Inc., 1212 New York Ave. N.W., Washington, DC 20005, phone (202) 898-0662.

Senior Media Directory. More than 900 special news and marketing media covering 65 million people over the age of 50 are in this special directory. Newspapers, magazines, newsletters, syndicates, daily newspaper supplements, columnists, radio and TV shows that are directed to senior citizens are included. Media represent every major market area. Cost is $45 plus postage and handling from GEM Publishing Group, 250 East Riverview Circle, Reno, NV 89509, phone (702) 786-7419, fax (702) 786-7856.

Society of American Travel Writers Directory. This contains the names, business addresses and telephone numbers of over 500 of the top newspaper and magazine travel editors and writers, syndicated travel columnists, freelance writers, photojournalists and radio and television broadcasters who cover the travel industry in the United States and Canada. In addition the directory lists more than 300 executives in public relations who handle tourist attractions; domestic and foreign tourist offices; air, sea and rail carriers; and hotels; as well as public relations agencies that handle travel accounts. The book is available for $95 from the Society of American Travel Writers, 1155 Connecticut Ave. N.W., Suite 500, Washington, DC 20036.

Travel, Leisure & Entertainment News Media. Another guide from Larriston, this volume allows the professional to target media in this specialized field. The book costs $155, a computer disk $255 or both purchased at the same time $355. Labels are available for $140 or a set of four for $475. Contact Larriston Communications, P.O. Box 20229, New York, NY 10026-1518, phone (212) 864-0150, fax (212) 662-8103.

Working Press of the Nation Feature Writers, Photographers, & Professional Speakers Directory. Lists 4,000 leading free-lance writers and free-lance photographers, their areas of expertise and home addresses and telephone numbers. Also lists hundreds of professional speakers with addresses, association membership, principal topics and typical audience. Available for $165 from National Register Publishing, P.O. Box 31, New Providence, NJ 07974-9903, phone (800) 521-8110, fax (908) 665-3560. Available on IBM-compatible magnetic tapes or diskettes in a label program or for data base use. Cost savings are offered for purchase of other directories.

Federal, State and Local Government Directories

Congressional Directory. The official, 1,200-page publication of the United States Congress, this comprehensive directory lists all members of Congress, committees and staffs, and key aides in the administration, from the White House to the federal agencies. Available for $27 in hardcover thumb-indexed, $20 hardcover and $16 softcover from the Superintendent of Documents, United States Government Printing Office, Washington, DC 20402.

Congressional Pictorial Directory. Photographs and contact information are included on all members of Congress in this handy pocket-size directory. Cost is $15 hardcover and $5 softcover from the Superintendent of Documents, United States Government Printing Office, Washington, DC 20402.

Congressional Staff Directory. This comprehensive publication has detailed biographies of all members of Congress and biographies of more than 3,200 staff members. Committees and subcommittees and staffs are included as well as home state and district office addresses, telephones and staff. It is published each May and October for $69 from Staff Directories, Ltd., P.O. Box 62, Mt. Vernon, VA 22121-0062, phone (703) 739-0900, fax (703) 739-2964. Also available on both 5¼-inch and 3½-inch computer disks for $450.

Congressional Yellow Book. This 750-page compendium of Congress lists all senators and representatives and their staffs, including photographs and biographical information. Included are jurisdictions, membership rosters and key staff aides for the more than 300 congressional committees and subcommittees. Published quarterly, the price is $225 for the four-edition subscription. Available from Monitor Leadership Directories, Inc., 104 Fifth Ave., 2nd Floor, New York, NY 10011, phone (212) 627-4140, fax (212) 645-0931.

County Executive Directory. This source covers 27,149 officials in more than 3,100 governments throughout the United States. Special features include vital statistics for counties with populations greater than 25,000 and complete listings of county council members and their office phone numbers for counties with populations over 50,000. The 375-page reference is updated and published in full twice a year. Cost is $140 from Carroll Publishing Company, 1058 Thomas Jefferson St. N.W., Washington, DC 20077-0007, phone (202) 333-8620, fax (202) 337-7020.

Federal Executive Directory. This directory combines the executive and legislative branches of government in one volume with information on more than 35,000 key officials. Committee assignments and biographical profiles for members of Congress are included. This book is updated and published in full six times a year and is purchased by subscription for $197 from Carroll Publishing Company, 1058 Thomas Jefferson St. N.W., Washington, DC 20077-0007, phone (202) 333-8620, fax (202) 337-7020.

Federal Regional Executive Directory. Another Carroll publication, this book provides complete contact information for more than 19,000 non-Washington-based executive managers in Cabinet departments, Congress, the courts and administrative agencies. Special listings include Federal Regional Depository Libraries, Federal Information Centers and agency abbreviations. Updated and published in full twice a year, it costs $140. Order from Carroll Publishing Company, 1058 Thomas Jefferson St. N.W., Washington, DC 20077-0007, phone (202) 333-8620, fax (202) 337-7020.

Federal Staff Directory. This guide contains 1,464 pages of detailed information listing 33,000 key federal executives and military leaders who draft regulations, interpret and implement policy, disseminate information, contract for goods and services, and make government decisions in general. Information is contained on the various federal departments, independent agencies and the executive office of the president. There are more than 2,600 biographies. Published in March and September at a cost of $69 each from Staff Directories, Ltd., P.O. Box 62, Mt. Vernon, VA 22121-0062, phone (703) 739-0900, fax (703) 739-2964.

Federal Yellow Book. This 900-page directory lists administrative and policy-making appointees and staff from the White House to federal agencies in Washington and across the United States. Lists key direct-dial telephone numbers within federal departments and agencies as well as names, titles and phones and office locations of top officials and key staff aides. Published quarterly, the price is $225 for a four-edition subscription. Available from Monitor Leadership Directories, Inc., 104 Fifth Ave., 2nd Floor, New York, NY 10011, phone (212) 627-4140, fax (212) 645-0931.

Judicial Staff Directory. Information on more than 1,300 federal judges and their staff in 207 federal courts appears in this 944-page directory. There are more than 5,000 individual names, job titles, addresses and telephone numbers and more than 1,900 biographies of federal judges, magistrates, circuit executives, clerks of court, probation officers and public defenders. Listings include staffs of all federal, circuit, district and bankruptcy courts as well as national courts such as the Supreme Court, Claims Court, Tax Court and others. Published annually in November for $69 from Staff Directories, Ltd., P.O. Box 62, Mt. Vernon, VA 22121-1062, phone (703) 739-0900, fax (703) 739-2964.

Municipal Executive Directory. This directory lists more than 33,000 elected, appointed and career officials in 7,200 cities, towns and villages across the United States. An information capsule for each municipality with a population over 15,000 includes population statistics, county, locator phone number and municipal personnel. The book is updated and published in full twice a year. Cost is $140 from Carroll Publishing Company, 1058 Thomas Jefferson St. N.W., Washington, DC 20077-0007, phone (202) 333-8620, fax (202) 337-7020.

Municipal Yellow Book. Published semiannually, this is a who's who of leading city and county governments and local authorities with names, titles and phone numbers of nearly 25,000 key decision makers in local governments. In 700 pages are comprehensive listings of all departments, agencies, subdivisions and branches. New editions are completely updated twice a year. Cities and counties are indexed by population. Price is $170 for the two edition subscription from Monitor Leadership Directories, Inc., 104 Fifth Ave., 2nd Floor, New York, NY 10011, phone (212) 627-4140, fax (212) 645-0931.

State Executive Directory. More than 92,000 entries list more than 37,000 people, functions and offices of state governments in all 50 states, the District of Columbia, Puerto Rico and the American territories. Special listings include governors, legislative sessions, state supreme courts and state offices in Washington. Updated and published in full three times a year. Cost is $170 from Carroll Publishing Company, 1058 Thomas Jefferson St. N.W., Washington, DC 20077-0007, phone (202) 333-8620, fax (202) 337-7020.

State Yellow Book. Another *Yellow Book* from Monitor with lists of more than 35,000 leaders of 50 states, the District of Columbia and four U.S. territories. Provides a wide range of historical, statistical and geographical data, profiles on all 50 states and helpful information on counties. Published quarterly, the cost is $225 for four editions. Contact Monitor Leadership Directories, Inc., 104 Fifth Ave., 2nd Floor, New York, NY 10011, phone (212) 627-4140, fax (212) 645-0931.

U.S. Department of State Diplomatic List. This directory lists, alphabetically by country, the names, addresses and phone numbers for all the diplomatic missions in the United States. The name of the ambassador, his or her spouse and key staff are contained in this booklet. Available for $1.75 from the Superintendent of Documents, U.S. Government Printing Office, Washington, DC 20402.

U.S. Department of State Key Officers of Foreign Service Posts. This 100-page, pocket-size booklet is alphabetized by country and lists the U.S. ambassador and key staff as well as consular posts throughout the world. U.S. mailing addresses, local addresses and telephone and telex numbers are included. Cost is $4.50 from the Superintendent of Documents, U.S. Government Printing Office, Washington, DC 20402.

U.S. Government Organizational Manual. This official handbook of the U.S. government provides comprehensive information on the agencies of the legislative, judicial and executive branches. It also includes information on quasi-official agencies, international organizations in which the United States participates, and boards, committees and commissions. A typical agency description includes a list of principal officials, a summary statement of the agency's purpose and role in the federal government, a brief history of the agency, including its legislative or executive authority, a description of its programs and activities, and a Source of Information section. This last section provides information on consumer activities, contracts and grants, employment publications and many other areas of public interest. Available for $21 from the Superintendent of Documents, U.S. Government Printing Office, Washington, DC 20402.

Washington Representatives. More than 14,000 key personalities and firms, as well as key executive branch lobbyists in the federal government, are listed in this 900-page guide to Washington, D.C. Listings are both by the representative firms and the organizations which are represented. The book lists employees, legal counsel and special consultants to more than 11,000 U.S. and foreign organizations, and it is indexed by subject and foreign country. Price is $70 from Columbia Books, Inc., 1212 New York Ave. N.W., Washington, DC 20005, phone (202) 898-0662.

Public Relations Resources

The J. R. O'Dwyer Company publishes a number of newsletters and directories, including *O'Dwyer's PR Services Report,* which includes an annual buyer's guide. Information is available from the J. R. O'Dwyer Company, 271 Madison Ave., New York, NY 10016, phone (212) 679-2471.

4

HOW TO USE SPECIAL DISTRIBUTION SERVICES

Getting the message out is one thing. Having it received is completely another. Once almost all publicity releases were sent by mail. In a few metropolitan areas and depending on the urgency, they may be hand-delivered by messenger.

Today there are as many different distribution service organizations as there are sophisticated delivery systems and state-of-the-art computer and electronic technology that one can use to get the story to the media. Many newspaper editors do not even open obvious publicity releases—or, when opened, do not read the story. The practitioner needs to be just as creative and selective in the organization and method of distribution used as in preparing the campaign and the message to be told.

Some of the available systems include:

- Private public relations wire services
- In-house computer delivery system
- Facsimile (fax) transmission
- Specialized mailing services
- Syndicated public relations release services
- Photo distribution services
- Overnight courier or special messenger

PUBLIC RELATIONS WIRE SERVICES

The electronic transmission of news releases to news media was pioneered by PR Newswire in New York City in 1954. At first regarded as a novelty and used primarily to issue general citywide and entertainment news and memos, the new network soon gained acceptance from editors and public relations practitioners as a unique and reliable method of high-speed, simultaneous news release distribution. By the time the "go-go" stock market of the early 1960s arrived, PR Newswire and other services patterned after it had become vital distribution tools for those involved in financial and investor relations. Business and financial news soon accounted for more than half of all the releases flowing across the country's public relations wires.

The Securities and Exchange Commission, various stock exchanges and other regulatory agencies require timely disclosure to the news media of information that could affect the market price of, or an investor's decision to buy or sell, a company's stock. This information includes announcements regarding earnings, acquisitions and mergers, or major contract awards.

Until private public relations wire services such as PR Newswire, Business Wire and others were established, newspapers, trade publications and radio and television stations subscribed to general wire services such as Associated Press, United Press International and Reuters. With no guarantee that any of the major wire services would use a company's financial publicity release, the private wire services guaranteed their customers that the message would be delivered promptly and simultaneously to those outlets required to comply with securities regulations and many more as well.

Based on the success of delivering stories to financial editors and having an established network of media throughout the country, PR Newswire and Business Wire expanded their services. Today both can provide instant access to almost any point in the world. Custom services include a range of distribution possibilities, from meeting minimum financial disclosure requirements to delivering a story to entertainment publications, sports media, environmental writers, energy news outlets and even international media and financial analysts. These two organizations provide one of the most efficient and cost-effective means of instantly distributing all types of news and information.

Both organizations charge an annual membership fee. Publicity releases are charged based on the distribution selected ranging from as low as $25 for a 400-word story transmitted to all media in Nebraska or Wyoming to $550 to reach more than 2,000 newspapers, wire services, magazines, broadcast outlets and security analysts across the United States.

PR Newswire

Headquartered in New York City, with its technical complex across the Hudson River in New Jersey's Harborside Financial Center, PR Newswire

(PRN) is the leading media distribution service in the world and the first public relations wire service. It has 21 bureaus throughout the country and affiliate relationships internationally. The company transmits some 100,000 news releases a year. Through its own high-speed, satellite-linked electronic communications network, PR Newswire provides immediate and simultaneous delivery 24 hours a day, seven days a week to thousands of media organizations, financial analysts and electronic news data bases around the world. The PRN Investors Research Wire, which carries all business and financial news releases, now is accessible on hundreds of thousands of terminals in the worldwide financial community.

PR Newswire has been a prime source of company news in virtually every major merger or corporate takeover in the last 25 years. Beyond carrying financial and business news for the majority of all companies listed on any stock exchange, thousands of public relations professionals have turned to PRN in moments of crisis. Consequently, PRN copy has included up-to-the-minute details of major disasters such as the nuclear incident at Three Mile Island; the deaths from chemical pollution in Bhopal, India; and the national debate over dioxin (Agent Orange) as well as attention-riveting events such as airplane crashes, hijackings and major drug busts (from public affairs officers of U.S. Customs and the Drug Enforcement Agency). PRN regularly carries news of significant product recalls and product tampering released by affected companies.

In addition to its two principal nationwide circuits, PR Newswire has four regional circuits—Northeast NewsLine, Southeast NewsLine, Midwest NewsLine and West/Southwest NewsLine—as well as selected state, local and special area distributions. Business, trade and special interest publications also are on the company's circuit and enable a client to send a news release to, for example, more than 335 high-technology publications, including 15 magazines covering the chemical and plastics industries and 14 that specialize in retailing (PR Newswire 1994).

Under an exclusive agreement with Reuters, an international news agency, PR Newswire first translates and then transmits news releases to more than 120 leading media throughout Latin America for a cost of $400 for 300 words. Special circuits also are available, such as the Andean Pack that reaches media in Bolivia, Colombia, Ecuador, Peru and Venezuela for $295.

The organization joined with Tass, the major news service of the former Soviet Union, to transmit releases to hundreds of media in the new Confederation of Independent States. These points include not only newspapers and radio and television stations throughout the 11 new republics but also influential government offices, ministries and trade and academic institutions across the continent. A news release distributed in Russian to some 1,000 outlets costs $370.

In association with a subsidiary of the Press Association of the United Kingdom, the PR Newswire international service also covers all of Europe,

Africa, Asia, Australia and New Zealand, the Caribbean and the Middle East.

Not all stories are breaking news or need instant disclosure as do financial releases. Consequently, PR Newswire began its Feature NewsLine to take advantage of its in-place satellite distribution network. At 7:30 a.m. each weekday it moves a package of feature stories to more than 1,500 news points. The Feature NewsLine reaches newspapers, television and radio stations, major magazine publishing houses and magazines at a subscriber cost of only $230 for up to 400 words.

Reaching Data Bases. Data bases have become a prime source of information for journalists, corporate librarians, attorneys, investment analysts, researchers and others. The full text of all PR Newswire releases can be accessed from both domestic and international data bases. All releases sent over any PRN circuit are stored in NEXIS, Dow Jones News/Retrieval, DIALOG Information Services, Knowledge Index, Knight-Ridder's Press Link, Vu/Text and a score of other data bases. Releases sent internationally can be accessed on Reuters Textline, Reuters Company Newsyear, Quick, Telekurs and more than a dozen others. Some of the data bases have every news release transmitted by PRN since 1981 on-line.

Marketing Entertainment. PR Newswire started EntertaiNet, a dedicated communications network that transmits entertainment news directly to hundreds of entertainment editors at newspapers and broadcast and trade media throughout the country. The full network reaches major daily newspapers, 113 radio stations and 19 state, regional and national radio networks, 700 televisions stations, 50 television network bureaus, 11 international television networks and key consumer and trade publications.

Coverage can be selected to distribute a release to any of five regions or even more locally, such as just the major entertainment media in New York and Los Angeles. Other special circuits include print and radio, only television or more than 200 television stations in America's top 50 markets.

Specialty Distributions. The company's NewsLeads and FeatureLeads services send 200-word or 300-word releases to 770 television newsrooms for only $100. Distributors of video news releases can issue a 400-word Video Alert that goes to the same newsrooms with VNR satellite coordinates and two satellite daybook entries.

The U.S. Hispanic NewsLine reaches 300 journalists at all the leading Spanish-language newspapers, magazines, radio and television stations, networks and feature services. It can be used nationally or regionally.

PRN's Capital NewsLine is a way to reach the Washington, D.C., media and the news systems of the U.S. House of Representatives and Senate. The D.C. Pack adds additional distribution to 300 foreign, domestic and trade news bureaus in the National Press Club Building and Press Club Rack.

E-Wire goes to 250 leading environmental, science and medical writers.

E-Wire also is active on Internet, reaching several thousand environmental groups around the world including Greenpeace, Friends of the Earth International, Sierra Club, World Wildlife Fund and Consumers Union of Japan.

Other services include: NewsGrams, a mailing service that sends a printed release to any number of selected publications the same day it is transmitted over a PRN circuit; Pronto Direct, a high-speed, high-capacity facsimile distribution service; and Pronto On-Call, a system that stores information that can be retrieved by fax by calling a toll-free number. PRN operates the largest fax facility in the world dedicated to public relations applications (PR Newswire 1994).

Business Wire

Business Wire was established in 1961 by public relations executive Lorry I. Lokey. Based in San Francisco, the organization has 16 regional offices and a system of simultaneous electronic delivery to more than 2,500 news media and 500 investment firms and affiliates in Canada, Europe, the Far East, Australia and Latin America.

It has a National Circuit, Eastern Circuit and Western Circuit, 11 regional circuits and numerous local and state circuits. Business Wire's U.S. Super Pack costs $550 for a 400-word story that goes to its Eastern and Western Circuits, Analyst Wire and any of eight regional circuits. The U.S. Pack, for $475, includes only four regional circuits, while the combination of Eastern and Western Circuits costs $260.

Rates for Business Wire Features are less than the cost of priority releases and still less than the cost of mailing a publicity release. The National Circuit is priced at $135 for 400 words and as low as $50 for a specific geographic area (Business Wire 1994a).

There is a National BroadcastWire as well as optional circuits that reach the top 30 national television markets.

Special Business Wire Circuits. The Tri-Continent High-Tech Circuit is for distribution of news of interest to media in key computer markets in the United States, Japan and Europe. In this country, coverage includes Associated Press and United Press as well as the entire computer and high-tech trade magazine circuit. In Europe, nine-country coverage includes Associated Press and Dow Jones in Paris with service news points throughout the continent, the 20 leading computer and electronic publications and the company's entire TRIM English-language network. In Japan, the wire sends releases to 50 media outlets that include all leading computer and high-tech publications (Business Wire 1994a).

EntertainmentWire. This service electronically delivers entertainment news to film, television, radio and entertainment editors, writers and producers at newspapers, radio stations, television newsrooms, entertainment trade publications and news wire services. Included are such specialized entertainment media as *Variety, Hollywood Reporter, Billboard* and "Entertainment Tonight" (Business Wire 1994b).

EntertainmentWire also makes the availability of satellite feeds, video news releases, B-roll, movie trailers and video opportunities known to hundreds of television newsrooms across the country. Targeted distribution is available to a city, state or regional area as well as to the top 100 television markets.

BW SportsWire. BW SportsWire is a separate division that distributes sports-related news releases to sports writers, routing the copy directly to the sports desks of 850 media points across the country, including newspapers, specialty publications, wire services and television and radio stations. It is used by sports public relations professionals, sports information directors, sports marketers, professional teams and organizations, sanctioning bodies, sports facilities, sponsors of sporting events and many other sports professionals.

The information goes directly into the computers of the sports editors along with other breaking sports news of the day. Media that are not equipped to receive by computer get the publicity release copy by the organization's high-speed printers. Distribution can be made nationally or on various regional, state or metropolitan area networks (Business Wire 1994c).

Special Circuits. Business Wire's Entertainment/Gaming Circuit has special relevance to the gambling industry. News releases are directed to appropriate editors, both entertainment and business, on circuits in Los Angeles, Las Vegas, Miami, Atlantic City and New York, as well as the trade publications that cover the industry.

The North America Energy Circuit is a comprehensive distribution package for energy-related public relations news. It combines media available in the Southwest Energy Circuit with daily newspapers in New Mexico, Colorado, Wyoming, Montana, Utah, Southern California, Alaska and Alberta. The circuit also includes key trade publications in the United States and Canada. The Southwest Energy Circuit is a more limited network of daily newspapers and trade publications in Texas, Louisiana and Oklahoma.

Business Wire Data Bases. The same as PR Newswire, Business Wire sends its news releases to a number of electronic retrieval services. Even if the story might not be printed by a particular publication, it is available on several dozen data bases to more than one million subscribers worldwide. The data bases include Business Dateline, DIALOG Information Services, InfoMaster Electronic Library, NEXIS, Dow Jones News Retrieval and Vu/Text (Business Wire 1994a).

PHOTO WIRE SERVICES

Both PR Newswire and Business Wire provide a way to send high-quality black-and-white or color news or feature photographs to newspapers. PRNewsFoto sends its images on the Associated Press PhotoExpress service, which transmits the same photo file to most AP member newspapers. The service also includes automatic electronic storage of the photo in a data base free to all newspapers for a year.

BW PhotoWire is a high-speed, national electronic satellite distribution system linked to a growing list of daily newspapers in key markets. Photos, charts and graphics of any kind go directly to the editorial offices of newspapers in 28 cities in 20 states.

A new Corporate PhotoFile service from Business Wire supplements issues of the photo sheet exclusively for profiling corporate newsmakers, logos and corporate headquarters. Portraits of key company executives and other corporate photos are periodically grouped on special issues of the FeaturePhoto sheet and sent to editors.

MEDIA DISTRIBUTION SERVICES

Media Distribution Services (MDS) is the nation's largest public relations media, mailing, faxing, printing and graphics services company. For more than 29 years this New York City-based company has produced, faxed, assembled and distributed public relations materials for its clients. These materials have included press releases, photographs, press kits and even personalized correspondence (MDS 1994).

The cornerstone of the MDS operation is its Mediamatic System, a computerized data base that provides access to more than 150,000 reporters, editors, broadcasters, syndicated columnists and security analysts in the United States and Canada. This information is updated daily. Mailings are made to the individual by name rather than being addressed to a department or editor title.

The company has 10 offices and service centers in major cities. The breakout on its media lists is extensive. For example, under "Textile Manufacturing" a release or package can be sent to the general editor, chemical editor, cloth manufacture editor, synthetic fibers editor or yarn manufacture editor in subcategories such as female apparel manufacturing or boys' apparel. Other breakouts are specialized to target groups including senior citizens, singles, gays, widowed people, farm youth, Protestant preteens, Catholic girls and Jewish intellectuals. MDS has virtually every type of editor or publication reaching any type of audience in its computerized media lists.

BURRELLE'S MEDIA LABELS

Burrelle's is the world's largest press clipping service and the publisher of numerous media directories. It has a data base of names and addresses of more than 160,000 editors, publishers, radio and television station managers, and advertising and circulation executives at over 40,000 newspapers, magazines, radio and television stations, cable systems, colleges and wire services (Burrelle 1994).

The company can provide printed pressure-sensitive labels, do mail-merged letters and mailings, prepare telephone and Rolex cards and even provide a computer diskette with a custom data base. Arrangements can be made to have the diskette updated on a monthly or quarterly basis. The media can be selected based on over 300 subject terms; by 100 top ADI markets; by state, county or city; by 250 different editorial and key management positions; by circulation range, from 100 to over 10 million; or by frequency of publication or broadcast power.

BACON'S MAILING SERVICES

Bacon's is the Chicago-headquartered company that publishes several popular media directories that were described in the previous chapter. The company will do printing and assembly, photo reproduction and mailing. It will inventory materials and maintain customized lists for mailings or labels. The firm also will provide customers with labels or diskettes of its mailing lists on a one-time rental basis.

Addressing options from Bacon's Media Bank include 175,000 editors at U.S. and Canadian trade and consumer magazines, every U.S. and Canadian daily newspaper, every U.S. weekly, every commercial U.S. television and cable station and every U.S. radio station. The list also includes news services and syndicates, syndicated columnists, newspaper Sunday supplements, African American and Hispanic presses, county home extension agents and others (Bacon 1994).

Bacon's also will fax a press release to the media. Its Publicityfax service is available with a standard same-day service using the original letterhead of the client to send to broadcast media. Premium-quality service digitizes the letterhead and has the release word processed before transmittal. Each release is sent with a cover sheet directing the information to the proper contact.

NORTH AMERICAN PRECIS SYNDICATE

North American Precis Syndicate (NAPS) of New York City is a feature release service that gets the publicity message to suburban and city newspapers and radio and television news and talk shows. Of the more than 10,000 newspapers in the United States, only 1,645 are dailies. Two out of three of the daily newspapers have 25,000 or less circulation.

NAPS sends its news releases as camera-ready art to 1,000 dailies and 2,800 weeklies for a cost of $2,900. The company estimates that one of its newspaper releases will result in between 100 and 400 placements. The client decides on a story and either writes it or sends the information to NAPS to rewrite in a way that will get the best media pickup. The release is then sent out in camera-ready format. Many of the releases sent out by NAPS are printed intact and often include a logo or other corporate identification in a headline or photograph.

To reach television news and talk shows the company sends out its TV Takes slide and script releases to 325 broadcasters. NAPS contends that it gets better results this way than with video news releases because the stills are used on a screen inset beside or behind the announcer. For a cost of $2,950 it estimates results of between 40 to 80 placements, half of them from stations in the top 100 television markets.

Radio Roundup is the name of the script service sent to 3,000 radio station writers. The cost is $2,650, and North American Precis estimates an average success rate of 200 to 300 placements.

NAPS provides its customers with newspaper clippings, usage cards from the television and radio stations, computer printouts with circulation and audience data and usage maps. Typical feature stories include offering a free booklet with product or service information that can be obtained by mail or by calling a toll-free telephone number. For companies that did not want to bear the expense of printing and mailing a brochure or booklet, some have taken the information in the booklet and divided it into a series of from four to eight stories or columns and achieved the same message delivery. Gerber Products Company did a series, "Bringing Up Baby," bylined by a physician-nutritionist with a series of questions and answers. All the columns mentioned the company and specific Gerber products.

NAPS suggests that helpful hints on health and homemaking, news about the environment and travel issues, and releases keyed to various holidays also get good results. Any latest development tends to look modern when described with copy on its historical antecedents. Tips on increasing safety and saving money also are popular. GTE Electrical Products did a multimedia release that included a "Hints for Homemakers" newspaper feature with tips on lighting a home, a 97-word, 38-second radio release and a television script with four slides showing various types of lighting ideas. All told consumers they could write GTE for a free copy of the book.

Using radio and print ads, the Tea Council promoted the use of tea in several ways. One script said, "Today athletic directors and authorities on sports medicine recommend that even 'weekend athletes' can benefit from drinking tea—hot or cold—as a fluid replacement that is easy to digest, non-carbonated and without calories." Another script made an implied link between tea and weight loss: "In the 18th century, tea moved into the home and was served to 'ward off that sinking feeling' which occurred mid-afternoon. Since then dieters have found that a cup of tea will still hunger pangs and curb the appetite."

ASSOCIATED RELEASE SERVICE

Chicago-based Associated Release Service (ARS) began in 1950 as a one-stop publicity production and distribution service for all media—newspapers, trade and consumer magazines, radio and television. Its services are similar to those of North American Precis Syndicate (ARS 1994).

Its individual press-ready mat and offset releases are camera-ready repro proofs and can be sent to 8,100 small daily and weekly newspapers, to the 6,000-plus most frequent users or to any market or combination of markets selected by the user. ARS also distributes two or more releases with a common theme together, often under a running headline such as a syndicated column. A minimum order costs $550. A one-column story 7½ inches deep sent to 1,000 newspapers costs $970 compared to a three-column story for $1,220.

Associated Release Service handles reproduction, distribution and reporting of airplay for every type of release accepted by radio and television stations:

- Radio scripts
- Records
- Open reel tapes
- TV slides and scripts
- Videotape (1-inch Hi-Band)
- Videocassettes

The staff of ARS track radio and television stations to identify users of publicity material so that its known user list ensures the most cost-effective pickup of a client's message. Distribution can be selected by type of station (music, news and sports; classical music; talk radio), station power (watts), market area or any other criteria. A market can be saturated or releases can be sent only to those most likely to air the message. The service has pinpointed 3,000 of the more than 8,000 radio stations in the country that frequently use scripts or recorded releases. A one-page script sent to 1,000 women's and drive-time program directors costs $865 compared to a three-page script sent to 3,000 radio stations for $2,605 (Chelvin, 1994).

Extension Home Economists

For nearly 40 years Associated Release Service has pioneered and developed publicity distribution to 3,200 U.S. government extension home economists. As part of the Cooperative Extension Service established in 1914 by the U.S. Department of Agriculture, there is one extension home economist in every county in the country. They originally were required to acquaint rural Americans with better farming and homemaking methods, but since then the role has expanded tremendously.

Today's home economists function as mass media, conveying all kinds of information to millions of people in urban and suburban as well as rural areas through a variety of outlets. They meet with families, community groups and school classes and provide information at demonstrations, at county fairs and through individual counseling. Many write regular columns for their local newspapers or act as frequent contributors. More than 1,100 of them appear on radio or have regular programs. Some 200 appear on television in their communities.

Federal, state and local governments jointly fund the extension program. Each state's land grant colleges of agriculture and home economics have a role in the program. The home economists can and will use any type of publicity release that offers solutions to homemaking problems and promotes lifestyle improvement. They particularly like a regular flow of related material. Some of the topics ARS says they are interested in receiving include:

- Clothing: care, style, sewing, patterns, fabrics
- Community affairs: transportation, sanitation, crime, social service agencies
- Education: preschool, schools, scholarships
- Food: new products, recipes, appliances
- Gardening: tools, landscaping, flowers, vegetables, chemicals
- Health: adult, teen-age, child, senior citizen
- Home decoration: furniture, draperies, floor coverings, paint, accessories
- Home employment: opportunities, tax considerations, management, techniques, tips on coping
- Home entertainment: toys, books, games, hobbies, crafts, outdoor equipment
- Home remodeling and repair: wall coverings, heating and air conditioning, building plans and materials
- Housekeeping: cleaning equipment and materials
- Personal finance: bank accounts, credit cards, personal loans, financing for homes, autos, appliances, or vacation travel
- Safety: around the home or farm, on the job, traveling

Most of the ARS clients include reply cards in their mailings to ask for details on use of the materials and suggestions for future material. The cards also are a means for the extension home economists to order booklets and other literature as well as product samples. As with other distribution services, this group can be covered nationwide or in target states and counties. The 3,200 extension home economists can be reached for as little as $1,440 plus postage (ARS 1994).

Special Media Outlets

ARS regularly sends publicity materials to 220 important daily and weekly newspapers with a combined total circulation of more than two million serving the African American community as well as 200 newspapers with a combined circulation of more than 1.6 million serving the Latino population. As an extension of a regular mailing the add-on cost is 90 cents per newspaper for a two-column release and $1 for a three-column story. A mailing to the African American press would cost $550. Releases sent to the Hispanic media, in Spanish, cost $695 plus postage.

The company also can help companies reach approximately 1,600 of the nation's leading colleges and universities, which publish student-edited newspapers that use outside publicity material. These also can be selected by geographic location (ARS 1994).

NEWS USA

News USA is a company based in Alexandria, Va., that nationally syndicates columns and features for its clients to daily and weekly newspapers, radio and television stations and the Spanish-language media. News USA distributes its material to more than 10,000 newspapers, including every daily in the United States and most of the weeklies. Distribution is made camera-ready in a publication as well as by computer disk using Macintosh and IBM formats on CD-ROM and by high-speed computer feed. The service includes providing story ideas, writing, editing, typesetting, printing, distribution and postage as well as tracking the stories to provide clients with clippings and readership reports (News USA 1994).

Print rates run from $2,300 for a one-column feature between 200 and 250 words to $3,500 for an extended feature of 450 to 650 words to $8,800 for a full tabloid page. There are discounts for prepayment and for volume, with a monthly column cost of $1,700 to a weekly release of $1,500.

Burson-Marsteller used the service for Arm & Hammer with a series of feature stories on the environment and cooking. One story recommending baking soda as an alternative household cleaner was published by 248 papers and read by more than 11 million people. The American Kidney Fund did a series of health columns written by a physician and educating the public on early warning signs and what to do about kidney diseases. One column appeared in 244 papers with a readership of nearly six million. One health series released by the National Association of Retail Druggists appeared in 3,020 newspapers with a readership of more than 83 million (Scharf 1994).

The company recommends that clients consider one of its Special Events Pages which focuses on holidays, seasons and specials like Children's Day, Crime Prevention Week or Car Care Month. The service also has been used for op-eds—opinion pieces to be placed opposite the editorial page.

Radio USA

Radio USA is a division of News USA. Scripts in 30-second, 45-second and 60-second lengths are sent to 6,000 stations in the top 260 markets as ranked by Arbitron. The company says to expect more than 4,000 airplays per script. The basic cost is $2,900 with discounts for prepayment and volume. Clients' news and feature stories are rewritten and prepared by the service's journalists who are experienced in radio and television (News USA 1994).

Latino USA

This is an add-on service by News USA and can be included with a 50 percent surcharge on any package. A 200- to 225-word story costs $1,150 and a radio script $1,450, including translation. The material is sent to 345 Spanish-language and bilingual publications throughout North America and more than 200 Spanish-language and bilingual radio stations.

Blast-Fax

A new service from News USA, Blast-Fax offers customers same-day distribution and proof of usage to reach radio stations. The stations can be selected by station format, area code, state or size of audience. The broadcasters fax back proof of usage, usually within 24 hours. The company says its average response is more than 5 percent—nearly triple the national direct mail response rate. It is recommended for background materials, scripts and media alerts for in-bound media tours.

SPECIAL MAILING LISTS

A number of companies provide special mailing lists. Ad-Lib Publications of Fairfield, Iowa, has specialized lists for newspaper and magazine editors and radio talk shows and top television shows that do interviews. The lists can be purchased on labels or on IBM-compatible or Macintosh computer disks. Breakdowns for editors include food, fashion, health or medical, sports, science, travel and many other categories (Ad-Lib 1994).

ESTABLISHING YOUR OWN COMPUTER NETWORK

Texas A&M University's Office of University Relations was a pioneer in the use of personal computers to transmit news releases. It is believed to be the first non-media entity to make widespread use of the electronic technique to disseminate such information to newspapers and wire services, beginning in 1979.

Lane B. Stephenson, who headed the news bureau operation, then known as the Office of Public Information, built on an idea first employed by a staff member of East Texas State University. The ETSU staffer, who also served on the staff of the athletic conference to which the regional institution belonged, used a Texas Instruments "Silent 700" portable unit to transmit sports statistics. He outlined his procedures at a district meeting of the Council for Advancement and Support of Education, and Stephenson seized on the concept and applied a significantly expanded version to establish Texas A&M's own "wire service."

The concept was ideal for the university, which, while located between three of the 10 most-populated cities in the United States (Dallas, Houston and San Antonio) and the state's capital (Austin), is somewhat isolated geographically (Chicago World Book 1994). In 1979 it was considered even more remote, yet viewed by the media as a significant source of news. Key editors at major metropolitan newspapers and the main offices of Associated Press and United Press International in Texas were receptive to the idea of granting Texas A&M's new bureau the unprecedented privilege of transmitting news stories to them by computer.

Personal computers then were in their infancy. In fact, they were called microcomputers, and the first one used by Texas A&M came in a box and had to be assembled by an accommodating director of the university's central computer center. It was made by Vector Graphics, an early rival of then-fledgling Apple Computer, which then also catered to the build-it-by-the-numbers crowd.

Hardware was one thing; software was quite another. Nothing that would do the job was available off the shelf. Everything had to be written, one program at a time, a separate one for each newspaper and wire service outlet being served by the system.

The university's computerized operation was considered state-of-the-art at the time and attracted several visitors and numerous requests for information. A videotape was prepared to help explain it to interested personnel throughout the state and nation.

Texas A&M's Office of University Relations is now in its second generation of computers—various models of IBM and compatibles—and third generation of custom software. Having its own wire service enables the university to place its news and information directly in the computer of a newspaper or wire service.

Instant Media Access With Computers

In January 1992, Texas A&M's Office of University Relations took advantage of computer technology to provide another service for the media. Previously a 300-page sourcebook of some 800 experts and company representatives was published each year and sent to all interested media. The various members of the university's faculty and administration who were noted in their fields were listed by various categories along with their titles and business telephone contacts. Some names and phone numbers were out of date the day the publication was put in the mail.

A new software program called Gopher, developed by the University of Wisconsin, made it possible to computerize the sourcebook and keep it current. Media are given a toll-free telephone number and can access this sourcebook 24 hours a day, seven days a week—an important capacity for breaking news stories on evenings, holidays and weekends when the office may be closed. Now home telephone numbers are being added for most of the experts; in the twin cities of College Station and Bryan, Texas, few people have unlisted telephone numbers. All experts can be accessed by the user simply entering in a name or keyword search such as "Political Rhetoric," "Petroleum Engineering" or "Bosnia/Croatia." The office also added more than 80 fact sheets with information about the university; its colleges; selected departments, centers and agencies; traditions; and the new George Bush Presidential Library Center. Depending on the computer accessing the information, the fact sheets can be printed out by the user if a hard copy is desired.

When a user calls in on the 800 line the screen says, "Welcome To Texas A&M University—Office of University Relations" and then displays a menu:

A - Experts and Spokespersons
B - University Information and Fact Sheets
C - Help

The new program has been accessed an average of 1,000 times a month and also saved the university more than $25,000 in printing production and mailing costs. More important, the information in the system is always current and available.

RESOURCES

Here is the contact information for services discussed in this chapter.

Ad-Lib Publications
P.O. Box 1102
Fairfield, IA 52556
phone (515) 472-6617 or (800) 669-0773
fax (515) 472-3186

Associated Release Service
2 North Riverside Plaza
Chicago, IL 60606
phone (312) 726-8693

Bacon's Mailing Services
332 S. Michigan Ave., Room 1020
Chicago, IL 60604
phone (800) 621-0561, in Illinois (312) 922-2400
fax (312) 922-3127

Burrelle's Media Labels
75 E. Northfield Ave.
Livingston, NJ 07039-9873
phone (201) 992-6600 or (800) 631-1160

Business Wire
44 Montgomery St., Suite 2185
San Francisco, CA 94104
phone (415) 986-4422, outside California (800) 227-0845
fax (415) 788-5335 or (415) 986-4522
telex 34-728

Media Distribution Services
307 W. 36th St.
New York, NY 10018
phone (212) 279-4800
fax (212) 239-8208

News USA
4601 Eisenhower Ave.
Alexandria, VA 22304-4868
phone (703) 461-9500 or (800) 355-9500
fax (703) 461-9506

North American Precis Syndicate
201 E. 42nd St.
New York, NY 10017
phone (212) 867-9000

PR Newswire
1515 Broadway, 32nd Floor
New York, NY 10036
phone (212) 832-9400 or (800) 832-5522
fax 212) 832-9406
telex 1-2284 or 12-6217

REFERENCES

Ad-Lib Publications. 1994. Information package. Fairfield, Iowa.

Associated Release Service. 1994. Information package. Chicago.

Bacon's Mailing Services. 1994. Information package. New York.

Burrelle's Media Labels. 1994. Information package. Livingston, N.J.

Business Wire. 1994a. *Your Conduit on the Information Highway.* San Francisco.

___ 1994b. *EntertainmentWire* information package. San Francisco.

___ 1994c. *BWSportsWire* information package. San Francisco.

Chelvin, Ben J., vice president, Associated Release Service. 1994. Letter to author. April 14.

Chicago World Book, Inc. "Cities." *World Book 1994,* 4, p. 516.

Media Distribution Services. 1994. Information package. New York.

News USA Inc. 1994. Information package. Alexandria, Va.

PR Newswire. 1994. *PR Newswire Distribution Directory.* New York.

Scharf, Anna, senior account executive, News USA Inc. 1994. Memorandum to author.

5

HOW PUBLICITY AND HOW IT WORKS

Publicity is the basic tool and workhorse of marketing public relations. It is the mass promotional vehicle that professionals should consider first and use most to direct the message to the target audience. Publicity can be in the form of a news release. It can be a feature story. It can be a magazine story or a column item that came as a result of a suggestion to an editor or writer. Publicity can be a sound bite from a radio or television interview. It can be a captioned photograph in a newspaper or magazine. It can be a video news clip. It can be a record or audio tape for radio. It can be a letter to the editor or an op-ed piece. And it can be the spoken or written word as a result of a press conference or news or special event.

Publicity comes in many forms and can be as diverse as the marketing communications professional is creative. Its primary objective is to communicate the story. A story appearing in a newspaper or magazine is more believable to the reader than a paid advertisement is. It can reach many more people who may read a story but who may not read the full advertisement. As a result, it can have a strong impact on public awareness at a much lower cost than advertising. (Advertising is any paid form of promotion by a company or organization. The message can be completely controlled in content and scheduling for appearance.)

HOW TO TARGET THE AUDIENCE

It is essential to determine the audience and be selective in how to communicate to that audience. In defining the audience, it may be necessary to segment it into submarkets or several audiences. Know your market and what you want to accomplish from publicity exposure in the media that reach that market. Here are some examples:

A Bolt Manufacturer with a Select Audience. A machine screw manufacturing company has developed and plans to introduce a new high-tech bolt made with sophisticated, state-of-the-art materials. The outlets for a news release on this item would be limited to the trade magazines and newspapers read by the wholesalers and distributors and to the industry publications that reach the end user of the new high-tech bolt.

The first announcement of the new product would be in the form of a new product publicity release. If design is an additional factor and the bolt is visually different from others available, a captioned photograph would be appropriate to send with the release. The sender should be familiar with the publications or have carefully screened their editorial requirements in one or more of the available publication resources.

A New Home Appliance and a Broader Public. A manufacturer of a new, small home appliance such as a blender, food processor, or other similar device would find a much broader audience. Not only would the release and captioned photograph be sent to the industry trade publications read by the buyers at leading department stores, chain stores and appliance stores responsible for distribution of the product, but also to the consuming public. The story should be directed to the home service and shelter magazines and the cooking and gourmet magazines as well. If it is suitable as a gift item, special seasonal sections (Mother's Day, Father's Day, Christmas) of magazines including *Playboy, Esquire* and *Cosmopolitan* should be targeted as well as the food sections of leading newspapers.

Guest chefs who regularly appear on television talk shows should be made aware of any new appliance and encouraged to use it when appearing on programs such as "The Today Show," "Good Morning America" or "Regis and Kathie Lee." Cooking shows in local markets, syndicated and on cable television networks, also should be targeted.

This product has many more possible outlets for publicity than that of the bolt manufacturer. Additional outlets would include a column item about a celebrity using the product or placement of the item in a television sitcom or feature motion picture. If the appliance has application in the food service industry, then publications reaching this market should be placed on the mailing list.

Targeting the Hometown Media of Members of Congress. In some cases, a business could be impacted by possible federal regulatory or legislative action—which, depending on the action, could either impede the sale of a line of products or tremendously increase it. Such a business would add another dimension to its campaign. Cigarette manufacturers and producers of beer, wine and distilled spirits long have been faced with state and federal issues affecting sale of their products.

The legislative decision could be environmental or related to a trade agreement. Companies in this category could include U.S. domestic-based automobile manufacturers; producers and exporters of citrus fruits; and lumber companies and manufacturers of wood building materials.

In addition to building coalition and grass-roots support, the company may want to target, for editorial board meetings and op-ed pieces, the major metropolitan newspapers in the hometown or home state of the members of the congressional committees responsible for legislation or oversight of the regulations.

Marketing to Mixed Audiences. The Wine Institute, a marketing cooperative of all California wine producers, launched a major marketing communications effort in the 1960s to convince Americans that drinking wine is a part of good living and that California wines compare favorably in quality and value with other wines around the world.

The comprehensive program involved a number of targeted audiences. The consuming public was reached through articles written by wine columnists in major metropolitan newspapers and shelter and gourmet magazines. Personal letters with story outlines were sent to certain editors and writers, and publicity was mailed directly to many others. The message was that serving wine at a meal or as an aperitif or with dessert is a proper thing to do.

The retail trade and the hotel and restaurant industry were reached through stories in important trade magazines. Here the message cited a growing trend of Americans buying and serving wine and how profitable it would be for business.

To increase the image of California wine, an effort was directed at the White House and to First Lady Jacqueline Kennedy, the paragon of good taste and etiquette. Until this effort, the White House wine cellar was predominately French. It was during the Kennedy years that California wine became an important part of state dinners and social functions at the White House. This story was widely publicized to all print and broadcast media. Every year a congressional wine tasting was held in Washington, D.C., and hosted by the California congressional delegation to get the message across to break down barriers prohibiting the marketing of wine.

A wine expert was scheduled for radio, television, newspaper and magazine interviews throughout the country. He would help the audience overcome the fear of selecting the wrong wine and tell the reader or listener how and when it is appropriate to serve wine. This person also conducted wine tastings before important groups.

Other special audiences for this promotional program included young adults, college students of drinking age and various ethnic communities. The medical profession was targeted regarding wine's many health values, and publicity was released on hospitals that offered wine as an option to patients.

The Wine Institute even offered consumers a correspondence course to become "a wine expert." A booklet telling the reader everything there is to know about wine included a self-test. When returned to the Wine Institute, the "graduate" was sent an attractive certificate attesting to the completion of the course.

The campaign was comprehensive, coordinated and made maximum use of publicity (Posert 1994).

PUBLICITY FOR A NEW PRODUCT INTRODUCTION

After three years of research and development, Tree Top, Inc., a grower-owned fruit processing cooperative in rural eastern Washington, became the first company to extract pure fiber from apples in a form uniquely useful as an ingredient in processed foods and pharmaceuticals (Rockey Co. 1994).

Research played a vital role in the product introduction. Test calls to journalists helped determine the best way to describe the innocuous-looking brown powder to the consumer press. A search of scientific literature helped decide what claims could safely be made about the dietary benefits of apple fiber. A study of various food industry events helped determine the best platform for a formal introduction of the product.

Jay Rockey Public Relations of Seattle positioned Tree Top as *the* major fruit fiber researcher and manufacturer. It sought to increase its client's visibility as an innovator in a competitive marketplace, attract major nationwide news coverage, achieve public and industrial acceptance of fruit fiber and launch successful sales of the product.

The goals were achieved—Tree Top received the most massive publicity in its history and within 16 weeks had completely sold out its supply.

The campaign was directed to multiple audiences, including food processors, the pharmaceutical industry, health-minded consumers, the Washington state business community, consumers in Eastern states, and grower-members, employees and friends of Tree Top.

A news conference formally introduced the fiber at the industry's major conference of the year, the convention of the Institute of Food Technologists in Atlanta. Journalists covering the convention, as well as Atlanta area media, were invited. A Tree Top snack bar featured a variety of apple-fiber cookies and juices.

Early "backgrounder" letters alerted Seattle-area media of the upcoming announcement. Media kits were tailored to several categories of target media and kits individualized for each of the target publics. Media calls arranged interviews with company executives and researchers.

More than 60 journalists and potential fiber buyers attended the Atlanta kickoff conference. Nationwide newspaper coverage resulted from wire stories on Associated Press and United Press. There was extensive coverage in virtually every trade publication in the processed foods industry. This case provides a good example of successful publicity for a new product introduction.

HOW TO GET RESULTS WITH A WRITTEN RELEASE

To reach the media that reach the audience, you have options of using a written press release, an audio tape or record, or a video news release or television clip. Ideas on how best to use the electronic media are discussed in other chapters in this book.

The written release is one of the most efficient and economical in achieving a wide distribution of facts and data. Follow these rules to maximize the use of the written release:

1. The release should be clearly written.
2. Incorporate all facts and data that are relevant, accurate, and truthful.
3. Answer all of the five Ws—who, what, where, when and why—and how, if possible.
4. Check to be sure there are no typographical, spelling or syntax errors. Don't rely completely on computer software spell-check programs because a word, while properly spelled, could be misused.
5. The release should be double-spaced. (With computers and incremental spacing of less than 2.0, 1.5 is acceptable and will save space.)
6. If you are preparing a release for distribution exclusively for broadcast media, triple-spacing of the copy is preferred.
7. Duplicate the release on only one side of the piece of paper. If you need two pages for the release, then use two pieces of paper. Never use the front and back of a sheet of paper for the publicity release.
8. The news release should include a dateline or release date. For a feature story it is not necessary to specify a release date unless you have a good reason to do so.
9. A contact person or company should be listed on the release, with a telephone number the editor can call if more information is needed.
10. Follow a consistent style such as that prescribed by the Associated Press's *AP Stylebook.*
11. Be sure the release is delivered to the proper person by the proper time.
12. Keep releases to no more than two pages. The shorter and more concise, the better. No story can be too short if it contains all the vital information.

13. Keep paragraphs short. Long paragraphs inhibit the editor's as well as the public's desire to read what has been written. Generally speaking, keep paragraphs to a maximum of 60 words.

14. Try not to break a paragraph, and certainly not a sentence, to the next page.

15. Do not hyphenate words. Let lines run longer or shorter.

16. At the bottom of the first page, write "*-more-*" if the copy is to be continued.

17. At the top of the second page, repeat the first part of the headline and note that it is page 2.

Be sure the release is correct before it is mailed. A New York journalist faulted one leading public relations firm for misspelling *Huntington* three times and *hosiery* once, misnaming a mall and making a total of 15 mistakes in three paragraphs—all in one release. There is no faster way to have a release thrown in the trash than to send an editor one that is pointless, overstated or pure puffery.

The news release can be duplicated on plain white bond paper or on a letterhead. Many companies have specially prepared news release letterhead that includes the address, phone number, fax number and, where applicable, telex. Public relations agencies that use their own letterhead will generally indicate the name of the client for whom the release has been prepared with a line such as, "FOR: Standard Computer Systems, Inc." A one- or two-color letterhead will have no more impact on the use of a story by an editor than one prepared on plain white bond. The substance of the release and its news value are the determining factors.

Don't be intimidated by corporate attorneys. Never use characters such as TM for trademark or ® for a registered name or capitalize or italicize brand names. Many corporate attorneys will insist on this being a part of a news release, but it is the quickest way to make an editor throw away the release. These marks are not used by the media. If the attorney insists, counter by asking the attorney to produce evidence of use of such marks by a magazine or newspaper.

Radio and Television Releases

Releases specially prepared for radio and television will maximize chances with these media. Write succinctly and with liveliness, which is good advice for all releases but imperative for broadcast.

Remember, that announcer will have no more than one minute, and probably considerably less, to say what you want him or her to say. You must include something interesting to go along with the commercial message. Simplicity of sentence structure is essential when writing radio and television releases. Here are some simple rules:

1. Avoid the use of commas. "Michael Johnson, president and CEO, United Industries, said today that..." should read, "United Industries president and CEO Michael Johnson said today that..."

2. Spell out all numbers. In "The event will begin at 8:00 p.m." the time should read "eight p.m." and "at 7:00 tonight" should read "at seven o'clock tonight." If a company has "500 employees" it should be spelled out "five hundred employees." When using numbers in excess of one million it should read: "two (m) million," or "five (b) billion." The (m) indicates million is correct and the (b) indicates billion is correct.

3. After you have written your release, test its readability by reading it aloud to yourself—and time it. If it doesn't sound right, change it. Put the time prominently at the top and triple-space the release.

4. Be careful when referring to relationships. "James Appleton, lawyer for Peter Harrington, said..." should be rewritten, "Peter Harrington's attorney James Appleton said..." The public will be hearing and not reading this release and could very well associate the statement with the last name heard.

Have a Stylebook in Your Library

While certain newspapers and magazines may have their own specific editorial styles, as do publishing companies, the most universally used style is that of the Associated Press. The *AP Stylebook* is a soft-covered (spiral-bound optional), 300-page book of rules of capitalization, abbreviation, punctuation and spelling. The Associated Press calls it "the complete guide to newspaper journalism." Many bookstores carry it, or copies can be ordered for $9.75 plus $2.50 for postage and handling from Associated Press, 50 Rockefeller Plaza, New York, NY 10020, phone (212) 621-1500. The stylebook also is available on IBM-compatible or Apple diskette at $65.00 a copy.

The Associated Press also offers two other helpful publications: *The Word: An Associated Press Guide to Good Newswriting,* which costs $5.00 plus $1.00 postage and handling, and *The Picture: A Guide to Good News Photography,* which sells for $8.95 plus $1.00 postage and handling. Order from the aforementioned address.

United States Government Printing Office Style Manual is a comprehensive, 480-page book that is an excellent reference manual, but it should not be used as a guide for any editorial style for capitalization, abbreviation or punctuation. It is not consistent with—and in some cases is contrary to—the rules of Associated Press or those followed by most media. It does, however, have good suggestions on job planning and content for books and pamphlets as well as reports of a scientific or technical nature, proofreader marks and general instructions on printing.

There are excellent sections on commonly used foreign words and with diacritical marks essential to correct spelling (résumé, pâté, exposé, and such); compound words; signs and symbols; useful tables, including metric tables and conversions; geological terms; physical divisions of the United States; principal foreign countries with titles of chiefs of state and names of legislative bodies along with nouns and adjectives denoting nationality; a listing and spelling of all counties in the country; plant and insect names; proper congressional style for reports, documents and hearings; and 17 foreign languages plus Latin and classical Greek, complete with alphabet, pronunciation guide, special characters, vowels and consonants, combinations of vowel sounds (diphthongs), cardinal numbers, months, days, seasons, time and abbreviations.

The *GPO Style Manual* sells for $15.00 hardcover and $11.00 softcover and is available from the U.S. Government Printing Office in many major cities or by writing the Superintendent of Documents, U.S. Government Printing Office, Washington, DC 20402.

WHAT MAKES A GOOD PUBLICITY RELEASE?

John DeFrancesco of DeFrancesco/Goodfriend Public Relations in Chicago defines publicity as "soft" news rather than "hard" news. He says there are two types of soft news stories: (1) natural and (2) created or manufactured (DeFrancesco 1994). Following are his examples of natural news:

- Transitions within the company, such as appointments, promotions, new accounts, awards, new lines, services
- Anniversaries and milestones
- Office relocation, expansion and ground breaking
- Case studies of successful programs
- Attendance at a convention
- Response to other news: letter to the editor or essay for the opinion page
- A business profile story, trend, tips
- Human interest

Here are examples that DeFrancesco gives for a created or manufactured news story:

- A survey on a business topic or trend
- A speech
- Involvement in community affairs (such as a car dealer who bought a bus and used it as a loaner to charity and community groups for good will)
- Holding or sponsoring an event
- A contest

- A grand opening or an open house
- A unique photo

HOW TO DEVELOP THE COPY PLATFORM

It is essential that the overall marketing public relations campaign be cohesive, comprehensive, coordinated and selling a common concept. Because publicity is only one part—though a very important part—of the effort, it is important that it stress the key words or themes of the overall campaign.

The copy platform also uses the same five Ws and How as in writing a publicity release. *Who* is the target audience. *What* is what is to be said. *Where* is where the message is to be communicated. *When* is the timing of the message. *Why* is the objective. *How* is the means of communication.

Research, or just common sense, will have previously determined the target market. Both demographics and psychographics should be considered when defining the audience and outlining the copy platform. *Demographics* means grouping the target market by age, sex, race, national origin, geographic location, income level, education or any other quantitative degree of measuring or identifying the audience. Consumer needs, wants and purchasing frequency are closely associated with demographics. *Psychographics* is the qualitative or attitudinal segmenting of a market based on behavior preference. The benefits sought, user status, image and loyalty are psychographic motivators for purchase of a product or service.

In many instances the theme of the advertising and its copy may drive the entire program. It is certainly advantageous to use some of the same key words in a publicity release to further reinforce the advertising. However, this must be skillfully and carefully done to make sure the news release still contains its news value and does not become a commercial that will not be printed or read.

The message should be one that will influence or motivate the targeted audience to respond by buying a product, using a service or supporting an issue. It should make the product, service or issue more desirable than any competing or alternative product, service or issue. The message must be believable and persuasive, and it must tell the audience how and why the product, service or issue is better.

Key words, key phrases and one or more themes should be identified and selected to be used in the publicity effort. Different words, phrases or themes may be necessary to communicate to various audiences, because of either demographics or psychographics. Flexibility with continuity is the important consideration.

Within the outline of the overall theme or subthemes, news and feature story possibilities then should be outlined. Some of these stories could be originated in-house to be distributed to the media. Other concepts could be ideas developed working with the media and in which a pitch letter would be sent to an editor, writer, columnist, producer or reporter with one or more ideas that would be written or produced in collaboration.

EDITORIAL BOARD MEETINGS

Editorial board meetings can be an effective way for a new company or organization president to get acquainted with the media, or to make a point on a particular issue. While editorial board meetings generally are scheduled with the executive staffs of major metropolitan newspapers, they also can be effective with selected general interest, business news or industry trade publications.

Generally the most important editors, reporters and columnists who would be writing about the company, its products or issues would meet with the company representative. They should be sent an information kit and be fully prepared for the meeting with advance background information.

This is not a news conference where a specific announcement will be made, but a meeting that will lay the groundwork for future stories with, it is hoped, a much better and clearer understanding of one another by the participants. Sometimes soon after an editorial board meeting, the newspaper may publish an editorial, which may not always be advocating or supporting what the company wants.

HOW TO MAKE USE OF THE EDITORIAL AND OP-ED PAGES

Editorial pages should be carefully screened not only in important daily newspapers, but also in general interest and business news magazines and trade publications. Companies and organizations should be prepared to respond quickly when it is in their best interest to do so.

Op-ed page (the page opposite the editorial page) exposure is something else. This can be timely or a piece prepared that would be as interesting several weeks from now as today. Op-ed pieces can be sent unsolicited to a newspaper, or the editor of the section can be queried regarding possible interest in a piece. When a publication is targeted, the op-ed piece should be written in the style, format and length preferred by the publication.

In some campaigns it may be more effective to recruit a third party to advocate the issue of the company. This person also may be better known than an officer of the company or organization would be, particularly in certain local markets. If a campaign has several supporting themes, certain people may be more qualified to write about one theme more than another. In this case several op-ed pieces may be written by several different individuals and scheduled for distribution over a several month period.

HOW TO PRODUCE A SUCCESSFUL PRESS CONFERENCE

Press conferences are generally overdone. Avoid a press conference unless the subject matter and speaker are so newsworthy that what is announced at the event will have major impact. If the decision is made to schedule a traditional press conference, then do so, but do not call it a press conference. Many public relations and communications professionals today prefer to use the terms *news event, media event* or *news conference* rather than press conference. The reason is implicit in the terms. The purpose of bringing the media to one place is to provide news. A second reason is that the word *press* refers to print media, and the broadcast media often can be more important than the print media.

The most important factor to consider when deciding to call a news conference is whether the news you are going to disclose is worthy of gathering the journalists together, or whether the interest of the news media couldn't be just as well served by distributing a news release. Realize that reporters have to spend their time where and when it is most profitable. It takes time to go to a news conference and to return to the newspaper or radio or television station. The presence of a reporter and an electronic news crew with sound and camera is expensive. Sometimes a live remote truck is required and becomes an even more expensive additional cost for the station.

The individuals addressing the news conference must be articulate, knowledgeable and thoroughly conversant with the subject to be announced. Prior to the conference the participants should have a dress rehearsal and be briefed on every conceivable question reporters may ask. Good preparation is essential to the success of a news conference. There should be no surprises and no crises.

Peter Ueberroth, who ran the 1984 Olympic Games in Los Angeles and went on to become commissioner of Major League Baseball, was coached intensively the evening before the press conference was held announcing his appointment as president of the organizing committee. A water polo player in college, he was a successful, self-made millionaire who headed a major publicly held travel industry business. However, he had not been involved at all in the effort that brought the Olympic Games to Los Angeles and was not familiar with the structure or politics of international or Olympic sports.

An exceptionally fast learner, he quickly grasped the substance of the issues he would be expected to discuss and be questioned on the next morning. As the evening grew long, he objected to answering one specific question and started to argue with his coaches that it was not necessary to answer this particular question "because no one would ever ask that question." His coaches insisted he answer it. The answer he gave was wrong. After several minutes of work he came up with the right answer.

As the news conference began the next day, the question Mr. Ueberroth did not want to answer in training was the first one he was asked. As he correctly answered it, he acknowledged, with a wink, thanks to his coaches in the rear of the room. As he continued to correctly respond to every question asked, not one was asked that had not been rehearsed the prior evening. The conference was a success.

The Right Time and Place

Of equal importance with the choice of speaker are the choices of time and place for the news conference. In most instances, the best time is in the morning between 10:00 and 11:00. Carefully check upcoming news or special events when considering the time and date of a news conference to avoid any conflicts that could diminish attendance at the event.

Try to limit the conference to no more than 45 minutes, including a question-and-answer period. Keep the conference as short as possible and try to start on time. While it often is difficult, in no event begin more than 15 minutes after the scheduled start.

After the major announcement at the event, arrange for the key participants to be available for one-on-one interviews with reporters who may want a personalized story. This is especially vital to the broadcast media.

The morning hours allow the assignment editors to schedule the story into the overall news picture for the day. Such timing also permits the reporters to get the videotape back to the station for editing and for use on the early evening news.

For certain stories you will hope an affiliate may send it to the network, or the network itself will cover the story. In such cases, there always is a chance that it could make the affiliate's feed. Each afternoon the networks transmit via satellite to their affiliates selected stories a producer believes would be of interest for network stations to use as part of their local news. This practice provides the source with even greater exposure.

The best days of the week for a news conference are Tuesday, Wednesday or Thursday, unless any are legal holidays. Monday is not a good day because many newspeople may have carryover assignments or stories that broke over the weekend and require follow-up. Also newspeople who are to be invited, or their editors or assignment editors, should be called at least the day before, which typically can not be done on the weekend. Friday is considered unsuitable because Saturday newspaper circulations are lower and if follow-up is necessary, it is often difficult for the media to locate the necessary people over the weekend.

The selection of the site also is important. The size of the room should be in direct proportion to the number of people expected. It also should be central to the media and highly accessible and familiar to the media.

How to Set Up the Room for the News Conference

When setting up the room, individuals participating in the conference should be placed on a level with the television cameras. If a stage or raised portion of the room is used, risers should be used to accommodate the television cameras, which should have an unimpaired view of the speakers.

Chairs should be set up theater style and angled back from the front of the room, the podium, and where the focus will be directed. This is where members of the print media should be seated. Visitors and guests should be seated behind the print media. Be sure that the vision of members of the print media is not blocked and they don't feel like second-class citizens. A space should be allotted between the participants and the seated media to allow still photographers room to shoot and so that they will not impair the vision of either the seated media or the television cameras.

Check the room for electrical outlets and be sure the circuits can handle the load requirements for the lighting. Determine those outlets most accessible for use by television.

There are differing views on whether to use a mult box (for multiple access to the audio signal), which is an electronic device into which radio and television stations can plug their audio recording devices. When a mult box is used, generally there are only one or two microphones at the podium and the sound is fed through the mult box to all the other reporters covering the event. However, some companies prefer to have the film and photographs show a dozen or more microphones to give a picture of the extent of the coverage of the event.

How to Get the Media to a News Event

The invitation should be specific as to time, place and participants. The subject matter should not be revealed except in the most general sense.

To get attendance by representative media it may be necessary sometimes to be more specific. Whatever is done will be a matter of judgment and based on your knowledge of the media being invited. You may choose to reveal the specifics as background only and not for release, or release just the essentials if you are sure that releasing them will not preclude attendance at the news conference.

Here is a typical media alert:

> MEDIA NEWS EVENT—THE TELEVISION OF TOMORROW
> New Concept Electronics will unveil its new HDTV interactive compact disk television system on Tuesday, June 5th at 10:00 a.m.

The new system is all-inclusive and is a complete package with digital stereo audio, HDTV interactive video, computer companionship and a 20-hour compact disk system that permits home recording.

The system will be in retail outlets throughout the country early next year.

Fred Anderson, president of New Concept Electronics, and Dr. Helen Nagy, who headed the research team, will make the announcement.

VISUAL OPPORTUNITIES—The system has been set up so reporters can interact with the system in several areas: playing golf, doing an automobile engine tuneup and preparing a gourmet dinner.

DATE: Tuesday, June 5
TIME: 10 a.m.
SITE: Century Ballroom
The New Plaza Hotel
1400 Central Parkway
RSVP: Mark Smith
MS&A Consultants
212/555-1010

This release should be mailed out five to seven days in advance of the events. When setting up a rush event, use faxes, mailgrams or messenger or personal delivery service. For the most important media, follow up with personal telephone calls.

Also be sure the event is listed by wire services that will further get the message out, such as the daybook of Associated Press or local-regional wire services such as City News Service in Los Angeles.

In New York, Chicago, Los Angeles, Washington, D.C., and other cities where the networks have their own news bureaus, contact the assignment editors of the networks as well as the network-owned and -operated stations.

Plan to have suitable visual props to avoid a "talking head" press conference for television and to get further identification for the company, product, service or cause. Banners or signs should be within range of the cameras. They should be non-glossy to avoid reflection. Keep in mind that television and the still photography of the print media are visual media, and play to that aspect. You may wish to place a company logo or other visual over the name of the hotel, which already is affixed to the podium or lectern. Be prepared for last-minute problems and have tape handy to hang a banner, because it may not be available from the banquet and catering department of the hotel.

Have a full news release on the subject matter of the news conference with any appropriate supporting information. If it is appropriate you may want to give the media an information kit.

A News Conference Checklist

General and Advance Items

- Invitation list?

• Notice of the event? How sent? Date?
• If appropriate, reply cards enclosed?
• Follow-up notice, inquiry? Date?
• Agenda and program prepared?
• Location selected?
• Meeting and conference room chosen?
• Luncheon room or dinner room needed?
• Coffee service, soft drinks, rolls, to be provided in room during conference?
• Visual props, banners?

Location
• Easily accessible?
• Adequate parking? Free? Valet?
• Reservations confirmed? By whom? In writing?
• Name of contact at location with phone number

Meeting or Conference Room
• Size of room? Length? Width? Height?
• Anticipated attendance?
• Seating arrangement accommodating radio, television, print media and photographers?
• Use of head table? Lectern? Podium? Is the table skirted?
• Television cameras accommodated? Risers necessary?
• Still photography accommodations?
• "Green room" or pre-conference meeting room for participants?
• Registration table? Who is assigned to table?
• Guest book?
• Name tags? Made ahead and ready for distribution? Provisions for making them on the spot? Blank tags and pens available?
• Is canned music piped into the room? If so, is there a control switch in the room to cut it off? Or, can music be quickly cut off at a central control board?
• Is the room adequately lighted for general purposes? Where and what are the lighting controls? Can the room be blacked out for slides or films?
• Does the room have mirrors that must be covered to prevent light reflection problems?
• Is it an outside room where draperies should be drawn? Does this create a lighting problem?
• At what time will the principal room be available for setup?
• What is the immediately preceding event in this room? At what time? Scheduled completion?
• Will there be staff available to help with the setup?
• Can equipment be set up prior to the meeting?

- Equipment needs—who provides? Delivery?

Television set	VCR unit
35mm carousel projector	Spare bulbs
Overhead transparency projector	Video projector
	Mult box
Extension cords	Projection screen
16mm projector	Projection stands
Public address system	Speakers

  Microphones: lavaliere, hand-held, cordless?
- Easels? Other display items?
- Is the public address system adequate?
  Is it built in throughout the room?
  Is it self-contained?
  Are there lectern mikes? Stand mikes?
  Is the system tested for acoustics, kickback and clarity?
  Will the system need to be rented?
  Where are the system controls?

Luncheon or Dinner

- Seating—round tables? Square tables? Number needed? U-shaped arrangement with head table?
- Head table—elevated platform or on floor level? Number of seats needed at the head table?
- Lighting and lighting controls?
- Public address system?
- Menu and price confirmed? With whom? Copy in writing?
- Bar service set up? Waiter service? Hosted?
- Guarantee and final confirmation date on number? Number to be confirmed? Price-per-plate guarantee?
- Can room be easily served without disturbance? Deadline for room setup?

ADDITIONAL TIPS FOR MEDIA COVERAGE

The DeFrancesco/Goodfriend firm suggests that practitioners be creative in generating media coverage. Here are some techniques they recommend (DeFrancesco 1994):

Review Editorial Calendars. Anticipate the editorial needs of media people. Review the annual editorial calendars published by many trade and business journals and some consumer magazines. These calendars pinpoint the major topics planned for coverage in each issue of the magazine. Some might indicate specific types of products that will be spotlighted in an issue or general concepts and trends that will be a focus.

Take Advantage of Trade Show Appearances. If a company exhibits at a trade show, there are great opportunities to foster press coverage. Nearly every trade show is attended by the media that cover the industry as well as consumer media. Activities that can be conducted include providing trade publications with information on any new product or service that will be exhibited; developing a media information kit on the company and its products for placement in the press room at the show; building relationships with the media by scheduling appointments with editors to visit the exhibit and meet with top executives.

Create Your Own News. Just attending a trade show makes news to some local newspapers. Other types of created or manufactured news releases include giving a speech at the convention, receiving an award or releasing a survey on a trend.

The Media Bandwagon. There are occasions when one media outlet covers a story and because of it, others will hop on the proverbial bandwagon and pursue the story. If you are not in the first story, be sure you are before the parade goes by.

Media Monitor Other Media. Media watch, listen and view themselves. Coverage in a trade journal that covers consumer electronics, for example, can provide the added benefit of reaching the electronics reporter at *The Wall Street Journal.*

Offer Story Ideas to Media Not Associated with Your Company or Client. When you spot a situation with good story potential, even if the prospective story has nothing to do with your company, let the reporter or editor know about it by a phone call, fax or letter. If the editor likes the idea, chances are he or she will be more receptive the next time you pitch your story idea.

Build Relationships with Key Target Media. Know what your media targets cover and the stories they have done, and keep them informed with background information. When appropriate, even if it doesn't pertain to a specific story idea, go to breakfast or lunch with him or her just to keep the editor filled in on industry developments.

REFERENCES

DeFrancesco, John. 1994. DeFrancesco/Goodfriend Public Relations. Information package. Chicago.

Posert, Harvey P., vice president of communications and industry affairs, Robert Mondavi Winery. 1994. Memorandum to author. Oakland, Calif. April.

The Rockey Company. 1994. Memorandum to author. Seattle. April.

6

HOW TO MAKE A PRESS KIT WORK FOR YOU

Whatever you call it—a press kit, media/information kit or information package—this can be one of the most useful and multipurpose tools in your marketing public relations campaign. Properly used, it will be an invaluable part of your program.

An effective kit should be designed for many uses. For publicity purposes it can be used at news conferences or media briefings. It is an excellent information piece to give to editors prior to, during or after an interview regarding the product or service being sold in the campaign. It can be used with a cover letter to solicit an interview. And it can be used as a briefing book for media and participants in a meeting.

Once the basic materials are prepared, additional copies can be printed and the contents adapted for many other uses. For example, use the basic kit with additional product information and prices and it can become a part of a sales presentation to a potential buyer. Add basic pro forma cash flow and financial information and the kit also can become an integral part of a financial presentation to a lender or banker.

The kit also can be used by the human resources department as an orientation and information package for new employees by adding additional information to the core kit. The cover itself has many uses and can be the focal point of a meeting information package.

The kit can be adapted for general use as well. When supplemented with specific information, it can be a corporate or product backgrounder for a government organization or congressional committee.

WHAT SHOULD THE KIT CONTAIN?

The kit should incorporate any information about the company and the products or services it is selling that will be of general and specific interest to the press. Fundamental contents of a press or information kit should include the following:

Basic Fact Sheet. This is general background information written in either a text or an outline format. It should answer all of the Who, What, Where, When, Why and How questions. Questions can be posed and answered with the fact sheet. It should talk about the campaign being announced, what is new with the product, what the company is doing differently—basically the key elements of the campaign. The fact sheet can be double-spaced, single-spaced or spaced 1.5 lines, depending on individual preference and corporate style.

Supplemental Fact Sheets. These supplement the basic fact sheet and should be concise, single-sheet outlines that segment products, services and geographic regions. A supplemental fact sheet becomes a modular element in the overall kit.

Biographies. Detail in text form, the background of the company or organization, when it was established, how large it is in relation to the industry and its competitors, its successes and innovations and its leadership role. In effect, stress the selling points you have in your copy platform. Next, include biographies on the leading company executives such as the president, chair, CEO and those involved in the program. With single pages prepared and kept on file on all leading executives, the individual biographies can be important modular elements and customized for each specific use.

Be sure to include honors won; membership, participation and involvement in professional business, government and industry organizations; and colleges and degrees.

Photographs. Include black-and-white, glossy photographs of the leading individuals whose biographies are contained in the kit. Preference by editors is glossy and a 5-by-7-inch size. Be sure to get quality prints of the individuals in minimum orders ranging from 25 to 100 copies for as low as 25 to 30 cents each.

Where relevant to tell the story, other photographs should be included that would illustrate products, services or facilities. These are preferred in an 8-by-10-inch size. Reproducible graphics also can be included and printed on glossy, printed stock or glossy, photographic stock. These can include logos, charts and graphs.

Be sure to identify all photographs. For individuals there are several ways to do this. You can have the name of the individual set in type and included as part of the photograph when quantity prints are made. Newspaper editors prefer a label on the back of the photograph with the person's name and title and the name of the company. All photographs should have captions and on those 8-by-10s also include the name, address and phone number of a company contact.

If color photographs of the black-and-white pictures in the kit are available, note this and let the editor know the format in which they are available, such as 35mm, 4-by-5-inch transparency, and so on.

News Release. When the press kit is used for a press conference, where a meeting is called, and where media are invited to attend, have a news release about the announcement being made. Tell the story succinctly, answering all of the journalistic Ws—Who, What, Where, When, Why—and How.

Feature Story. This is a type of news release that does not involve an urgent time element. It is as newsworthy a month from now as it is today. Feature stories are included in press kits to give editors ideas of the types of stories they can write about you, your organization or the product you are selling. They also can use excerpts from the feature story, with attribution to your company or an individual you may quote.

The feature article can contain statements of opinions, predictions and forecasts, or excerpts from speeches given by management. It also may be directed at different audiences and can be modified with statistics or information to a target group of media.

Quotes. Where appropriate, some press kits can contain one or two pages of "quotable quotes" that editors can lift and use in stories they may be planning. Such quotes already can be contained in a news release or a feature story that is in the press kit, but the quote page allows them to find an excerpt with a minimum of effort.

Speeches. If the press kit is to be distributed at a major convention or conference or where a company executive is giving a speech, then copies of that speech could be included in the press kit. Also have an executive summary of the speech and key quotes that can be excerpted, such as the way the broadcast media would edit for sound bites.

Pamphlets and Brochures. These are printed material that will highlight or further help tell the story. They can be produced by your organization or copied from other associations and organizations.

Reprints. Important stories that have been written about individuals or the organization, or in which company officers have been quoted as business and industry leaders, should be reprinted and included in the basic press kit. Reprints are especially important because they are third-party "endorsements" of the firm and its leaders.

Keep the information kit to the subject. Do not overkill. Keep it brief, otherwise the important issues will get lost with the superfluous, and its value to the editor—and to you—will be diminished.

CONTENTS FOR MULTIPURPOSE KITS

Always have a generic kit assembled—one that will be the nucleus of information representing the company or its products and services or issues for any type of audience for which it may be used. For a sales presentation, detailed product and pricing information would be included. If used for a meeting, you would include an agenda and other supporting documentation.

For employees, an employee handbook with company rules and regulations would be combined with the generic kit with the biographical information about the company, biographies on the key executives, important reprints, appropriate pamphlets and brochures and other information that would further tell the company's story and provide a proper orientation for the employee.

PACKAGING THE PRESS KIT

There are many ways to package your press kit, depending on your budget and what you want to accomplish. Some companies have put the press kit inside a plastic pouch or folder, or even a vinyl or leather zipper case or portfolio cover, to make it a nice gift for the recipient.

Remember that the contents and substance of the kit are what matter, not how they are presented. Simply putting the modular elements in a manila envelope is sufficient. However, some items are nice mementos and appreciated by the media and others.

Mechanically Producing the Cover

First determine the quantity of covers you expect to use during the coming year. Check with other corporate officers regarding their anticipated use of the cover to determine an overall quantity.

Custom covers can be expensive, but any cost is amortized over the term of the use. You also must consider the importance of image and what you are selling. The cost will include design, typography, graphics and printing. Printing alone can range from $1 to $2 each depending on the quantity, type of paper stock chosen and the design—the number of colors and whether it will be embossed or hot-foil stamped. Generally it is not economically feasible to print fewer than 500 custom folders, and quantity cost breaks do not begin until there are orders of 1,000 or more.

Ready-made covers are available from stationery stores. They can be "customized" by applying a label. Cost ranges from 45 cents to $1 depending on quantity. There is a good selection available in different types of paper stock, from matte to a high-gloss plastic finish, in a variety of colors. You may only need a small quantity; this case would warrant buying stock covers. Costs are prohibitive otherwise. Ask your art director or designer, a printer or your public relations agency for their thoughts. Many excellent stock folders are already available for such purposes.

Consider multiple uses for the cover. Some companies have taken an overrun of an embossed or multicolored press kit cover and trimmed it to be a single sheet and cover for a custom presentation folder, sales information flyer or employee manual where the design is the same. This makes a custom kit cover more cost-effective.

If you already have a design, then discuss the costs of printing with a printer. If not, you need to have the image you want designed by a commercial artist. Be specific with regard to what you want and how much you want to spend.

Every press run is a cost. Each time the paper stock passes through the press—whether it is printing a color or not—it adds to your cost: embossing, steel-die engraving, each color used (black plus others), foil-stamping, scoring, die-cutting the paper stock to make the folder, folding the pockets, gluing the pockets, or lacquering or varnishing the cover.

Special Considerations for the Kit Cover

Everyone has personal preferences. Consider the pros and cons of cutting slits in the pockets or flaps so a business card can be inserted. Or would you prefer to have certain information printed on the flap? Or you can leave the flap without any information, which would be contained with name, address and phone contact on the fact sheet and news and feature releases.

Certain colors and inks, especially black and metallic finishes such as silver, need a coat of clear lacquer or varnish to prevent smudging. This is an extra press run and cost.

If you want certain users to retain the press kit in a file, design the kit cover with a tab to encourage filing. This would only be a nominal additional cost if you wanted to split the press run and have some covers printed as regular folders without the tab.

While on the press, single-sheet copies of just the cover can be run at nominal costs. This is an excellent opportunity to consider using the cover for an employee manual, as a proposal or for other purposes. It can be especially useful for quick, in-house presentations and proposals where there is access to velo-binding or spiral binding.

Be sure to select a paper stock heavy enough to carry items to be included in the kit—probably at least 80-pound, if not 100-pound, cover stock. Be sure the pockets are deep enough to hold all the materials to be inserted in the kit.

The finish is important. Remember that some stocks do not always emboss well or will not take hot stamping well. Your art director or printer will give you advice on this. Be careful on the gluing of certain coated stocks that need special glues. Sometimes printers make mistakes, and it is always safe and correct to ask.

On the finished art work, or mechanical, which is being sent to the printer to produce the kit, spell out all details on the reverse side. Often your art director or designer will have a stamp or form that will ensure you get the job you are ordering. This information will spell out the paper stock, press run quantities and colors, and it is an easy way to avoid any misunderstanding later between you, the printer and the artist. Be sure to have written bids in advance from both the printer and the artist. Generally it is wise to get bids from more than one printer. Many do not do this type of work because of the embossing and binding operations and will only contract out to another job printer, taking a profit on the markup and costing you more money.

QUANTITIES FOR THE COMPLETED KIT

The cover is the envelope or shell for the kit. Because of the cost of the covers, print a good quantity. However, you do not need to print a quantity of all the modular elements. Keep on hand an ample supply of generic kits; this quantity will be determined by use. Depending on your reproduction facilities, you will know how long it will take you to assemble various types of modular kits. The contents can always be duplicated on a high-quality photocopy machine.

Stay flexible so that the biographies, fact sheet and other information can be continually updated. Keep master copies of the various finished kits so you have a basic generic kit, and kits marked A, B, C, and so on, depending on use. Keep the basic kit updated with current reprints, pamphlets, statistics, speeches and quotes.

Always plan to have additional copies available, even for a press conference. You may plan to have 100 media representatives attend, but you should have extra copies for those who may be unable to attend. Most of the ingredients of the kit will not be wasted. The kit covers are always usable as is much of the contents. These can be included in a newer and currently updated kit. Don't prepare 500 if you only need 100, but a few extras won't hurt.

THE ELECTRONIC PRESS KIT

Some companies and organizations are now distributing their press materials by computer, by either sending the information directly to the media with a disk or having the media access the information electronically. When Marsha Robertson, a Hollywood entertainment executive and former vice president of national publicity for MGM/UA Film Company, was working as a project director for the film *Sneakers* at Universal Pictures, she and her colleagues produced the first interactive picture computer press kit for a motion picture. Robertson says it may be primitive by today's standards, but it was produced on a 3-by-5-inch floppy disk for IBM-compatible computers and featured an interface menu that could take the editor to several branches: color stills from the film, production notes, credits and a puzzle to be solved with an anagram. The anagram was a takeoff on one of the film's plot devices. She says the innovation broke new ground for movie-related publicity and proved to be quite popular with the press. It even resulted in publicity about the novelty of the computer disk press kit.

Keep File Copies

Always keep a master file copy of each press kit or other type of kit assembled, including all contents. Be sure to date each and keep the sample so marked in a master file. You never know when you will need to refer to it or to compare even a generic kit to one done in a previous year.

To prevent someone giving away a file copy, you can draw a red diagonal line through the cover and each page and photograph in the kit.

WHAT TO DO WHEN THE KIT IS READY

This is when the kit's value starts giving you a return on its investment. What was the purpose in the first place of preparing the kit? To hold a press conference? To market your company to the local and regional media? This is your objective.

If you are marketing to the media, consider this. Develop a list of the media who would be interested in hearing your story—the business editors of local newspapers; radio and television talk show hosts; editors of local, regional and national trade publications read by your potential customers.

Prepare a concise, to-the-point letter to each, introducing yourself and explaining why you are sending the press kit. Suggest a meeting, then follow up within a week with a phone call. If the editor is not interested in a story now, or does not have the time to meet with you, encourage the editor to keep your information on file and share it with associates. Ask that he or she call you whenever the media outlet does plan a story on this or any related subject. Let the editor know what you are most qualified to talk about and to be interviewed and quoted on.

Remember that the press conference or news conference is the most abused of all publicity and public relations techniques. In the major media centers of the United States—New York, Los Angeles and Washington, D.C.—there are many conferences scheduled and few that merit extensive coverage. Don't abuse the opportunity of holding an event. Do not overpromise, for you want support from the media if you ever hold another conference.

7

HOW TO USE PRINT MEDIA

In the beginning and before radio or television, the only available medium for the early pioneers of public relations and publicity was print. Then it was limited primarily to local and regional newspapers and general interest magazines.

Today's practitioner has a wide selection of print media to use—all types of newspapers and magazines, vertical interest trade publications, company publications or house organs and newsletters. A news or feature story placement with a columnist or even an op-ed piece are not the only exposure opportunities with print media. All too often the use of a photograph, chart or graph to tell the story is overlooked. Sometimes just a photograph alone is all that is needed to deliver the message.

KNOW WHAT THE EDITOR WANTS

Before you send information to a publication, be sure you know its format. Don't send color photographs to a publication that does not run color. Don't send a release on a new product or literature if it won't fit the editorial format. Become familiar with the publication and have a feeling for what the editor wants.

News USA, a national syndicated feature service, conducted a survey of 6,200 newspaper editors. From a list of 36 topics, the 10 most requested were:

1. Health, 62.4 percent
2. Senior citizens, 61.4 percent
3. Medicine, 56.4 percent
4. Agriculture, 50.5 percent

5. Environment, 50.5 percent
6. Food, 49.5 percent
7. Education, 45.5 percent
8. Consumer issues, 44.6 percent
9. Recreation, 43.6 percent
10. Finance, 41.6 percent

While 48.5 percent of those responding said to send a story of any length, nearly 30 percent said 250 words was the preferred length (O'Dwyer 1993).

THE PITCH LETTER

More than with any other medium, the pitch letter is not only very effective, but often the only way to get that important story sold to an editor of a print publication. The pitch letter is just that—telling an editor the story idea in 100 words or less (figuratively, not literally). Pitch letters are a necessity with magazines and for major newspaper feature stories. If the editor likes the concept, the process begins. The editor will begin by asking for additional information and possibly interviews.

An effective pitch letter writer will develop several story outlines or themes and tailor these proposals to the editor and the publication. The story should be proposed on a first exclusive basis, meaning that the periodical that initially publishes the story will be the only one to carry it. Good story ideas are continually recycled.

Entire campaigns have been built around pitch letters, with almost no publicity releases developed, written and distributed on a non-exclusive basis. Pitch letters also are a most cost-effective means of creating awareness and recognition for a product or service.

Squash is not an easy sport to sell. And *The New York Times* is not considered an easy publication in which to place a story. Here is how Don Smith, of Don Smith Consultants approached this problem (Smith 1994):

> Mr. Dave Anderson
> Sports Columnist
> THE NEW YORK TIMES
> 229 West 43rd Street
> New York, N.Y. 10036
>
> Dear Dave:
>
> Jahangir Khan!
>
> The name doesn't mean much to you, does it?
>
> Let's see, how can I describe Jahangir Khan? If he had taken up baseball, he'd be Hank Aaron. If he played basketball, they'd call him the "Big O." In the NFL he'd be Joe Montana. If he rode race horses, he'd be Eddie Arcaro aboard five Derby winners. And if he played the cello in his spare time, he'd be Pablo Casals.

Jahangir Khan is none of these people but he is all of them.

Quite simply, Jahangir Khan is the greatest squash racquets player to play this demanding and exciting racquet sport. He is, at the tender age of 25, already a living legend, a scion of the famed Pakistani clan that has, over the past century, produced a long line of world champions. Indeed, he overshadows the feats of even the incomparable Sharif Khan, his cousin, about whom they said, "Nobody will ever play the game better!"

But Jahangir, incredibly, *does* play it better. He is unbeaten and unchallenged in world competition. He is as close to invincible as any athlete has ever been in his sport. He is squash's "fastest gun in the West."

A few years ago, Dave, you did a column on Sharif Khan. I think you might be interested in doing one now on the young player who has made us all forget Sharif, impossible as that seems. He will be in town next week for the annual Chivas Regal Shootout and I would be happy to set up an interview, either by phone or in person.

Let me know, okay?

With warm regards,

DON SMITH

The first response was, "Nobody could be this good," to which Smith answered, "Yeah, well come and see for yourself." It resulted in a column by Anderson in *The New York Times.*

Smith did a shorter version the year before about Sharif Khan to make a television pitch:

Mr. Marv Albert
Sports Director
WNBC-TV
30 Rockefeller Plaza
New York, NY 10112

Dear Marv:

Sharif Khan wants you. Bad!

Sincerely,
DON SMITH

This worked, too. Albert called Smith to see who Khan was and went on to give the tournament and the athlete more than one minute of airtime, which can be an eternity in New York.

Guidelines for Pitch Letters

John DeFrancesco and Gary Goodfriend of DeFrancesco/Goodfriend Public Relations in Chicago suggest the following tips for writing a pitch letter (DeFrancesco/Goodfriend 1994):

Be Brief. Try to limit the letter to one page. Media receive dozens of these letters a day, and their reading time is at a premium. Create eye appeal for your letter by writing concise sentences and short paragraphs; use bullet points to enhance readability.

Write the Story Lead as the Start of the Letter. Many effective pitch letters often provide the right framework for the story that you hope will be written ultimately, or the television segment that will be produced eventually. By doing this, you're graphically showing the editor how your idea comes to life.

Provoke the Reader. One way to accomplish this is to begin a pitch letter with a question, or a startling statistic. (Note above how Don Smith did this with Marv Albert.)

Don't Oversell or Make Your Letter Sound Like a Commercial. Remember, you're not trying to run an advertisement. The letter must spell out why the story or segment will benefit the media outlet's audience.

Know What the Reporter Has Been Covering and Tie Your Idea to It. Investigate what the target media person has been reporting recently, and reflect this knowledge in your pitch letter. You will appear "involved" in the journalist's activities. Even if the reader declines your pitch this time, the person may be more amenable on your next effort.

Send Background Materials. A company brochure, a news release, a photo or even an article published in a non-competing media outlet (for example, a trade magazine story if pitching a newspaper) may be enclosed with the letter to provide additional background, if appropriate.

Close the Letter by Stating You Will Follow Up by Telephone. Your call will be to discuss the story idea with the editor or producer.

NEWSPAPERS

There are a number of types of newspapers, including national dailies, metropolitan dailies, suburban dailies, weeklies, and ethnic and foreign-language publications.

A few newspapers are considered national in scope, not only because of their coverage and circulation or distribution, but also because of the impact they have on the general public in the way news is treated. Such national daily newspapers would include *USA Today, The Wall Street Journal, The Christian Science Monitor, The New York Times* and *The Washington Post*. The latter two newspapers have their own syndicated news services, which can result in even broader mass coverage.

An international newspaper is the *International Herald Tribune,* which was founded in the United States but ceased publishing in New York City in the 1960s. Now published in Paris, the newspaper not only can be purchased from newsstands throughout Europe, it is seldom more than one day delayed for mail delivery in the United States.

There are important regional newspapers including *The Los Angeles Times/Newsday, Chicago Tribune, The Dallas Morning News, Atlanta Journal-Constitution, Boston Globe* and *Denver Post.* Because of the prestige and circulation of these daily newspapers, their editors are inundated with publicity materials and always have far more information and story ideas than available space.

When you have a story for a daily newspaper, be sure you have an idea where it will be used in the newspaper. Is this a breaking news story that should be in the main news section? Or in the state or metro section? Is it a feature story or sidebar that might be appropriate for a lifestyle section? Is there a business news angle? Even sports?

Know the editors of your important outlets. Know what they want and in what format they want a story idea. Get to know their styles, preferences, pet peeves and idiosyncracies. Some prefer to have a pitch letter or the idea outlined in writing. Others prefer to be called and discuss the story idea on the phone. If you have a story for a special section that may appear only in a Sunday edition, such as a real estate, calendar or entertainment section, know the deadline for that section. Because of deadlines some section editors are busier on certain days than others. Avoid calling on these days for a friendly discussion.

Wire services including Associated Press (AP), United Press International (UPI) and Reuters are effective ways of reaching the major newspapers in this country. However, just because a wire service carries the story gives you no insurance the newspaper will run the story. Distribution services such as Business Wire and PR Newswire that were described in Chapter 4 also provide a means to deliver the story to the publication.

There also are regional wires that serve their media customers in ways similar to AP and UPI. One is Los Angeles-based City News Service, which provides news to media throughout Southern California. This is a very important outlet if you want to alert Southern California newspapers and radio stations to a media event, photo opportunity or press conference as well as to get a story told.

Syndicate feature services and syndicated columnists also are vehicles to reach newspapers. Paid release distribution services and local and regional leased public relations wire services provide another excellent alternative.

Be familiar with the editorial style of the newspaper you want to run your story. Not all newspapers follow the style of the Associated Press. Often you can purchase the stylebook of a newspaper. If the story is not being mass produced, but targeted for a particular newspaper, deliver it to the editor in a format that follows the newspaper's editorial style.

Create exposure opportunities for your product or service by looking beyond the obvious. If you have a book on baseball, don't just send it to the editor of the book review section—get it in the hands of the sports editor or one of the leading sports columnists. The same is true for a cookbook. While the book editor may run it in the book review section, the food editor may be interested in doing a much longer feature story on the author.

While the business editor may profile a corporate executive, there may be additional exposure opportunities for the company with a human interest piece on the executive's spouse in a lifestyle or Sunday magazine section. Most stories can be approached several different ways with different themes, leads, substance and concept. The public relations practitioner has to be creative and know how to structure segments of the story to be of interest to all possible publications.

If you write an op-ed, opinion piece or guest editorial for a newspaper's editorial page, be sure you know the editor's ground rules. Some want exclusivity on the work for a specified number of days and for a particular geographic area. If you give *The New York Times* an op-ed or opinion piece, it will expect nationwide exclusivity. Other regional newspapers may only want exclusivity for the state or city. Op-ed pieces generally are 750 words in length, and an opinion piece is generally 1,000 words long. A good, creative writer can take the same piece and recycle it a number of different times to newspapers in different markets without breaking any ground rule.

Tips for a News Release

John DeFrancesco and Gary Goodfriend suggest these basic reminders when writing an effective news release:

1. The content should be written in the inverted pyramid style, with the most important information in the lead and the next couple of paragraphs and less-important facts covered later in the release.
2. Follow the newspaper style that answers the five W's and H—Who, What, Where, When, Why and *High*. Cover these high up, or early on, in the story and expand on points with more detail later in the release.
3. Like the pitch letter, write concisely and keep the paragraphs short.
4. The release presentation should be in a format acceptable to the media. This means the first page on company letterhead; a contact name and phone number positioned in the right or left top corner of the first page; a headline; a release date; double-spaced; enough room in the left and right margins for editors to make notes.
5. Write in an objective style. When referring to the company, don't say "our company" or use the word "I" unless this is in a quote. It should read "the company." Avoid puffery, jargon, technical terms and editorial opinions. As Sgt. Joe Friday on "Dragnet" used to say, "Just the facts, ma'am."

6. To help organize the release, first develop an outline.

7. Read the release out loud. Often it is easier to hear awkward-sounding phrases than to look for them on paper.

8. Proofread, proofread, proofread. Be sure that the release does not contain a single typo, that names are spelled correctly and that phone numbers are accurate and not transposed.

9. Make sure the news release actually contains news. Remember that news for one media outlet may not be news in another. What is newsworthy for the *Daily Herald* may not warrant a mention in the *Tribune.* An announcement on a new food product for a trade journal such as *Vending Times* or *Snack Food* may not make it onto the food pages of *Family Circle* or *Good Housekeeping*.

Weekly Newspapers

Exclusivity generally is not something you have to be concerned about in getting exposure through weekly newspapers. Weekly newspapers are a tremendous outlet for news that is truly local—that is, the individual written about in the news release is from the community. In reaching the masses served by the nation's weekly newspapers, the big question comes down to budget and how can you be most cost-effective in getting the desired audience reach. Paid feature release services are an important and cost-effective way to reach weekly newspapers.

Sunday Newspaper Supplements

Sunday supplements are nationally distributed magazine sections that are part of a Sunday newspaper. Examples include *Parade* and *USA Weekend.* The circulation and audience reach is tremendous with these publications. A pitch letter is the best way to start. The story must be provided on an exclusive basis. Before making the pitch, become familiar with the types of stories the editors want.

MAGAZINES

There are many categories of magazines—general interest (*Life*), news (*Time, Newsweek, U.S. News & World Report*) and special interest. Special interest includes business magazines (*Business Week, Fortune, Forbes*), women's magazines (*Elle, Self*), home and family service (*Better Homes & Gardens, Family Circle, Woman's Day, Good Housekeeping*) and as many categories as people have special interests (*Road and Track, JazzTimes, Cross Stitch*). There also are important ethnic publications (*Ebony, Black Enterprise, Hispanic, Noticias del Mundo*).

As with the newspapers, know the publication and the types of stories it uses. All good practitioners should always be on the lookout for new magazines and seeking to discover new publicity outlets. Doctors' waiting rooms and airlines are two good places to quickly find and scan magazines that one normally does not read. Another way to do simple research is to browse at the magazine section of a newsstand and purchase several publications that have opportunities of being a publicity outlet. The publication's masthead will even provide the names of the editorial staff.

Because of the advance lead time needed in magazine publishing, find out from the editors what types of stories they want for future issues. Many will have special holiday editions and shopper's sections that provide an opportunity to give exposure to a new product. Stories also can be developed not only around holiday issues, but to appear in the issue of the publication in the month of the holiday, such as July for Independence Day or February for Valentine's Day. Ask your editorial contact for an advance copy of the annual editorial schedule with themes and special editions.

TRADE PUBLICATIONS

Trade publications can be both newspapers and magazines. They may be published daily, weekly, monthly or at some other frequency. These are considered vertical interest publications because of their narrow editorial focus concentrating on just one industry. One of the leading daily trade publications of national interest is a newspaper, *Women's Wear Daily*. In the entertainment industry there are two leading daily magazines, *Hollywood Reporter* and *Variety*. There also is a weekly edition of *Variety* that is published in New York, on the opposite coast from its daily of the same name.

There is a trade publication for every conceivable interest. Some are national in coverage while some are local or regional. Some have controlled circulation and there is no subscription charge, but the recipient must be a qualified member of the profession covered by the magazine. (Chapter 3 lists the various reference publications available to identify important trade publications.)

COMPANY PUBLICATIONS OR HOUSE ORGANS

There are thousands of important publications published by companies and other organizations for their employees that use public relations information unrelated to the product or service of the company. Examples include household tips, travel ideas and suggestions, financial concepts or information about certain new products.

There are reference directories (see Chapter 3) that help identify leading company house organs. Companies also can be reached through feature release services. The numbers of American readers reached is tremendous. If you are promoting a consumer product or service, you should consider that everyone is a potential customer, regardless of the publication in which the story appears.

PHOTOGRAPHS AND GRAPHICS

Newspapers and magazines are always looking for good photographs. In News USA's newspaper survey (1993), 70.3 percent of the editors said they are interested in receiving graphics and 65.3 percent said they would like to have photographs.

Too many firms budget dollars are spent for ribbon cuttings, ground breakings, hand shakings and people posed almost as rigid statues. Good photography is an art, and it takes a professional to see the opportunities. Consider adding a line item in the budget every year to bring in a leading photojournalist who can walk around the facility and look for photo opportunities. Too often great photographs come from things you see every day and take for granted.

The Associated Press will transmit color and black-and-white photographs. Services also can be purchased using PR Newswire and Business Wire.

Look for opportunities in a story where the information can be supported with a graph or chart. Graphics further encourage use of the story by a newspaper or magazine. The publication may not use what you have sent, but the concept of the graphic to illustrate the story may help get the story used. *USA Today* has prompted a new look at and use of graphics by newspapers.

Public relations executives at Home Box Office, a New York City-based Time Warner Entertainment Company and television cable network, have been exploring the possibility of making publicity stills and press releases for original television programming and still photographs for some motion pictures available to newspapers on a CD-ROM disk. Not all newspapers have the capability to use this new computer technology, and the service is still under consideration.

MARKET YOUR RESULTS

Reprint clippings and purchase reprints of important magazine stories to help market your results. A cover story or major feature story in an important trade or consumer publication is virtually a third-party endorsement of that company's product and service.

Residential community developers and home builders have effectively used cover stories about the project that were published in building and construction trade publications as sales brochures for prospective home buyers. A story in a leading industry publication also can enhance a company's image and reputation for its lenders and bankers.

ESTABLISH MEDIA RELATIONSHIPS

As you get to know the beat reporters or editors who cover the business, industry or profession you represent, keep them informed of developments in your area and maintain periodic contact. Let them know that you are available and will help them when they are doing roundup stories or basic, generic stories about a particular subject. This may not mean instant exposure for your product or service, but it will pay off with big dividends (in the long run) because the editor or reporter knows you are a source to depend on and who delivers. You will be sought out as a source for future stories.

Editors and reporters network their sources among themselves, but you can network with them to ask for an introduction to a reporter or editor of a newspaper, magazine, wire service or other outlet who does not know you.

CHECKLIST FOR PRINT MEDIA

1. Is this a breaking news or feature story? Or an announcement or media alert?
2. Should it be pitched exclusively? Or use selective, mass distribution?
3. How should it be distributed? In-house? Using PR Newswire or Business Wire? Or a feature release service?
4. What about my timing? When should I distribute the release?
5. Has the mailing list been reviewed? Are all opportunities covered? Special interest and ethnic publications? Foreign publications? Trade publications?
6. Is the story going to the right person at each media outlet?
7. Is there a graphic possibility? Photograph? Illustration? Chart?

REFERENCES

DeFrancesco/Goodfriend Public Relations. 1994. Notes from professional presentation.

News USA Inc. 1993. News release. Alexandria, Va.

O'Dwyer's Washington Report. 1993. Vol. 3, no. 12. June 7.

Smith, Don. 1994. Letter to author. New York: Don Smith Consultants. March 1.

8

HOW TO GET THE MOST EXPOSURE ON RADIO AND TELEVISION

The shrinking number of newspaper, magazine and print media outlets, a shift of the country's preference to obtaining the majority of its information in sound bites from the airwaves, a declining literacy rate and the need to rapidly convey information to a mass audience all have contributed to the increasing importance of the electronic or broadcast media: radio and television.

This latter medium is becoming increasingly important as the number of television households in the United States continues to grow each year. In 1991, 98.2 percent of all households in the country had television, totaling 93,100,000 television households.

In 1993 there were 1,477 television stations throughout the United States, broken down as follows: 553 VHF (channels 2-13) commercial, 571 UHF (channels 14 and higher) commercial, 124 VHF public/educational and 229 UHF public/educational.

There were 10,889 radio stations in the United States in 1993, of which 4,987 were AM, 4,442 were FM and 1,460 were public/educational. Some 77 percent of the population, or nearly 157 million people, listen to the radio on an average day, and 95 percent of all automobiles and 99 percent of all households have radios. There are 551.8 million radio sets in use every day.

Cable television continues to increase. As of 1993, there were 9,575 cable systems throughout the country, and 56,072,270, or 60.3 percent of all households, have cable television (NCTA 1993).

Television sets are turned on 6 hours and 53 minutes a day in the average American house (Rieger 1994). Viewing time is broken down as follows:

Men, 3 hours, 51 minutes
Women, 4 hours, 28 minutes
Teens, 3 hours, 15 minutes
Children, 3 hours, 18 minutes

WHAT TV RATINGS AND SHARES MEAN

The life expectancy of a television program, especially in prime time (8 p.m. until 11:00 p.m. Eastern and Pacific time, 7 p.m. until 10:00 p.m. Central and Mountain time) depends on its rating or share of market which equates to the number of viewers watching the program. A television rating point represents a viewer audience of 931,000 television households. A 10 rating would indicate that 9,310,000 households watched a particular program, a 20 rating would indicate 18,620,000, and so forth.

Share is the percentage of television households watching television at any particular time who watched a particular program. If 50 million households were watching television, a 50 share would be 25 million, or 50 percent of 50 million, for that particular program. It is possible to have a higher share of audience and a lower rating. This would happen if a program had the same 50 share but only 30 million households were tuned in at that particular time; thus, the 50 share would be 15 million viewers rather than the 25 million in the first example.

AREAS OF POTENTIAL EXPOSURE ON RADIO AND TV

Radio and television offer myriad opportunities for the creative professional seeking exposure for a company, organization, product, service or cause.

Here are some examples of television opportunities:

Talk Shows. Network ("Good Morning America," "The Today Show," "CBS This Morning," "The Tonight Show With Jay Leno," "Larry King Live," "Late Show With David Letterman," "Sunday Today"), syndicated (Donahue, Geraldo, Oprah, Regis and Kathie Lee, Maury Povich, Sally Jessy Raphael, Jenny Jones), local and cable.

Magazine Programs. Network ("60 Minutes," "20/20," "PrimeTime Live"), syndicated ("Working Woman"), local and cable.

Public Affairs. Network ("Face the Nation," "Nightline," "This Week With David Brinkley," "Meet the Press"), syndicated, local and cable.

News. Network, syndicated, local and cable.

You also can produce a video news release for distribution to television and produce vignettes and programs for distribution to radio and television stations. Ways to do this effectively are covered in upcoming chapters, along with suggestions for syndicated and bartered and informational programming.

Radio is primarily a local-market medium, but there are opportunities with talk shows, public affairs programming and news. Carefully research the programs you want to target for exposure opportunities. Use the directories that are available and discussed in Chapter 3. Monitor newscasts, local talk shows and public affairs programming on networks, syndicated and local programs. Do your homework and research the audience. Pay particular attention to the overall editorial content of a news show. Each news program has its own identity. Identify the feature reporters who specialize in various areas such as consumer, education, health, environment, business, sports and entertainment. Develop your customized, personal list complete with contacts for each of the targeted areas with the name, title, address and phone number of the contact, what type of material is preferred and deadlines.

The most important thing to consider for television is to think in visual concepts that will translate into story possibilities. On both radio and television the story must be told clearly and concisely in as brief a time as possible. For radio it also must be told so that it will be visualized and understood by the listener. Most of all, tell the story so that however it is edited, there is a sound bite that gets the message across.

Whether you are seeking out a program for an interview for your company representative, or a program has sought you out and wants to interview one of your executives, be sure that you are familiar with the program. If it is radio, record it several times over a period of several weeks. Do the same thing for a television program. Study the types of questions asked and how the host handles the interviews, and be certain that the concept you suggest for the interview will conform to the format of the program.

WHAT DO RADIO STATIONS WANT?

News USA (1994) surveyed station managers of 6,300 radio stations, and the 10 most requested script topics were:

1. Health, 70 percent
2. Consumer, 67 percent
3. Education, 64 percent
4. Environment, 63 percent
5. Medicine, 56 percent
6. Entertainment, 52 percent

7. Safety, 51 percent
8. People, 50 percent
9. Senior citizens, 49 percent
10. (Tie) Sports and Taxes, 48 percent each

A 30-second script was preferred by 72 percent of the respondents, followed by 37 percent for a 60-second script and 14 percent for a 45-second one. The survey also showed scripts were the preferred format by 67 percent of the stations, followed by 47 percent for cassettes and 18 percent for actualities.

HOW TO PITCH A TALK SHOW OR PUBLIC AFFAIRS PROGRAM

Once you have determined the program you want to target for an interview, find out who makes the decision on guests. The exact title may vary with different programs, but generally the decision makers for these shows are the producers and associate producers. In some instances, the host of a show also serves as the producer. Check the show's credits at the end of the program or call the production office for their names.

Outline a theme or concept that coincides with the overall strategy and copy platform of the campaign. Then prepare a letter for the decision-making individual outlining ideas in visual and editorial terms. Follow up the letter in a few days with a call, and be prepared to take "no" for an answer. Editors and producers work under great deadline pressure and resent arguing with a public relations person over what is or is not a story. Courteous acceptance of their judgment may result in a positive response the next time.

Consider this example. The manufacturer of protective headgear who has a major share of this market would benefit from any increased sale of helmets, for whatever reason. Encouraging more people to wear protective headgear for safety could be one of the theme elements of the overall campaign.

Here is a letter that might be appropriate to send to a talk show or public affairs program producer:

> Ms. Susan Smith
> Associate Producer
> The Morning Show
> XYZ Television Network
> Hollywood, CA 10000
>
> Dear Ms. Smith:
>
> Every 15 seconds, someone receives a head injury in the United States; every five minutes, one of these people will die and another will become permanently disabled. A survivor of a severe brain injury typically faces five to 10 years of intensive services; estimated lifetime costs can ex-

ceed $4 million. The economic cost alone of head injuries is nearly $25 billion each year.

Each year more than 50,000 children in this country sustain bicycle-related head injuries, and more than 400 of these children die. In most cases their injuries could have been prevented or minimized by wearing a helmet or protective headgear.

Fred T. Jones, president of the National Helmet Co., is someone who can address this issue. We hope you will consider him as a guest on your program.

Enclosed is a videotape showing the impact of someone hitting the pavement and how protective headgear prevented a serious head injury. Also enclosed is a photograph and biography of Mr. Jones, plus further background information on this increasingly serious problem.

I look forward to talking with you soon.

Very sincerely,
JANE JOHNSON

Instead of a company source, consider having a third-party spokesperson, such as an officer of one of the bicycling organizations like the League of American Wheelmen, or a neurologist, physician or official from a health-oriented organization, such as the National Head Injury Foundation. If you have any good visual materials, be sure to include these with your letter.

USING RESOURCES TO PROMOTE YOUR REPRESENTATIVES

Placing a listing in the *Yearbook of Experts, Authorities & Spokespersons* is one way to quickly let the media know you have someone who can speak on a subject. This 840-page directory is a researcher's tool for the media. It is an encyclopedia of sources available for stories or interviews arranged in a topic index, geographically and by participants.

According to Mitchell P. Davis, editor of the yearbook, some 17,000 copies are requested by all types of media including newspapers, radio, television, business publications, magazines, wire services and syndicates, and cable television, along with professional writers, international journalists and speaking coordinators. Examples of copies requested by the media include 94 by Associated Press, 63 by ABC News, 35 by *The New York Times,* 50 by Cable News Network, 38 by Reuters, 24 by CNBC and 18 by *USA Today.* In 1993, the most requests by area came from Washington, D.C., followed by the states of New York, California, Virginia, Maryland, Illinois, Florida, Pennsylvania, New Jersey and Texas.

Cost for reference listings range from as low as $325 to as high as $870 for a full page, 7 by 9 inches. Purchase price for this who's who directory is $49.95. For information contact Broadcast Interview Source, 2233 Wisconsin Ave. N.W., Washington, DC 20007-4104, phone (202) 333-4909.

HOW TO GET COVERAGE ON A NEWS PROGRAM

When it comes to selling your story for the evening news, always approach the assignment editor of a news program with your story idea. Only in rare circumstances does a television reporter have the editorial authority to make a story and news crew commitment. On radio, the reporter has more freedom to pursue a story since the only equipment needed is a tape recorder.

View the television news program in the same light as the daily newspaper, and note numerous story possibilities. The major difference, however, is that for television news the story must be told in pictures. The best television news stories that have the most impact are the ones with simple but action-oriented visuals.

Make it a point to get to know the assignment editors of the stations in the markets most important for you. Find out what they are looking for. It is always beneficial to call an assignment editor between 7:00 a.m. and 2:00 p.m. They usually plan the next day's stories after 2:00 p.m. The early evening news, the late news and the weekend news programs all may have different assignment editors. Weekends generally have fewer crews available to cover events.

You can make the pitch by phone, fax or letter, depending on the urgency of the breaking news. Animals and babies are always good for news. For example, if you happen to represent a dairy and one of its cows gives birth to triplets, here—because of its great visual impact—is both a good photo opportunity and a story for the evening news. In this case all you have to do is relate the facts, offer some statistics regarding the odds of a cow giving birth to triplets, and provide information on where the calves can be "interviewed."

Human interest and behind-the-scenes stories also can be good news. People working to prepare a float for a the annual Rose Parade or who are getting a site ready for a major public event also can be news. If a manufacturer of a new cellular telephone is providing the important communications link for either the parade or the event, then here is an opportunity to expose the product being used.

THE NEWS CONFERENCE

A news conference or media event is a great way to get radio and television coverage. Be sure you carefully schedule the event so that it does not conflict with another event that might take away the coverage. Also be sure that it is scheduled at a time convenient for the media. Mid- to late-afternoon events are generally problems because the reporter cannot get back to the station in time to edit the material for the evening news. (Review Chapter 5 for specifics related to a news conference.)

THE RADIO PROMOTION

If you have a product or an event with something that can be given away to a listener, there is an opportunity to arrange a promotion with a radio station. The prizes the station gives away to listeners will increase its audience. If you find a station with strong ratings, chances are you can package your own promotion.

This was done a number of years ago for the Magic Pan restaurant chain. With crêpes being one of the restaurant's specialties, an all-expense paid trip was arranged for a lucky listener to get free lessons at one of the greatest chef schools in the world, Le Cordon Bleu in Paris. The most expensive part of the package was airfare. The restaurant paid for the tuition and room at a nearby pension, and because of the in-store and radio promotion, Air France donated the tickets for the trip.

Some radio stations now charge a fee for promotions, which can range from several hundred dollars in a small market to as much as $10,000 in a major metropolitan market. However, it is a good value if the numbers are delivered. In addition to product, the sponsor can provide the radio station with promotional T-shirts or other such giveaways.

Mark Hart, an account supervisor with Public Communications, Inc., a Tampa, Florida-headquartered public relations firm, believes the effectiveness of a radio promotion can be improved by making it the foundation of a larger public relations effort (Hart 1994). He cites the following examples:

Stage a Remote or Live Radio Broadcast at a Location Outside of the Studio During the Promotion. A popular shopping mall where the client's products or services are available is an ideal site. Distribute collateral materials or free samples to shoppers during the remote, possibly from a temporary display booth.

Conduct a Media Tour by a Representative for the Client During the Promotion. Include a public appearance and autograph-signing session in the tour if the spokesperson is a celebrity.

Link the Promotion to a Local Charity. For example, solicit contributions to the charity during the promotion, or pledge contributions from the client based on the numbers of listeners who participate in the promotion.

Enlist Another Media Outlet as a Co-Sponsor of the Promotion. This could be a newspaper, local or regional magazine or even a television station.

Hart (1993) adds that radio promotions might not be the right strategy for all clients and situations, but they can complement other techniques focused on a given market. "In addition, by offering promotional considerations to other participants in the promotion, as well as using the client's existing public relations materials, it can be cost-effective strategy as well."

ALWAYS TELL THE TRUTH

From 1958 to 1967 a popular prime-time television program was "To Tell the Truth." Three contestants claimed to be the same person when in fact two were impostors and only one person was telling the truth to a panel of celebrities asking questions.

When one is working with the news media, one rule must be followed: always tell the truth and never mislead your interviewer.

Time and time again, outstanding investigative reporters such as Mike Wallace, who has been with "60 Minutes" since the program first aired in September 1968, have completely discredited people when they do not tell the truth. You can be absolutely certain that if Mr. Wallace or one of his colleagues asks a question about a report, a memorandum or a document, they already have a copy and have reviewed the contents. If the interviewee denies such a document exists and lies on camera, the producers of "60 Minutes" will follow the statement by showing a copy of the item in question, proving the lie and completely discrediting anything that the person has said on the program.

If "60 Minutes" or a similar program calls and wants to talk with a company representative, consider the producer and the reporter adversaries but treat them as friends. If a company or organization is on the defensive, it is generally put in a no-win situation whether it agrees to or declines the interview. Any refusal to appear in person on the program could be perceived by viewers as an indictment of guilt by absence. On the other hand, a spokesperson who is inarticulate or not adequately prepared can easily create a real disaster.

For programs like "60 Minutes," the producer and the investigative reporter generally will work together as a team so the person being interviewed has the odds against him or her to begin with. The producer and reporter will have rehearsed the questions, which often are transferred to index cards. As the interview develops, the producer shuffles the cards and hands the questions in order to the reporter. The person being interviewed has no help whatsoever. The speaker is outnumbered two to one and is alone in front of the camera. He or she is inaccessible to someone who could likewise hand over cards with suggested answers or responses.

Sometimes this can become an advantage to the person being interviewed. There is a classic story of the president and CEO of a company who was being hounded by a leading network news television program for an interview. Against the advice of his public relations counsel, the company head agreed to the interview. "Why not? [Name of television reporter] is an old family friend for more than 20 years. He lives virtually across the street from me. Our wives are best friends. We play golf together. He would never do anything to embarrass me," the president told his public relations counselors as he dismissed any need for media training or intensive preparation for the interview.

As the parties met just before the interview got under way, there was a swapping of old stories and their friendship was obvious. It ended only a few minutes later. After a couple of warm-up questions, the producer handed out tougher questions and the investigative reporter took off the gloves and started pounding away at his longtime friend and neighbor.

Not anticipating anything like this at all, the president and CEO became flustered as the questioning continued. He lost his train of thought and was missing important rebuttal points. To try to help his client, the public relations adviser quickly wrote out several key points for his client to use as a response, got down on his hands and knees out of view of the camera and started crawling to the desk.

As the CEO took the notes in his hand from his adviser and was ready to respond in a more prepared manner, the reporter asked (with the cameras still rolling), "Why is your press agent on the floor under your desk and would you share with us the notes he is handing you?" The company president responded, "Why, [reporter's name], I'm amazed. I've seen your program so many times and I always considered you one of the best television journalists in the business, but I thought they were your questions. Now I see you have a helper not only giving you the questions to ask but telling you when to ask them. I think I deserve the same kind of help. If you're going to show your audience the tape of my public relations adviser seeking to get me this information, it is only fair that the viewers at home see the producer giving you the questions you have been asking me. Now I have a couple of questions I want to ask you."

The CEO's quickness in responding the way he did caught the producer completely off guard, flustered his old investigative reporter friend, and rendered the tape of the public relations man crawling on the floor an outtake. The tenor of the interview quickly changed and the session ended, as did the long friendship between the reporter and the corporate executive.

NEVER SAY "NO COMMENT"

There are many ways to respond without saying "No comment." A "no comment" response is abrupt, coarse and rude and often can be perceived as arrogant, discourteous and impolite as well as an implied confirmation if the question involves some wrong doing. Never offend the reporter asking the question or make an enemy of that person. When attorneys, who are never at a loss for words in a courtroom, do not want to respond to the media, their favorite response is "no comment." Typically this is how they advise their clients to respond. Yet, if you want to neutralize an adversary and perhaps even gain an advocate, be polite to the reporter. There are many ways to respond. For example:

• "Under the circumstances, it would really be inappropriate for me to discuss that with you at this time."

• "I really would like to answer that, but as you heard the judge instruct us, at this point in the hearings we have been asked not to discuss this in public."

• "That's a good question, but I really can't go into all of the details at this time."

• "I am sorry, but we are in a situation at this time that I am unable to either confirm or deny what you ask. Please just bear with us a while longer."

• "It would just not be prudent to answer your question at this time. I hope you will understand."

Regardless of how hard the reporter or group of reporters press for an answer to a question, be calm, stay as relaxed as possible, smile, and be polite. The same question may be posed again and again, but try not to repeat the same answer; respond with something similar or say, nicely, "I just told you all that I can tell you right now on that subject, and please, I hope you will respect my response as much as I respect your eagerness to elicit an answer."

If the reporter nonetheless becomes rude or arrogant while you remain nonplussed, the viewers will sympathize with you as being picked on. It will be the reporter, not you, who loses face.

HOW TO PREPARE FOR THE INTERVIEW

Any person who may represent a company on radio, television or in public should be professionally trained. Most executives today in business, industry, associations, non-profit organizations and government at some time will be in front of a camera; a microphone; a reporter with a pen, notebook and tape recorder, or a public audience.

Many executives prepare with communications enhancement training before a news conference, talk show interview or major speaking engagement or prior to testifying before an important committee of Congress.

John Martin Meek, a prominent Washington, D.C., public relations counselor who heads HMI, Inc., has trained scores of top business, government and political executives to enhance their personal communications with the media, Congress and speaking audiences. He says that even experienced spokespersons can improve with assistance (Meek 1994).

Meek cites an example of a man who came from a prominent American family, had served as a governor and a high federal official and had even run for national office. In his law practice he was asked to appear on a major network television show representing his client, a controversial foreign government. Before appearing, he agreed to an afternoon of training to test his knowledge of the show's topic. During the on-camera practice session, three training interviewers questioned him about his client's policies.

During the interview critique, the man received pointers on how to present his client's position more clearly, rather than on the substance of what he said. He immediately became defensive, but he also carefully listened to the criticism. Later he conceded that during the afternoon's session he learned more about appearing on television than he had ever known before, and he left the training session confident and grateful.

Meek also tells about training a Japanese executive, a managing director of one of Tokyo's largest banks, who was invited to Washington to testify at an important U.S. Senate committee hearing. In an effort to enhance his ability to make a good impression at such a significant event, Meek assembled a mock "committee" for the executive to testify before one day prior to his scheduled appearance before the Senate.

Under questioning by one of the "senators," the executive momentarily lost his temper and demanded to know why he was being asked a particular question. Meek carefully explained to him that the question was not intended to embarrass him, but to prepare him for facing those senators who would play adversarial roles in the next day's hearing. The executive understood and continued the session.

Meek said that the following day his "student" testified in impeccable English. Then came the questions, including the exact one that had angered him in the training session. He answered it calmly and left the hearing with praise even from his adversary.

The individual being trained should not be made aware in advance of the questions being asked. Brainstorm and anticipate the worst possible questions and have the panel of "reporters" include both friendly and adversarial members. Training sessions should be videotaped, played back and critiqued. Professional counselors and trainers like Meek will look for eye movement, body movement and facial expressions when the executive is being questioned. When asked a difficult question some people bite their lip, others move their eyes away from the camera, and still others have personal ways to telegraph their feelings to the viewer. It is critical to keep eye contact with the camera to present a positive and believable image (HMI 1993).

In a talk show or public affairs program, two or more cameras will be used. The red light on the camera lets the host know which camera the director has selected for the program's video. Sometimes the guest may be caught in a situation where the camera will show more of a profile than desired. This can happen if the guest is looking directly at the host. To prevent this, the guest should split the difference between looking into the camera and at the host. However, always focus on the host more than the camera.

Be prepared as possible before the interview by watching the host or interviewer in action to get an idea of his or her style and technique. Is the person aggressive? Does the person interrupt and not let the guest always finish an answer? Is it a friendly and relaxed approach? If you are going to be on a panel or with other guests on a talk show, will any be adversaries? If so, have background information on your adversaries and competition.

THE 30-SECOND ANSWER

Be candid and brief. Keep your answers for both radio and television brief, and make your main points in 30 seconds or less, or no more than about 120 words. Keep your language simple; avoid technical terms that the audience may not understand. Do not overanswer or overqualify your answers. During the rehearsal and pre-interview training, anticipate the questions that may be asked and prepare and practice 30-second answers on subjects you expect to discuss. Know how to turn a tough question into a positive answer.

During the 1988 presidential campaign, then Vice President George Bush agreed to a live television interview on the "CBS Evening News" with Dan Rather. Bush was carefully prepared and coached by his media consultant, Roger Ailes, in the event that the situation got difficult. (Taped interviews are one thing. Being live is something else.)

Rather was supposed to question Bush on his candidacy and his policies. Instead the interview turned into one in which Rather was hammering at Bush for answers about the Iran-Contra Affair. Bush took control and refused to be bullied by Rather. Bush would not let Rather interrupt him until he was finished giving his answer. When Rather pushed too hard once, Bush asked him, "What if we judged your entire career on just one incident?" Everyone immediately recognized the reference to the time when Rather walked off a set and left the network dark because a tennis match resulted in the delay of his evening newscast.

In an interview on NBC's "Today Show," Senator Edward Kennedy took charge of an interview with Bryant Gumble, one of the best in the business. The senator refused to let Gumble get him talking about his recent problems resulting from an Easter holiday incident involving his nephew that took place at the Kennedys' Palm Beach residence. Instead, the senator hit home all points he wanted to make about national health care insurance. For example, here is some dialogue that happened well into the interview after the senator had made a number of points about national health care insurance (NBC 1991):

> *Gumble:* But what about you, Senator? Will you be able to—
> *Kennedy:* Well, we'll be battling along, and I think we've got a good

program. I think that we've had good meetings with our colleagues, in the Senate and also in our conversations with the leadership: Senator Foley, Rich Gephardt, and Danny Rostenkowski, Henry Waxman and many others. And I think we'll have a good program and I believe the American people are well ahead of the politicians on this one. After we pass that program, people, I think, are going to say why did it take you so long?

Gumble: Senator, do you think the view of the American people of Senator Ted Kennedy has changed?

Kennedy: Well, I'll have to worry about what their health insurance issues are. And I think they understand that they got some real important problems and I think we have a program that can address them and I look forward to the debate and the discussions.

Gumble: Senator, are you not going to talk about the Easter—

Kennedy: Well, I'm glad to talk about whatever you'd like to. I'd like to talk about health insurance but I'm glad, Bryant, to talk about anything you'd like to.

Gumble: Sir—

Kennedy: I enjoyed your speech up there in Providence College where you spoke up there, and my son graduated.

Gumble: Thank you very much, Senator. Let me ask you a couple of quick questions if I might. You have obviously taken a public relations pounding as a result of the Easter incident. What's your view of the way the media has handled this alleged incident and your role in it?

Kennedy: Well, I've been in public life for some 30 years. I think I've enjoyed more favorable stories than others, but I believe by and large I've been fairly treated and look forward to the continued work in the Senate.

Senator Kennedy continued to give positive answers and get the message across to the viewers that he wanted to give, whether or not they were answers to questions being asked by the reporter. The important thing is to stay in charge of the interview.

THE TAPED INTERVIEW

Most broadcast interviews will be taped and edited. If there are pauses in responding, these will be edited out. One should be aware when an interview is being broadcast live so there is no room for error.

Speak casually and as though just you and the interviewer are having a discussion. Broadcasting is a person-to-person medium, and your best voice is a friendly, normal, conversational tone. The most effective tone to take is the same one you would use in an after-dinner discussion in a friend's living room. Be casual and relaxed, even if making a formal statement to start a press conference or news event.

Being nervous and having "butterflies" before a television or radio interview or appearance can be expected and is just being human. Remember with absolute confidence that you know more about your subject than the reporter does. The rehearsal and training should have you well prepared. Several deep breaths before going on the set, or before the interview, will help increase your oxygen supply, slow your heart rate and help you relax.

If the opportunity permits, try to get to know your host before the talk show begins, or the reporter as the crew sets up the camera and lights before the interview begins.

Don't lose sight of your objective or let the interviewer intimidate you. Take charge and control the interview. Some interviewers interrupt and ask another question when they believe they have the answer they want. If you have not fully given the answer you want, then politely let the interviewer or host know that and complete your statement. If you are not absolutely sure how you want to phrase your answer, then talk a bit more slowly until you have organized your thoughts. Try to have what is called good "hang time," or the time during which you are doing the talking and getting points across. It is hard for an interviewer to dominate you when you're doing the talking.

If the reporter asks a question that places you on the defensive, quickly turn it around and positively state your position or policy. If the host or reporter makes a misstatement in the question, be sure to correct the misleading portion before going any further. Beware of multiple questions that are only a series of criticisms and disguised attacks. Stop the interviewer and request an opportunity to answer, then pick the question you want to answer.

Before the interview is over, make sure you have made the most important point you want to make during the interview and that you have told the viewing and listening audience the message you want them to hear. Even if the question you want asked is not, talk around a question you do not want to answer and get your story told. On a talk show, don't simply wait for the next question. Take the initiative sometimes and ask questions and volunteer information.

Never lose your temper on camera or get into an argument with the interviewer or another guest on a talk show. Don't be scornful or abusive of your critics. Appeal to both the emotions and the logic of the audience.

Always be aware of when a microphone is clipped to your lapel, blouse, shirt or tie. Microphones are highly sensitive and will pick up sounds very easily. Never touch the mike.

HOW TO DRESS FOR TELEVISION

The rule of thumb is to be basic and simple. Stay away from white shirts, bold patterns and flashy jewelry.

Men should avoid high-contrast clothes such as plaid. Medium colors such as muted brown are good, as is a combination of a gray suit, blue shirt and plain tie.

Women should wear a solid-color dress or a suit with a tailored blouse. For a panel or talk show, wear a skirt slightly longer than you generally might wear because the skirt tends to hike up when you're sitting. A full skirt may feel more comfortable if it is full enough to drape (HMI 1993).

In addition to voice control for confidence and poise, your body, gestures, facial expressions, posture, walking and movement should be as natural and relaxed as possible. Use your muscles freely, naturally and with sincerity. Let the audience see your interest and enthusiasm. Sit up and lean forward, not away from your host or interviewer. Insincerity in body movement usually is very identifiable and detracts from the credence of the presentation. When the words and the body action are inconsistent, the audience generally will discount the verbal message in favor of the body language.

Listen attentively and be aware that the director may take reaction shots of you as the host or another guest is speaking. Anything you do, any movement you make, could be caught by the camera.

DOCUMENT RESULTS

In most cases you will want to have a copy of what was aired on radio or television. Review the program with your professional trainer and see where any improvement could have been made.

There are special reporting services in all major cities that provide transcripts or tapes for you for a nominal charge. It is important to have both an East Coast and West Coast supplier for this service. In the event a program is missed in New York, there still is a three-hour time difference to make arrangements to record the program or interview in Los Angeles.

Firms including Burrelle's and its Video Monitoring Services of America, Inc., subsidiary; Luce; Audio Video Reporting Service; and Radio TV Reports will provide typed transcripts of radio or television programs.

You also may want to videotape comments, stories or interviews on the competition.

INTERNATIONAL MARKETS

No other country in the world has a level of television household saturation near that of the United States. In most of the countries throughout the world, radio is the most feasible way to reach mass audiences.

However, television is growing in a number of ways, especially in Western Europe (Andersen 1993, 1994). In some countries where the dominant network once was government owned, now licenses are being given for private-sector operation of television stations and channels. Cable television is making great inroads in a number of markets, including Western Europe,

Japan and Mexico. Where programming once was limited to only a few hours in the evening by a number of countries, programming time has been significantly expanded. There are not necessarily the same opportunities for exposure in overseas markets as in the United States, but each should be explored on a market-by-market basis.

REFERENCES

Andersen, Wies. 1993 and 1994. Interviews. Antwerp and Brasschaat, Belgium: Andersen Productions.

Hart, Mark. 1994. Interview and correspondence. April.

___. 1993. *Public Relations Quarterly* (Winter):43-44.

HMI, Inc. 1993. *Communications Enhancement Manual.*

Meek, John Martin. 1994. Interview. Washington, D.C.: HMI Inc.

National Cable Television Association. 1993. Public Relations Office.

NBC. 1991. "The Today Show." June 5.

News USA, Inc. 1994. News release. Alexandria, Va.

Rieger, Hank. 1994. Interview. Academy of Television Arts & Sciences. March.

9

THE WHENS, HOWS AND WHYS OF FILM AND VIDEO

The advent of television launched a whole new era in marketing communications. No longer was just film the primary vehicle used to visually reach grass-roots audiences. Television first created product exposure opportunities in live programs. Then came the video news release. The invention of the VCR, combined with the tremendous increase of television households and growth of cable television, marked another milestone in visual communications.

Since 1980, the number of cable television households has increased from 16 million to more than 60 million, and 75 percent of American families have a VCR. More than half of these families are connected to one of the 7,000 cable systems in the country.

With a proliferation of cable channels and programs to view, since 1975 there has been a steady decrease in prime-time network viewing. In less than 20 years, the network share of the viewing audience during the 8 p.m. to 11 p.m. (Eastern and Pacific times) time block fell from a 93 percent share to a 64 percent share (Williams 1989).

GROWTH OF THE TELEVISION MARKET

While television has been a source of entertainment, news and information for more than 50 years, its real growth did not occur until the mid-1950s. In 1952, only 9 percent of American families had television sets. There were

Table 9.1. Growth in U.S. household television ownership, 1952-93

Year	U. S. Households (millions)	Television Households (millions)	Percentage
1952	43.0	3.9	9.0%
1956	47.6	30.7	64.5%
1960	52.5	45.8	87.1%
1964	56.9	52.7	92.6%
1968	61.4	58.5	95.3%
1972	63.4	60.5	95.4%
1976	70.5	68.5	97.1%
1980	77.9	76.3	97.9%
1984	85.4	83.3	97.2%
1988	91.0	90.4	99.3%
1993	98.3	97.2	98.8%

Source: *Statistical Abstract of the United States,* 1994.

only 3.9 million television households in the country. From 1956 to 1964 there was continued significant growth until there was saturation and almost every household in the country had a television set. Table 9.1 shows this growth pattern.

FILM AND VIDEO PR TOOLS

There are a number of marketing communications tools to use in the broad area of film and video to reach various publics. They include:

- Video news releases
- Public service announcements
- Satellite media tours
- Sponsored films
- Sponsored videos
- Infomercials
- Satellite programming
- Digital interactive videoconferencing
- Product placement

There are scores of companies, large and small, that can provide creative production and distribution services for any of these tools. The important consideration is not which product is used, how it is distributed or whether it is shown, but whether or not the product was seen by the intended public.

Video News Releases (VNRs)

When television was in its infancy, public relations and publicity professionals sent black-and-white, dull-matte photographs to television stations to get exposure for individuals or products. Innovators quickly recognized that television was a moving medium and began to provide stations with 16mm black-and-white film clips. As color began to become popular in the 1960s, the news and feature film packages were produced in color.

With the increased use of videotape, the video news release, or VNR, has become the standard visual press release for placement with television. A backup with the VNR is called a B-roll, a secondary video with additional materials, quotes or sound bites and background information that the television producer can edit to prepare a custom story. A B-roll does not have graphics or narration.

Whereas the film packages and early VNRs were first hand-delivered or sent by overnight air express, today the most popular distribution system is by satellite. As television stations have increased news programming and there has been an increase in the number of independent stations and cable networks, there has been a growing need for news footage and VNRs.

Today a typical newsroom in a major city or network could receive as many as 10 to 15 VNRs in a day. Only the best-produced and most newsworthy get on the air, and even then, chances are the VNR will not be used exactly as sent.

When well produced and properly distributed and promoted, a VNR can have tremendous impact and reach a huge audience. Medialink, the nation's largest distributor of VNRs, cites one produced by Edelman Public Relations Worldwide in Chicago for its client, StarKist Seafood Company. This VNR, talking about dolphin-safe tuna, was viewed by 81.2 million people. A VNR about Iraq's invasion of Kuwait, produced by Hill and Knowlton of Washington, D.C., for Citizens for a Free Kuwait, was seen by 61.4 million people. Even one featuring Michael Jackson talking about a new ad campaign for L.A. Gear, produced by Bragman & Company of Los Angeles, was viewed by 21 million people (Medialink 1994).

Few VNRs will reach this many people. Many just do not have the news or feature value or technical quality that the news editors are looking for; either they do not get used or their pickup is limited to secondary markets and combined use is in the area of three to four million viewers. A story in *Public Relations Journal* quotes an anonymous producer who says that fewer than 250 commercial television stations use handout VNRs, and each station has less than two minutes of air time available each day for outside material. He notes that if all of these VNRs being sent to the stations were used, there would be precious little time for anything else.

The typical length of a packaged VNR is no longer than 90 seconds. Production costs from major producers can range from $7,000 to $20,000, with satellite distribution costing from $2,300 up. Some companies will do only the entire package which can vary from $10,000 to $25,000 (Medialink 1994).

Video News Release Checklist

• Production values and quality must be equal to the standards of the recipient.

• It must be news or a feature story of interest to the station or network.

• The length should be 90 seconds or less.

• Include B-roll with background information, quotes and sound bites of two to three minutes in length so the producer has an opportunity to repackage the VNR.

• Consider doing a miniseries if one VNR will not tell the whole story. Do not confuse the viewer by trying to include too many different points in the 90 seconds.

• Split the audio track with the voice-over announcer on one audio channel and the natural or wild sound on the other. This gives the user the option of stripping out the announcer's voice.

• Do not superimpose any titles or graphics on the tape. This can be included as part of the B-roll. Good graphics may help get the VNR on air. Slate at the beginning of the VNR to identify the location of sound bites and people. The local station or network will use its own style and format for titles.

• Stations want to show only their own talent, so do not have any reporter or commentator shown on camera.

• Be selective in distributing the VNR. Do not send a release nationwide if the story is of interest only regionally.

• Consider using hard copies and mail or overnight air express if distribution is only regional or the VNR is considered in the "evergreen" category—that is, it does not have to be used immediately.

• If the VNR has news or a feature of interest to an ethnic audience, consider special distribution. If of interest, for example, to Hispanic viewers, do a Spanish-language track for Spanish-language television stations or networks.

• Consider international distribution if this is an overall marketing public relations objective.

• If there are no in-house capabilities for broadcast-quality production, establish a budget and retain a professional producer experienced in television news.

• To maximize potential use of the VNR, and when it is of interest nationwide, consider using a professional company experienced in distribution and tracking results.

• Most of all, the story must be as non-promotional as possible.

Public Service Announcements (PSAs)

Public Service Announcements, or PSAs, cannot be used to promote a product per se, but they are used to promote or publicize information and issues of public interest and concern. Sometimes manufacturers who have a proprietary product will produce a PSA on an issue such as safety. Years ago, Volvo promoted automobile safety and the use of seat belts when it was the only automobile manufacturer providing seat belts as standard equipment on all of its cars.

PSAs can range in length from five to 60 seconds. Others can be in lengths of 10, 20 and 30 seconds.

Few PSAs get used in prime time when most viewers are watching television. Networks and stations most often schedule PSAs when they have not sold the commercial time and they can still take credit for providing public affairs time.

A well-done PSA will have longevity and will be aired not just over weeks, but months or even years. One very successful and well-done PSA was the Coalition for a Drug Free America spot that showed the egg in the frying pan with the voice-over, "This is your brain on drugs." The greater the production value of the PSA, the greater its chance to be used, used often and in a slot where it will be seen. Too many people waste money producing PSAs of talking heads that do not graphically illustrate the issue or concern. Others use graphics that are too amateurish.

Some corporations will actually underwrite a PSA if it benefits a charity or concern that they want to be identified with. Corporate backing also will help the PSA appear in a more favorable time slot. In its campaign for higher education, The Southwest Conference asked sponsors to provide spots in their purchase packages so the conference's PSAs could be shown during periods of larger audiences. Corporate sponsors were able to receive on-air identification for this support.

The public affairs director for the station is the person who decides whether a PSA will be aired on the station and if so, when and how often. For a PSA to be acceptable it needs to be sent to the station with a copy of the organization's tax-exempt status, such as that classified on federal forms 501(3)(c) or 501(6)(c). For national distribution it helps to have clearance from the Office of Philanthropic Services in the Better Business Bureau.

Satellite Media Tours

A satellite media tour places a company representative at a specific site, on location or in a studio, where he or she is then connected by satellite to a series of television stations, which tape-record the interview and edit it for their own program.

For example, the representative will be connected first to a station in Boston for a five-minute interview, then switched in succession to Philadelphia, Atlanta, Miami and other cities in one time zone, moving to West Coast stations later. This technique is convenient and highly effective if you have a representative you cannot send on tour in person or you want to show a site in the background. In just a few hours, the same impact can be achieved as with a multicity airplane tour requiring days or weeks.

Medialink Videobroadcasting Corporation calls the satellite media tour a kissing cousin of the VNR and believes they are powerful tools that shrink distances and compress the time and cost of doing business. The company believes this is one way to power the next promotional campaign, introduce a new product or explain a medical breakthrough. It says actual viewing audiences can range from more than one million to as high as four million, depending on the duration of the tour and the news value of the subject (Medialink 1994).

Medialink recommends transmitting a VNR, B-roll or raw footage as part of the tour to provide more visuals that help stations package the actual broadcast. The company has coordinated numerous media tours, including those for the government of Jamaica's Tourism Board after a devastating hurricane; the Shriners' Hospitals on free hospital care for children; the General Aviation Task Force for "Learn-to-Fly-Month" and Volkswagen and Mothers Against Drunk Driving for their alcohol and driving safety campaign.

This tool is especially helpful for crisis communications or when there is a small window of opportunity. Johnson & Johnson found a satellite media tour indispensable in controlling the company's Tylenol poisoning crisis.

Cost of a satellite media tour can be as low as $10,000 to as much as $25,000 for an extensive 50-city tour.

Sponsored Films and Sponsored Videos

Sponsored films and videos provide opportunities to reach millions of people at the grass-roots level. Once 16mm film was the principal tool used but videotape has become much more cost effective and projection equipment is almost universal today.

Modern Talking Picture Service is the world's largest distributor of corporate-sponsored communications. The company's catalog is sent to elementary, junior and senior high schools, community groups, clubs and organizations and television stations and cable networks.

The Modern catalog covers a wide variety of subjects, for example: "The Company We Keep," a 25-minute video produced by Deere & Company and partnerships it has forged around the world; "Sharing the Dream," an 18-minute look at great American Olympic moments from the past by the U.S. Olympic Committee; "The Food Equation," a 75-minute program Monsanto produced and had hosted by Kathleen Sullivan to talk about how 11 billion people will meet their most basic need in the year 2050; and "From Dreams To Reality," a 27-minute production of the U.S. Department of Commerce's Patent & Trademark Office in which Ossie Davis introduces viewers to outstanding minority inventors (Modern Talking Picture 1993-94).

Infomercials

This is an area that is expanding on commercial television and cable. According to people in this industry, nothing has proven to move product at the retail level as effectively as a successful infomercial. In just 30 minutes of television viewing, consumers can learn why they need a product, what benefit they can derive from it, how it will enhance their lives and why it outperforms the competition.

Compared to door-to-door selling, the infomercial has less trouble finding an excuse to get in the door. Most are listed in the television viewer guides as "Paid Programming." Advertising agencies or companies buy the time and air a commercial program selling a product or service. Between 1989 and 1992, advertising time purchased for infomercials increased from $159.7 million to $288.9 million. The measure of success for an infomercial is the number of orders received when the infomercial airs and the cost of the television time that makes the orders profitable (Infomercial 1993).

Infomercials are used for positive-response television or cause-related marketing. There is even a newsletter covering this field: *The Infomercial Marketing Report,* available from Steve Dworman & Associates, 11956 Gorham Avenue, Suite 14, Los Angeles, CA 90049, phone (310) 826-6301, fax (301) 826-1077.

The Citizens Against Government Waste aired a specially produced entertaining and informative half-hour television program that included commercials by well-known political leaders. Moderator and host of the program was former NBC network anchor and "Today Show" host Jim Hartz. The viewer was asked to call a toll-free number and make a donation to receive a free copy of the program. The difference between the money donated and the cost of the television time was profit for the organization. Studies show that infomercials also have been effective for motivational and fitness products and beauty and cosmetic products (HMI 1994). There are many media buying services and advertising agencies that specialize in this direct response marketing.

Satellite Programming

This is one way to call a press conference and simultaneously contact television newsrooms in cities throughout the country. The teleconference can provide two-way audio so people can ask questions of the individual or people in one studio. There also is the opportunity to have several speakers—for example, in New York, Los Angeles and Chicago—all connected for the teleconference. Technology can respond to almost any public relations need. Distribution can be international and programming can even be interactive, involving more than one country.

Some years ago Cyprus Mines Corporation of Los Angeles wanted to make a splash announcing the biggest ore discovery ever in the Yukon Territory. A luncheon held in Whitehorse, Yukon Territory, was televised and fed to Vancouver, B.C., and simultaneously transmitted to Los Angeles, New York, Ottawa and Frankfurt, with a delayed telecast into Tokyo. Luncheons were held in Vancouver and Los Angeles, a cocktail party and reception followed by dinner in both New York and Ottawa and a dinner in Frankfurt. Executives of companies in four countries were involved as well as certain cabinet-level ministers of government.

Digital Interactive Videoconferencing

This communications vehicle provides an economic way to hold videoconferences. Digital interactive television is actually compressed video that is transmitted by microwave rather than satellite. It is not of broadcast quality, but because it provides a two-way visual and verbal communications link between two or more locations, it is widely used for conferences, meetings, distance education, public affairs announcements and interviews.

The nation's largest and busiest network is the Trans-Texas Videoconference Network (TTVN) of the Texas A&M University System. Currently there are 24 locations throughout Texas for this system. In addition to two-way audio and video communications, each videoconference system features a variety of graphic, videotape, computing and facsimile transmission capabilities.

In 1993, the TTVN's connection to the Spring Meeting Channel provided videoconference service to Washington, D.C.; Reston, Va.; Danvers, Mass.; Atlanta, Ga.; and Research Triangle Park, N.C. There are many ways to link other systems. Live coverage of two visits to the Texas A&M University campus in College Station by former President George Bush was transmitted to various locations throughout Texas.

Product Placement

For years product marketers have seen the impact of getting a product or service exposed with brand recognition in a feature motion picture or on television. It used to be easy enough to get acquainted with the property masters at major studios and provide them with whatever they needed. Today it is more difficult: producers see new revenue potential by charging companies for this exposure. The practice also has created new businesses: some companies do nothing but make Hollywood placements of products and services.

If you start with a feature film, the first exposure for the product or service is in the movie theater. Then the film is released on videocassette for rental or purchase. Then the film is shown in foreign markets. Within a couple of years it airs on television to even greater audiences. And then the film becomes available to cable networks and international television. The impact can be spread over a number of years.

Clothing manufacturers seek to align their product with representative stars who provide a "silent" endorsement by wearing the clothes. The manufacturer gets a credit at the end of the program. Be sure to negotiate the credit received in any motion picture or television program. Credits sometime can roll so fast on a screen that if you blink, you've missed the credit.

MODERN TALKING PICTURE SERVICE

Modern Talking Picture Service began distributing corporate-sponsored films in 1937 for corporations, trade associations, government agencies and public relations agencies. Today the company has television and cable television distribution services; is involved in video news releases, public service announcements and satellite media tours; and became the first video media network serving the college marketplace (Modern Talking Picture 1993-94).

To promote distribution of its clients' sponsored films, Modern mails more than 1.5 million promotional brochures during a year to educators and group leaders throughout the United States. The company ships and recovers the videos and provides clients with a monthly report documenting the number of times the videos were shown and how many people saw the program. Modern also will ship collateral literature to be used with a program. The client is billed only for certified playdates of $9.10 each plus postage for the first 125 reported in a calendar month and $6.30 for those in excess of 125. A typical budget can be as low as $15,000 for 1,350 bookings reaching 125,000 viewers to $50,000 for 6,500 bookings and 780,000 viewers or as high as $100,000 for 15,000 bookings and 1.8 million viewers.

In addition to being a distributor, Modern also is a leading creator of high-interest, activity-oriented teaching kits that communicate an educational message. The sponsored teaching kits can deliver valuable educational information and provide an opportunity to create brand awareness or deliver a message that enhances corporate image or issue.

In 1993 Modern generated more than 100,000 telecasts on television stations and cable systems. Its staff contacts program directors by phone to promote available programs and send out a catalog to 3,500 program directors across the country. It claims that its average exposure reaches 50,000 potential households and that 22 percent of its placements are in the top 10 markets, 33 percent in the top 20 and more than 50 percent in the top 50 markets.

The company guarantees cable television exposure for its clients' programs through its *World in Motion* magazine that airs Monday through Friday on The Learning Channel. This service is carried on more than 1,400 cable systems reaching 22 million homes. The cost can vary from $600 plus $60 per running minute of the program for six daytime telecasts to $975 plus $100 per running minute for four evening telecasts in prime time. There also are combination daytime-evening packages.

Its MCTV network has freestanding kiosks in high-traffic locations at 160 colleges and universities. Total enrollment at the four-year institutions is more than 1.5 million students. The MCTV two-hour viewing loop is changed monthly, and each loop repeats four times daily. It has been used by clients for public service messages, advertisements and infomercials, video news releases, recruiting and career opportunities and special offers. Modern estimates that an individual spot will be aired 346 times per school during a month or 55,360 monthly broadcasts on the full network. The cost ranges from $5,625 for a 30-second announcement to $11,250 for a 60-second spot to $33,750 for three minutes.

Modern Talking Picture Service has offices in New York, Chicago, Washington and San Francisco and is headquartered at 5000 Park Street North, St. Petersburg, Florida 33709, phone (813) 541-7571, fax (813) 546-0681.

MEDIALINK VIDEO BROADCASTING CORPORATION

Medialink is the nation's largest distributor of video news releases and a major force in satellite media tours, public service announcement distribution and the staging of teleconferences. Its news wire now reaches nearly 700 television newsrooms to facilitate satellite delivery of VNRs.

The company's comprehensive usage monitoring system combines an exclusive service from Nielsen Media Research with written video summaries from two major television "clipping" services, Burrelle's and Luce. The reports include exclusive Nielsen station polling in addition to broadcast transcript summaries, direct mail responses, data base searches and telephone surveys by the Medialink stations relations staff. Each week Nielsen contacts between 125 and 130 television stations on a rotating basis about each video news release being monitored.

According to Medialink (1993-94), a recent Nielsen survey of 126 television news directors regarding satellite media tours revealed that 107 stations, or 85 percent, participated; 9 stations, or 7.1 percent, did not; and 10 stations, or 7.9 percent, did not respond. The same survey found that 76 stations, or 60.3 percent, preferred to tape a broadcast satellite interview; 16 stations, or 12.7 percent, went live; and 9 stations, or 12.7 percent, did both.

MONITORING THE RESULTS

Knowing whether or not your program or VNR was broadcast, the context in which it was used in a broadcast, exactly what was used and by whom and when is important in planning future programs. There are a number of local and national video monitoring services that can provide this information for a charge. Some include:

Burrelle's Information Services
75 E. Northfield Road
Livingston, NJ 07039
Phone (800) 631-1160

RTV (Radio/TV Reports)
41 E. 42nd St.
New York, NY 10017
Phone (212) 309-1400

Luce Press Clippings, Inc.
42 S. Center
Mesa, AZ 85210-1306
Phone (800) 528-8226

Video Monitoring Services
of America, Inc. (VMS)
330 W. 42nd St.
New York, NY 10036
Phone (212) 736-2010

REFERENCES

Informercial Marketing Report. 1993. Special sourcebook issue.
Medialink Video Broadcasting Corp. 1993-94. Information package.
___. 1994. *The Video News Release Handbook.*
Meek, John Martin. 1994. Interview. Washington, D.C.: HMI Inc.
Modern Talking Picture Service, Inc. 1993-94. Information package.
Williams, Marjorie. 1989. "The Eighties—The Fragmenting of Culture." *Washington Post.* December 13.

10

HOW TO USE SPECIAL PUBLICATIONS

A special brochure, pamphlet, newsletter or other type of publication can be an excellent way of keeping a company name, brand name, product or service in front of a potential consumer for a long period of time. A story in a newspaper is gone the next day. A magazine may have longevity for a week or a month. Radio is instant news unless repeated. The same goes for television. But a well-done printed piece may be kept for weeks, months or even years and can be very cost-effective as part of an overall campaign.

Cookbooks, for example, are a popular item for companies that market and sell fruit, vegetables, meat, condiments and other food products. The American Beef Council gives the consumer ideas that it hopes will increase sales of beef. So does the Dairy Council when it comes to milk and dairy products. Some will even include recipe tips as part of the product packaging.

DISTRIBUTION

Once you have an idea for a publication, a plan must be developed for its distribution, with a budget for the cost of distribution. One common way is to make the publication available free to the public by either phoning an 800 telephone number or writing to an address to request a copy. The availability of the publication can be announced with publicity or by a spokesperson talking about it on a media tour. Copies also can be promoted through product point-of-sale displays, on product packaging or by making it available where products are sold.

Some publications lend themselves to being an insert or pullout special section in a newspaper or magazine. Sometimes the advertising cost of the insert is cheaper than the cost of mailing out requested copies. With advertising in a specific publication, the delivery of a target audience can be virtually assured.

If a publication is of exceptional quality or content and covers a subject of real interest or public service to the consumer without being too commercial, it can be made available as a self-liquidating premium. This is one way to recoup the marketing public relations budget cost not only for distribution but for art and printing costs.

THE D.C. CONNECTION

Many Washington-based trade associations and organizations that provide services for companies with the agencies of the federal government, the administration or Congress will produce guides for members, customers and potential customers with tips on how to do business in the capital city.

Some publications have contact lists with names, addresses and phone numbers of various congressional committees, agencies and departments. The text covers information that will be helpful to someone who is not experienced at doing business "inside the beltway." Publications that provide such useful information have a long life span. Sometimes trade associations will recoup production costs by charging for copies.

HELPFUL HINTS AND PUBLIC SERVICE INFORMATION

There are myriad ways to use special publications to your company's advantage. Professional service organizations such as legal, accounting and public relations firms produce booklets or surveys on various subjects not only to obtain media exposure for their organizations, but also to give prospective clients an indication of the firm's capability in a particular area of expertise. Companies that provide services in the public relations area produce publications that cover dos and don'ts and how-to tips for use by customers and potential customers.

Commercial banks, thrift institutions and mortgage bankers make available books with monthly payments based on interest and amortization costs of loans. Lender trade associations also have published primers that explain how the secondary mortgage market works, and title companies explain the business of title insurance.

For Fuji Film Floppy Disks, Edelman Public Relations Worldwide developed "The Fuji Home Office Guide" to help solidify the company's leadership in the home office market. Press coverage alone generated 100,000 responses for this guide.

As a public service, Philip Morris Companies, Inc. published a series of directories helpful to specific ethnic markets or for people who wanted to target these audiences. The publications included the *National Directory of Hispanic Organizations,* a *Guide to Black Organizations* and the *National Directory of Women Elected Officials*.

Following are further examples of the successful use of special publications.

Glossary of Real Estate Words and Phrases. As a service to its clients and prospective clients, Kenneth Leventhal & Company, one of the major U.S. accounting firms, published a 42-page pocket-size directory of real estate terms and definitions. The publication was well received by both the industry and the media covering the industry. The publication was a giveaway at major industry conferences and conventions. As a result of the media writing about its availability, copies were sent free to those who asked.

The Low-Down on Roofs. This 24-page, 6-by-9-inch book was published by 3M Company to support the sale of asphalt roofing. 3M was the leading supplier of rock granules, which are used in the manufacture of asphalt roofing. The brochure discussed the history of roofs, the various types of architectural styles of roofs, care and maintenance of a roof and even a glossary. The importance of color in a house was in one section complete with a color guide with recommendations for the color scheme of the siding, doors, shutters and roof. The underlying sales pitch was in the section on quality and performance, which emphasized many of the proprietary features of asphalt roofing—fire safety, low maintenance, color, uniform quality and economy.

A chart was included in the book for the homeowner to use for both remodeling an existing house and buying a new house. The questions asked the reader to check for different types of roofing materials as well as different home builders. There were questions specific to the advantages of asphalt roofing. For example:

- Does the roof have the "UL" label for fire resistance?
- Is the roof installed over solid sheathing?
- How long is the roof designed to last?
- Is it guaranteed, warranted or bonded, and what are the material conditions?
- Is your house located in a potential fire danger area?

The company distributed the booklet through roofing manufacturers that purchased its rock granules and publicized it in newspapers and trade and consumer magazines.

Home Buyers Guide. This guide is everything you need to know about buying a home and was published by the National Association of Home Builders to encourage people to buy a new house. Sections discussed how much a family should spend on a house, how to determine what kind of house a family needs, how to select a builder and neighborhood, how to finance the house and the types of available mortgages, plus a checklist for inspecting the house before final purchase and even a glossary.

The public could obtain copies by writing to the home builders. Builders and builders' associations purchased copies for distribution in local markets.

How to Buy a Manufactured Home. The Manufactured Housing Institute published this guide in cooperation with the Federal Trade Commission's Office of Consumer & Business Education to promote the values of manufactured housing. The 28-page, 8-by-10-inch guide discusses construction and safety standards, the manufacturer's and retailer's warranties, appliance warranties, the placement and selection of a manufactured or mobile home and everything a purchaser should know before buying. The publication was available to consumers from manufactured and mobile home retailers or who could write directly to the trade association.

Vacation Homes Plans & Products Guide. Simpson Timber Company, a major producer of redwood, plywood, doors and other forest products, showcased some of its materials to customers in this 40-page, 8½-by-11-inch book of vacation-home plans. The plans could be purchased directly from the architectural firm responsible for the designs. All the plans specified a particular Simpson product or equal.

One section of the book was devoted to products. To offset the overall costs of the plans and products guide, Simpson solicited non-competing manufacturers—such as General Electric kitchens, Anderson windows and Congoleum-Nairn floor coverings—to participate in the project for a nominal fee. Each was given editorial information. These products were described and also specified in the architectural plans.

The guide was initially distributed as a special insert in *Building Products Guides* magazines, made available at a nominal cost to lumber dealers and builders of vacation homes and sold directly to consumers to partially recoup costs.

Tone-up for Tennis. Armour-Dial budgeted to distribute 100,000 copies of a promotional publication filled with tennis tips and exercises and, based on its success, had to reprint additional quantities to meet a demand in excess of 200,000. This printed piece was just one element of an overall campaign for the company's Tone soap.

The full-color, 6-by-9-inch self-mailer unfolded to an 18-by-24-inch poster of daily exercises and pregame warm-ups designed for tennis players. The promotional piece also included basic how-to tips from tennis pro Vic Braden. Arrangements were made to distribute the publication through the World Team Tennis League, so a complete league schedule was included.

One of the sections was on skin care and conditioning. It stressed the importance of using a moisturizing soap with cocoa butter (such as Tone soap) after exercise when the skin has been exposed to sun and wind, thus slipping in a plug for the sponsor.

The publication was promoted by Braden when he did a media tour for Armour-Dial. Color transparencies of the exercises were placed exclusively with *Tennis Magazine,* and the four-page spread mentioned how the publication could be obtained from Tone. To further ensure recognition for the product, the illustrated players demonstrating the exercises had shirts, skirts, headbands or wristbands in Tone soap colors and with the Tone logo.

Publicity about the piece was sent to tennis writers at newspapers and magazines across the country. After use by *Tennis Magazine*, the exercises were divided into 10 parts in black-and-white and mailed to newspapers to be used as a continuing series.

Enjoying Kings Hockey. Alta-Dena Dairy published this handy guide to hockey strategy and rules as part of a promotion with the Los Angeles Kings professional hockey team. The booklet explained the game of ice hockey in the simplest of terms. Alta-Dena wanted to build customers, and the Kings felt if more people better understood the game they would have more fans.

Copies were given to the Kings to use as a promotional giveaway for the first 6,000 fans who attended a game. The Kings in return gave free promotional time on radio and television for Alta-Dena and its products. The dairy also made the guide available free to its customers where its products were sold. The promotion was so successful that it was repeated the following season at two games.

Basketball Tips. In cooperation with the Los Angeles Lakers professional basketball team, Sunkist Growers produced a five-part series on basketball tips featuring the Lakers' coach, Bill Sharman. Printed both sides in one-color on 8½-by-11-inch stock and folded twice to 3¾-by-8½ inches, the tips were distributed through the Lakers organization at five games during the season to the first 5,000 fans who attended as well as to cooperating grocers who had a distribution rack in the produce section. A customer would have to shop over a period of five to 10 weeks to obtain all five parts of the set: (1) The Jump Shot, (2) Defense, (3) Free Throw Shooting, (4) Dribbling and Passing and (5) The Hook Shot. One panel of the printed piece had training tips by the Lakers' athletic trainer, Frank O'Neill.

How to Play Basketball the Lakers Way. This 24-page guide on basketball fundamentals was another promotional piece done in cooperation with the Los Angeles Lakers. The 6-by-9-inch booklet, published by Alta-Dena Dairy, was the first to show illustrations of athletes of color with authentic ethnic features.

In return for promotional spots and announcements during radio broadcasts and telecasts of the Lakers' games, Alta-Dena provided free copies of the booklet to the team to use as a giveaway to the first 6,000 fans attending a game. Copies also could be obtained at retail outlets selling Alta-Dena products. The booklet contained product ads and a team schedule.

Masterpieces from the Chefs of the Great Hotels of New York. In commemoration of its 75th anniversary, Sunkist Growers reprinted a limited edition of a booklet originally printed in 1920. The 4-by-7-inch publication was very Victorian in style and featured the recipes of chefs from 12 great New York hotels. All the recipes featured fresh oranges, the sponsor's tie-in. The chef from the Waldorf Astoria featured an orange-and-lettuce salad with Sunkist sauce. The Hotel Plaza featured Orange Grove Salad. Not all the hotels were still in business when the publication was reprinted, such as the Hotel Astor, whose chef featured Duckling Valencienne with orange sauce. Each two-page spread pictured the chef's presentation and also showed how fresh orange juice was served at that hotel. The booklet also had a two-page feature titled "Oranges for Health."

As part of a major press effort in New York, a morning media event was held with chefs from the hotels still in business and successors or relatives of some of the deceased chefs. For one month each hotel actually featured the recipe on its menu. Sunkist provided table-tent promotional pieces using illustrations from the booklet. New York food editors and restaurant critics were given copies of the book, and most did columns about the promotion. The limited-edition printing was given by Sunkist management to selective VIPs.

Visions of Glory. In cooperation with the U.S. Olympic Committee, and as a sponsor, McDonald's Corporation put together an Olympic education program directed at school students in grades four through eight. Called *Visions of Glory,* the program was a teacher's guide in a three-ring binder. The primary identification for McDonald's was a wall chart with its name and logo that saluted outstanding U.S. Olympic achievements. The poster was designed for an instructor to display prominently in the classroom.

The program had study guides, suggested reading, trivia and suggested tests, and it incorporated geography and history into the lesson plan. The education program was provided free to schools.

MAGAZINES

Edelman Public Relations Worldwide publishes a variety of magazines for its clients. *LINK* magazine is a key part of a program for the Yellow Pages Publishers Association. It is a paid-circulation trade publication distributed to more than 16,000 decision makers involved in the industry. For the National

Farmers Union the firm designs, prints and distributes the *British Farmer*, a monthly magazine for the 110,000 members of the union.

NEWSLETTERS

With the personal computer and hardware that makes it simple to do newsletters, the world has seen a proliferation of newsletters written and edited by people who have strong secretarial skills but no professional editorial training. More newsletters are published than needed or wanted, and this is one of the first areas any large company or organization should evaluate as a means of reducing costs.

Many newsletters are valid and serve a purpose. A good newsletter will provide important information or a service that helps accomplish the overall marketing communications objective. Newsletters with information on industry trends or surveys or that discuss a company's capabilities can help increase sales when mailed to prospective clients. Newsletters also are a way to get additional media exposure for a company or organization and its product or service. If the editorial content is interesting, educational and informative, it may be quoted.

Before any newsletter is begun, there should be an overall audit of all publications. It is important to determine whether the overall corporate objectives would be better served by having the editorial material in a proposed newsletter incorporated into an existing publication.

CHECKLIST FOR SPECIAL PUBLICATIONS

- What is the concept? Will it sell the product or service?
- Does it provide information that the reader will want to know? Does it serve a purpose?
- If the publication is a success, is there money in the budget to print more?
- How will it be distributed? Through publicity? A giveaway promotion? Some other way?
- Has a budget been included for the publicity effort to promote the publication's availability?
- Are there funds in the budget for additional distribution costs?
- Can a nominal charge be made to recoup costs?
- Can the publication be a self-liquidating premium?

11

HOW TO CREATE SPECIAL EVENTS

Special events have been a part of public relations and publicity programs and campaigns since public relations became a profession. However, special events only emerged as an important marketing tool as well as a major business in the early 1980s. While corporate sponsorship of cultural, art, entertainment and sports events was once limited, today corporations sponsor virtually every imaginable type of special event.

Sports sponsorship reached a new level with the financial and marketing success of the 1984 Olympic Games. By the end of the 16 days of competition in Los Angeles, corporate sponsorship of special events had become an $850 million industry. Today corporations spend more than $3 billion a year to sponsor community and promotional events, ranging from jazz festivals to triathlons and walk-a-thons to food festivals. Specific examples of sports marketing events will be outlined in Chapter 13.

The growth of cable television and the fragmentation of television markets, combined with rules and regulations related to the advertising and promotion of alcohol and tobacco products, helped drive many new sponsors into special events marketing. Advertising agencies found that by creating a new special event that would attract a targeted psychographic or demographic audience, they could be even more selective in selling a product or service. Special events became a way to effectively create lifestyle marketing.

A special event is not only a way to attract a particular audience, but also a means of gaining media exposure—and especially exposure on television, which, in some cases, could not even be purchased as advertising. At most sports events site signage is sold at a premium because it is in the line of sight of television cameras and seen time and again by viewers at home.

Special events create opportunities for the public to sample the sponsor's product. They also provide a business development opportunity by giving the sponsor a chance to entertain clients and potential customers. In other cases, special events give a company or organization an opportunity to contribute to a local community in which it does business or to help bolster the economic climate of the community.

The country's most authoritative source on special events is Lesa Ukman, whose Chicago-based company, IEG, publishes the industry's most informative newsletter, *IEG Sponsorship Report*, and also an annual directory of all major special events and sponsors, the *IEG Directory of Sponsorship Marketing*. Her company also produces conferences and seminars to help people who are interested in special event marketing.

Ukman believes that a well-executed event guarantees media coverage. She notes that there are so many facets to any given activity that it is not uncommon to see one event reported on entertainment pages, sports pages, metro pages and editorial pages. Because of the visual opportunities, television and live on-site radio broadcasts also are possible (Ukman and Ukman 1994).

Media are even becoming co-sponsors of many events, Ukman notes, citing the *San Francisco Examiner's* "*Examiner* Bay-to-Breakers" run, WJCT-TV's "Jacksonville and All That Jazz," in Jacksonville, Florida, and CFGM radio station's "CFGM/Molson Exports Summer Country Music Concert" in Toronto. Trade and special interest media are especially involved in sponsorship, such as magazines covering sports of skiing, tennis and bicycling that co-sponsor events in those sports with their important advertisers.

Ukman believes that because sponsorship offers cost-effective promotions that generate sales and good will and because it helps reinforce or create an image, event marketing today is as much of an element in the overall marketing mix as are advertising and public relations.

The line between a special event and other promotion techniques sometimes can be blurred. Ukman says that not all publicity generators are special events and cites the following elements that make an event special:

1. Generally it will fall in the category of sports or the performing arts.
2. The event begins and ends during a specific period of time and does not continue on like an advertising campaign does.
3. It involves some form of public participation, even if only being a part of the audience.
4. The sponsor expects a return on its investment and generally one where the expected results can be measured.
5. The event can stand alone with or without a sponsor.
6. Media exposure received is given the authority of a third-party endorsement, unlike advertising time or space that is purchased.

SPONSORING THE PERFORMING ARTS

As an alternative to sponsorship of sports events, many companies have turned to the performing arts. For nearly half a century Texaco has been a sponsor of New York City's Metropolitan Opera. Schieffelin & Somerset promoted its Johnnie Walker Black brand by sponsoring a 43-city tour of "City of Angels," winner of the 1990 Tony Award for best musical.

AT&T retained Frank Sinatra for a performance in Honolulu to promote its long-distance service. American Express sponsored a concert tour featuring Sinatra and Liza Minelli. L'eggs became a sponsor of the Ice Capades. Fuji Xerox sponsored a 24-show tour in Japan of "The Music of Andrew Lloyd Webber in Concert" to help celebrate its 30th anniversary. *Playboy* has its annual jazz festival at the Hollywood Bowl (*PRJ* 1991).

Corporate sponsors can be fickle, however. For years Brown & Williamson Tobacco Corporation sponsored the Kool Jazz Festival to promote its Kool brand of cigarettes, but when an upscale audience for the festival no longer matched the demographics of the Kool customer, the event was canceled.

According to Ukman's *IEG Sponsorship Report*, there has been an increase in spending on the arts. For the year 1993, she cites the following breakdown for sponsorship spending (Ukman and Ukman 1994):

Sports	$ 2.447 billion
Arts	$ 245 million
Causes	$ 314 million
Festivals	$ 333 million
Pop Music	$ 361 million

And the Winner of This Year's Oscar Is . . .

Andrew Stern and Margaret Nathan, principals of Stern, Nathan & Perryman, Dallas public relations counselors, in 1993 created an event based on the Academy Awards for its client, Price Waterhouse. The accounting firm is the one responsible for collecting and counting the ballots and keeping secret the names of the winners in sealed envelopes until announced on television by the presenter.

Stern and Nathan created an Academy Awards evening in Dallas that was entirely underwritten by Price Waterhouse. A private, black-tie screening of the television show was held with cocktails and dinner, and the $250 per couple contribution benefited the Dallas Theater Center and the Dallas Children's Advocacy Center. Guests also were given ballots to vote on best picture, director, actor, actress and supporting actor and actress, and six grand prizes were awarded to the winners (Stern and Nathan 1994).

The movie theme was carried out in detail, including the invitation being mailed in a Kodak 16mm or 35mm metal can. (These cans are quickly becoming collector's items because of recycling and a trend to plastic.) The mailing label replicated a slate. Not only was the event a success for Price Waterhouse and its clients and friends as well as the charities the event benefited, but it also resulted in positive media coverage for the firm throughout the Dallas metropolitan area.

The event was conceived for the following reasons:

Continued Name Recognition. While Price Waterhouse is typically No. 5 or No. 6 among the "Big 6" accounting firms, depending on whose survey is used, it has continued to have better name recognition than many of the "Big 6" because of its presence at the Academy Awards.

Improved Visibility. For many years, Price Waterhouse in Dallas had suffered from lack of visibility with a new managing partner coming to the city. It seemed an opportune time to reintroduce the firm to the business community through a big special event.

New Business. Both clients and prospective clients were united at the second annual event, held in 1994, which succeeded in developing four new potential client relationships.

LET'S HAVE A PARADE

For years Macy's has sponsored the annual Thanksgiving Day Parade in New York as a means of kicking off its Christmas holiday sales season—and it has become a major television attraction, letting the entire world know about Macy's. The producers of the parade get excellent cooperation and participation from celebrities, especially from those who are appearing on Broadway, because the television exposure helps promote their shows.

Every high school band in the country wants to be in the parade. Because they pay their own way, once selected, publicity for Macy's extends down to the grass-roots level in many communities. As a department store and a place where someone will want to shop, Macy's is presold before any tourist ever arrives in Manhattan.

There are other holiday parades throughout the country, perhaps none more famous than the New Year's Day Tournament of Roses Parade in Pasadena, Calif. Companies place their names on waiting lists to be considered a sponsor of a float because of the tremendous international television exposure and an opportunity to create sales incentives and customer promotions.

TOURING A HOUSE AS A SPECIAL EVENT

Because of its interest in architecture, housing and construction as a major appliance manufacturer, Whirlpool Corporation sponsored a nationwide tour of Frank Lloyd Wright's Usonian House. The house was built as a prefabricated house and moved to a city, assembled and a special event created. Arrangements were made with important museums in major cities to have the house on exhibit for the public.

The grand opening was at the Smithsonian's Museum of American History in Washington. In cooperation with the museum, Whirlpool hosted an elegant reception for the leadership of the museum, VIPs in Washington and important architect, home builder and appliance retailer customers.

SPECIAL EVENTS FOR A CEMETERY

The Stern, Nathan & Perryman firm that planned the Academy Awards party also represents Stewart Enterprises, Inc., a New Orleans-based, publicly traded company that owns and operates approximately 77 funeral homes and 57 cemeteries in 12 states. It is the third-largest funeral home–cemetery operator in the United States.

The company's Southwest division has 16 funeral homes and seven cemeteries or memorial parks in North Texas and Houston, including Restland of Dallas, the second-largest funeral home–cemetery combination in the nation.

Stern and Nathan recognized that in the United States, death is a sensitive issue compared to the way death is handled in many other countries. They note that the death-care industry has had image and media problems. For its client, Restland, they developed a seminar and conference called "Coping With Loss: A Seminar for Healing." It was designed to help people deal with the death of a loved one. The one-day seminar was free and open to the public and featured local and national grief experts as well as representatives from Dallas-area non-profit, mutual-aid groups.

The agency executives met with representatives from several well-established non-profit grief groups and the Greater Dallas Mental Health Association, which co-sponsored the special event, to get their input. The response was overwhelming. The cost of the entire conference was $15,000. Restland's visibility was limited to seminar "goodie bags," newspaper ads and collateral material. Representatives were at the seminar to answer questions about planning a funeral.

Another event, the Restland Festival of Lights Celebration, was created in recognition that the holiday season is usually the most difficult time of the year for family members who lost loved ones during the year. In early December letters were mailed to all the families Restland had served over the last two years, inviting them to come to Restland to hang ornaments on several special holiday trees, listen to a bell choir and enjoy cookies and cider. More than 500 people responded.

A 60TH ANNIVERSARY CELEBRATION

The Olympic, Seattle's first major hotel, was built in 1924 and extensively remodeled 56 years later. It reopened as the Four Seasons Olympic and the new management recognized a need to bring the hotel back into the fabric of Seattle and the Pacific Northwest. Jay Rockey Public Relations of Seattle saw an opportunity to do this in 1984 with a 60th anniversary celebration (Rockey 1994).

The primary planning objectives included the following:

- Reintroduce the hotel to area residents who have not used it since its restoration.
- Encourage those who use the hotel to continue to do so.
- Reinforce the idea that the hotel is a unique civic treasure.
- Stimulate use of guest rooms and restaurants.
- Execute the promotion in an upbeat manner, using the glamor and excitement of the past to promote the new hotel.

A five-day celebration was planned for the first week of December. A 60th anniversary crossword puzzle keyed on the fact that crossword puzzles first were popularized in New York Sunday newspapers in 1924. The special puzzle was published as an advertisement in the Sunday Seattle *Times/Post-Intelligencer*. Working in cooperation with the Museum of History and Industry, an exhibit of 1924 memorabilia from the hotel and Seattle was installed on the hotel's mezzanine. A historical plaque was unveiled by the descendants of owners of the original hotel property who gave it to the University of Washington, still the landowner. This event was followed by a luncheon for key university and downtown leaders.

Daily fashion shows included antique fashions. Special $19.24 meal prices bought lunch for two in the hotel's French restaurant and dinner for two in its seafood bar. A classic car exhibit was located in the grand entrance, with a new classic featured each day. Other events included a tea dance, free to the public, and an all-star jazz reunion that united musicians who played in big bands during that era.

The special anniversary theme was "1924—Tradition, Elegance, Style—1984." Anniversary events fliers were developed and distributed to Visa cardholders in Washington, Idaho and Oregon. Advance news releases were sent in midsummer to trade publications with long lead times. A 60th anniversary press kit was created. Mementos included lapel pins which were worn by all hotel employees and given to guests. A "1924 fun facts sheet" was given to the media daily. The anniversary kickoff was timed to coincide with the presentation to the hotel of the prestigious AAA Five Diamond Award.

The results showed that more people participated in the crossword puzzle contest than in the newspaper's survey, and of the 1,000 entries, about 45 percent were filled out correctly. The hotel's three restaurants were booked to capacity during the anniversary week. The daily $19.24 meal specials were so popular that they were used in other promotions.

The Four Seasons Olympic had its best December in two years, including a greater number of requests for Christmas restaurant gift certificates and weekend guest room packages. Special events were well attended. For example, 400 Seattle senior citizens participated in the free tea dance. Media coverage was significant and lengthy, with multiple coverage on all local television stations.

NOT ALL EVENTS ARE WINNERS

Auto racing can be a glamorous event, one that affords great employee and customer participation—and one for which a promotion can be ended before it starts. Some years ago one major financial institution sponsored two cars on the Formula One Grand Prix Circuit. The company had built a yearlong promotional campaign based on sponsorship of the cars and their drivers. The opening race of the season was in Monte Carlo. Before the first lap was completed, both cars were involved in accidents and virtually out for the entire racing season.

Sponsorship of a boat in the America's Cup yacht race backfired on Grenoble, France, entrepreneur Serge Crasnianski. The boat was named French Kiss after his company, Kis France. Kis' image had changed from a small firm with bold ideas to one that was perceived as a large, unsympathetic conglomerate with excess profits. The Kis firm selected yachting and the America's Cup as being the least expensive and most cost-effective sport for international exposure. (The firm had also considered soccer, bicycling, tennis and Formula One auto racing.) The French Kiss yachting campaign, which lasted for three years, cost less than a $10 million to $15 million per year investment in Formula One racing (Phillips 1993).

Crasnianski said he felt the sponsorship cost the company $70 million in business in addition to a *Business Week* story that reported that "Kis had engaged in questionable business practices, including false advertising and misrepresentation to prospective investors." The magazine also suggested that pending litigation in Europe and North America "could possibly put the company out of business."

IEG's Lesa Ukman calls the $12 million that Apple Computer spent on the US Festival as a major failure. "Apple was trying to reach young people through rock and roll, but found out that the young people weren't interested in computers," she said (Ukman and Ukman 1994).

CREATING AN EVENT FOR MEDIA EXPOSURE

Sometimes an event is just created to gain media exposure. French champagne maker Moët and Chandon has done this very effectively by creating a highly visual event. First, a six-foot-tall pyramid is built of crystal champagne glasses. Then a Moët executive uncorks a magnum of champagne using a saber and begins pouring the champagne into the top glass. As glasses overflow, the champagne cascades down into other glasses until all are filled. Then the guests are served. The event is such that it even allows participation by a television reporter, taking a lesson with the saber or pouring the bubbly.

One of the most outrageous and successful media events ever staged was by ICPR, a Los Angeles-based public relations agency, for its client, the American Song Festival. The agency's account group was given the charge of getting media exposure for the grand prize of $1 million that would be awarded for its annual contest. A number of ideas were considered that included delivering the prize money by hot air balloon and helicopter. The final decision was to have the money delivered in a Wells Fargo stagecoach pulled by a team of six horses, with four outriders riding security. Songwriter Paul Williams was dressed in a white sequined outfit and "rode shotgun" on top of the stagecoach—he actually carried a shotgun.

After considerable time in obtaining necessary clearances and permits, on a given cue, the stagecoach, horses and riders came full speed down Wilshire Boulevard heading toward the office building where the American Song Festival's headquarters were located. A 200-piece high school band, dressed in blue jeans and western shirts, played the theme from the "William Tell Overture" as the entourage made its way down the boulevard. The coach stopped in front of the building, and when Williams stepped down, the band broke into a medley of his songs. An antique chest was taken from the coach and opened to display $1 million in cash. Williams and the client made a few remarks for the media. Every television station and network in Los Angeles covered the event, all mentioning the client and the prize money. In his closing remarks, one reporter commented, "Why are we here? This event was just too outrageous to pass up!"

WHERE TO FIND THOSE HARD-TO-GET ITEMS

Anyone involved in special events should create a custom source file of suppliers. Keep on file any information received because it may be something needed next year. Chances are, many of the items needed can be found in the local area of the event, but for outdoor events there often will be a need for portable staging, portable restrooms and tents. One publication that can be an important source for suppliers is *Special Events*, P.O. Box 3640, Culver City, CA 90231-3640, phone (310) 337-9717 or (800) 543-4116, fax (310) 337-1041.

CHECKLISTS FOR SPECIAL EVENTS

At the end of this chapter are forms developed and used by Sharon Neelley in the Office of University Relations at Texas A&M University. The office is responsible for all special events held on campus. These forms can be easily adapted for use by any company, organization or consultant responsible for producing a special event.

RESOURCES

Following are publications from the International Events Group, 213 West Institute Place, Suite 303, Chicago, IL 60610, phone (312) 944-1727, fax (312) 944-1897. IEG provides discounts for subscribers and non-profit organizations. Information on special services can be obtained by contacting the company directly.

IEG Sponsorship Report, includes free copy of *IEG Directory of Sponsorship Marketing*, $390. This newsletter is published biweekly and covers news related to sports, arts, event and case marketing.

IEG Directory of Sponsorship Marketing, a 500-page directory listing 5,000 sponsors, 3,000 sponsorship opportunities, 500 sponsorship agencies and 800 industry suppliers organized by category, $175.

IEG Legal Guide to Sponsorship, a 498-page book that explores the legal issues surrounding sponsorship, complete with practical reference materials, a checklist for sponsorship negotiations and sample contracts, $89.

Sponsordex, a rotary file of individual cards with names, addresses and telephone numbers of more than 1,800 sponsors of festivals, sports, music and the arts, $985. Also available on computer disk.

International information publications are available from Hollis Directories Ltd., Contact House, Sunbury-on-Thames, Middlesex, Great Britain TW16 5HG, phone 0932/784-781, fax 0932/787-844. Hollis provides discounts for nonprofit organizations.

Hollis Sponsorship & Donation Yearbook helps identify and provides information to contact the top sponsors and donors in the United Kingdom. Tips are included with how-to advice. Price is 70 pounds.

Hollis Sponsorship Newsletter is published 10 times a year and provides information on the latest sponsorship industry news, views from industry professionals and expert analysis. Annual subscription is 195 pounds.

REFERENCES

Phillips, Angus. 1993. "Investment in French Kiss Boomerangs." *Washington Post.* January 1.

Public Relations Journal. 1991. (July):8.

Rockey, Jay. 1994. Interviews and correspondence with author. Seattle: Rockey Public Relations. April-May.

Stern, Andrew and Margaret Nathan. 1994. Interviews and correspondence with author. Stern, Nathan & Perryman. March-April.

Ukman, Jon, and Lesa Ukman. 1994. Interviews, correspondence with author, and informational material. International Events Group.

SPECIAL EVENT BUDGET FORM

Texas A&M University — Account # __________

University Relations — Job # __________

Event ____

Day/Date/Time ____

Contact: Name/Title/Address/Telephone/Fax ____

____

____

		BUDGET	COST
Site Rental/Preparation		______	______
Plaque		______	______
Building Letters		______	______
Portrait/Bronze		______	______
Invitations		______	______
Design	________		
Printing	________		
Address/Stuff/Stamp/Seal	________		
Stamps	________		
Programs:		______	______
Design	________		
Writing	________		
Printing	________		
Ceremony Setup	________		
Flowers and Greenery		______	______
Caterer		______	______
Traffic Officers		______	______
Custodial		______	______
Photographer ________; Photographs __________		______	______
Album		______	______
Gift		______	______
Video		______	______
Scissors/Shovels/Other		______	______
Travel		______	______

Following is the long form used by the university as a checklist for special events:

SPECIAL EVENT CHECKLIST

TEXAS A&M UNIVERSITY — Account #: __________

UNIVERSITY RELATIONS — Job No. __________

Attendance: __________

Event ____

____

1. Date ______________________________Time________________

Location ______________________________ Access for handicapped ______

Rain site ______________________________ Access for handicapped ______

A. Contacts:

1. Name ____

Title ____

Address ____________________

Telephone ____________________

2. Name ____________________

Title ____________________

Address ____________________

Telephone ____________________

B. Committee:

____________________ ____________________
____________________ ____________________
____________________ ____________________
____________________ ____________________
____________________ ____________________

C. On Calendars of:

_____ 1. Regents

_____ 2. President

_____ 3. Chancellor

_____ 4. Other ____________________

BUDGET COST

2. Plaques, Building Letters (order 12 weeks in advance)

_____A. Write words (attached) _____ _____

_____B. Design & order plaque _____ _____

(contact) ____________________

(account)____________________

date ordered____________________

_____C. Order letters _____ _____

(contact) ____________________

(account)____________________

date ordered____________________

_____D. Approval

(contact) ____________________

1. __________ 2. __________ 3. __________

_____E. Installation (work request if needed) _____ _____

(contact) ____________________

(account)____________________

3. Invitations: number (#); paper; ink; size. _____ _____

_____ A. Order:

_____ invitations # _____ P _____ I _____ S __________ _____

_____ envelopes # _____ P _____ I _____ S __________ _____

_____ parking cards # _____ P _____ I _____ S __________ _____

_____ maps # _____ P _____ I _____ S __________ _____

_____ reply cards # _____ P _____ I _____ S __________ _____

_____ reply envelopes # _____ P _____ I _____ S __________ _____

_____ account number ____________________

_____ B. Prepare mailing list:____________________

Approval____________________

_____ C. Arrange for addressing/stuffing/stamping _____ _____

____

____

(account)____
_____ D. Purchase stamps # _____ @ _____ Design _____ _____ _____
(account)____
4. Program
_____ A. Program order:
_____ Selections (musical) ____
_____ Aerial Salute ____
_____ "The Star-Spangled Banner" ____
_____ Presiding ____
_____ Presentation of Colors ____
_____ Invocation ____
_____ Welcome ____
_____ Introductions ____
_____ Remarks ____
_____ Remarks ____
_____ Unveiling of Plaque ____
_____ Presentation ____
_____ Acceptance ____
_____ Response ____
_____ Closing ____
Approval of program order:
1. 2. 3.
_____ B. Letters to invite speakers ____
_____ C. Speeches/Remarks

	Speaker/Needs	Responsibility	Due Date
1.	______________	______________	________
2.	______________	______________	________
3.	______________	______________	________

_____ D. Remarks prepared 1. _____ 2. _____ 3. _____
_____ E. Print program # ____________________Order paper__________ Weight ________
____
_____ Program printed __________ Due _______ _______ ______
(account)____
_____ F. Students to hand out programs
_____ 1. MSC Hospitality Committee
_____ 2. Department student organization
_____ G. Students to conduct tours
(contact) ____
5. Platform Party
_____ A. List of platform party including speakers
_____ B. Send letters to platform party
1. details of arrangements to speakers
2. invitation to sit on platform and details of arrangements to all others
_____ C. Platform seating chart
6. Publicity _____ _____
(Contact)____
Telephone ____
Account ____
_____ A. Advance news release _____ _____
(Contact) ____
_____ B. Radio _____ _____
(Contact)____

_____ C. TV _____ _____

(Contact)____

_____ D. Video _____ _____

(Contact)____

_____ E. Follow-up release _____ _____

(Contact)____

_____ F. Press Kit _____ _____

(Contact)____

_____ G. Press Conference _____ _____

(Contact)____

7. Ceremony Arrangements _____ _____

(account)____

_____ A. Location ____________________ _____ _____

_____ B. List VIPs and necessary protocol ____________

_____ C. Notify University Center ______________________

(Contact)____

Telephone: __________ Beeper: ____________

_____ 1. Platform/location ____________; size__________

_____ 2. Platform steps/location ______________

_____ 3. Podium; location ______________

_____ 4. Seal for podium ______________

_____ 5. Platform chairs # _____

_____ 6. Sound system

_____ platform

_____ floor mike

_____ 7. Press feeds # _____

_____ 8. Audiovisual needs

_____ 9. Background music______________

_____10. Backdrop/background ______________

_____11. Water setup

_____12. Easels #_____

_____13. Drapes: for easels # _____; other # ____

_____14. Chairs for audience # _____; other, # ____

_____15. Flags and holders _____ color guard ____

_____16. Signs, reserved seating # _____

_____17. Signs, directional # _____

_____18. Signs, platform party # _____

_____19. Guest register table _____

_____20. Standards for ribbon cutting or area blocking # _____

_____21. Tables; # _____ serving

_____ display

_____ handouts

_____ C. Flowers, Greenery, Site Preparation _____ _____

_____ 1. Contact: ____________________

Telephone: ____________________

Account:____________________

_____ 2. Prepare Physical Plant work request

_____ 3. Greenery _____ _____

_____ 4. Podium arrangement _____ _____

_____ 5. Corsages # _____; Boutonnieres # ______ _____ _____

_____ 6. Serving table arrangement _____ _____

_____ 7. Ribbon cutting setup _____ _____
_____ 8. Sprinklers turned off _____ _____
_____ 9. Fire ants; other _____ _____
_____10. Mow grounds _____ _____
_____ D. Notify Physical Plant (prepare work request)
(account)____
_____ 1. Sweep streets _____ _____
_____ E. Notify Parking and Transit _____ _____
_____ 1. Parking lot reserved; Lot #______
Inclement weather parking; Lot #______
Platform party parking; Lot #______
Handicapped parking; Lot #______
_____ 2. Request barricades for signs; #______
_____ 3. Map with location of barricades for Parking and Transit
_____ 4. Officers for traffic and parking control______ ______
_____ 5. List of individuals requiring reserved parking
Form of identification ________; #______
_____ list to Parking & Transit for distribution to officers working ceremony
_____ 6. Street or streets to be blocked ____
____
_____ 7. Notify List A if streets are to be blocked
_____ 8. News release if streets are blocked
_____ F. Custodial Services _____ _____
Contact: ______________________________
Telephone:______________ Beeper_________
Account:______________________________
_____ 1. Entrance
_____ 2. Ceremony area
_____ 3. Reception area
_____ 4. Platform assembly area
_____ 5. Catering assembly area
_____ 6. Rest rooms
_____ 7. Halls and other areas seen by guests
_____ 8. Attendant on duty ____________________
Telephone # _________________ Beeper #________________
_____ G. Notify University Police
_____ 1. Security: inside _______; outside ______
_____ 2. If dignitaries or public officials are attending
_____ 3. If protesters are a possibility

8. Platform Party Assembly
_____ A. Room designated for platform party _______________
_____ B. Coffee/water available _____ _____
_____ C. Pastries/cookies available _____ _____
_____ D. Distribute seating plan and programs
_____ E. Present corsages/boutonnieres
_____ F. Give gift to appropriate person for presentation

9. Reception
Account:____
_____ A. Select and reserve location ____
_____ B. Select and reserve caterer/menu _____ _____
____
____
____

_____ C. Order tablecloths and skirting; _____ _____
Color ____

_____ D. Students or staff to serve coffee and punch

10. Miscellaneous

Contact: ______________________________

Telephone: ______________________________

Account: ______________________________

_____ A. Photographer; color _____; black/white __________; contacts _____; proofs _____;
(account) ____

_____ B. Signs for streets ("Smith Naming Ceremony —>").

_____ C. Are hotel arrangements needed for special guests? _____ _____

Arrangements: ____

(account) ____

_____ D. Transportation arrangements ____
(account) ____ _____ _____

_____ E. Gift for honoree _____ _____
____

(account) ____

_____ F. Guest book pages and pen ____

_____ G. Portrait case (work request) ____
(account) ____

_____ H. Scissors and/or saber with bows ____
(account) ____ _____ _____

_____ I. Shovels with paint, decals and/or bows ______________________________
(account) ____ _____ _____

_____ J. Imprint album __________________
(account) ____ _____ _____

_____ K. Football tickets # _______
(account) ____ _____ _____

_____ L. Tickets for other events # _________
(account) ____ _____ _____

_____ M. Telephones: location ____

_____ N. Rest rooms: location ____

_____ O. Emergency Medical Personnel ______________________________

Location: ____

Telephone # ____

11. Luncheon or Dinner

Contact: ______________________________

Telephone: ______________________________

Account: ______________________________

_____ A. Prepare invitation list; Approval ______________________________

_____ B. Select and reserve location ____
____

_____ C. Select and reserve caterer/menu ______________________________
____

_____ D. Order invitations/envelopes and reply cards/envelopes; menu cards. _____ _____

_____ E. Head table ____
____

_____ F. Podium ____

_____ G. Sound system ____

_____ H. Seating charts/table numbers ______________________________

_____ J. Background music ____

_____ K. Centerpieces____

12. List team and individual responsibilities:

_____ A. Scan audience for individuals who should be recognized or acknowledged from the podium. ____

_____ B. ____

_____ C. ____

_____ D. ____

13. Following Week

_____ A. Write thank you letters for appropriate signature

_____ B. Order pictures for album ______ ______

Charge account: ____

_____ C. Prepare album and give to appropriate person for presentation to honoree.

TELEPHONE NUMBERS:

Emergency Medical Personnel	555-1525
Police Dispatch	555-2345
Theater Complex	555-8903
Pager 555-1611, Page #36	
Physical Plant Dispatch	555-4311
Bus Dispatch	555-9451

Following is a copy of a short checklist used for certain special events:

SPECIAL EVENT SHORT CHECKLIST

Texas A&M University
University Relations

Account # ___________
Job No. ___________
Attendance ___________

Event

____

____

1. Day/Date/Time ____

____

Location & Handicap Access? ____

Rain Site & Handicap Access? ____

2. Contacts: Name/Title/Address/Telephone/Fax __________________________

A. ____

B. ____

3. Plaques, Building Letters (place order 12 weeks prior)

___ words (attached)

____

___ design (source & contact) _______________________________________

___ order (source & contact) ____

___ approval: 1. ____________ 2. ____________ 3. ____________

4. Invitations: Printing Center, 555-5841

____ quantity ____; paper __________; ink ________; size ______; order # ____; Printer and service rep ____

____

___ inserts: map ____; parking pass ____; reply card/envelope ____; reserved seat ____; other_____;

____ prepare mailing list & secure approval
____ address/stuff/seal/stamp: 1. ____________ 2. ____________
____ stamps: # ____ cost ____
5. Program:
____ outline approval 1. __________ 2. __________
____ speaker & platform letters
____ printing: quantity ____; paper ____; ink ____; size ____; fold ____; order # ____; printer & service rep ____
___ students for distribution
___ remarks prepared 1.__________ 2.__________ 3.__________
6. Publicity: UR staff assigned
____

___ advance _____ TV coverage
___ follow-up _____ radio
___ press kits, quantity ______
7. Photographic Services, 555-2044. Photographer ___________
___ color neg; ___ color slides/transparency; ____ black & white
8. Archival video: 555-2369
9. Ceremony Arrangements: Theater Complex, 555-8903
____

____ platform size ____ sound ____ ribbon cutting
____ # platform chairs ____ mult box ____ unveiling
____ podium ____ floor mike(s) ____ signage
____ seal ____ audience mike(s)
____ # serving tables ____ flags
____ press feeds ____ # display tables
____ # audience chairs ____ easels ____ # guest book
____ table ____ # reserved chairs ____ drapes
____ water setup ____ other
____

10. Flowers, Greenery, Site Preparation:
Landscape Maintenance, 555-2379
____

_____ work request _____ centerpiece
_____ sweep street _____ ribbon cutting setup
_____ podium piece _____ fire ants
_____ podium greenery _____ mow
_____ corsages _____ boutonnieres
11. Parking and Transit: reservations, 555-9700
____

_____ reserve parking lot #_____
_____ platform party parking lot #_____
_____ # barricades & locations __________, __________, __________
_____ # officers & locations __________, __________, __________
12. Bus Operations: reservations, 555-1971 ______________________________
____

13. Security: _____ inside; _____ outside; University Police, 555-8058 ______________
____

14. Custodial: 555-5441 ____; on site ______________________________, __________________; telephone ______________________
15. Platform Party
_____ # on platform _____ seating chart & programs
_____ room # _____ _____ corsages/boutonnieres
_____ coffee/water _____ gift to presenter

16. Reception: caterer ______________________________, telephone ________________
______________________________ location ______________________________
Menu ____
____
____
_____ # guests _____ tablecloth/skirt _______/_________ color
_____ # centerpieces _____ # hostesses
Food Services: MSC, 555-1100; Commons, 555-3746; AFS, 555-8678;

17. Miscellaneous:
_____ album ____ scissors/shovels
_____ other ____
_____ gift ____ street signs ____________
_____ guest book _____ telephone locations ____________
_____ rest room locations ____
_____ tickets

18. Follow-up:
____ thank-you notes _____ album
____ order photographs _____ billing

Bus Dispatch, 555-9451
Physical Plant Dispatch, 555-4311
Emergency Medical Personnel, 555-1525
University Police Dispatch, 555-2345

12

How and When to Sponsor Existing Events

For every special event that a company creates, there are a countless number already available to sponsor. Sports events are obvious—the Olympic Games, New Year's Day football bowl games, and world cup and world championship events in practically every sport.

With competition increasing each year for available charitable dollars, non-profit and cultural organizations are looking for sponsors to help underwrite the cost of their special events so that revenues from ticket sales need not be used for expenses to stage the event. As marketing strategies of companies change from year to year and with changes in executive management, some event promoters and organizers discover that longtime sponsors can no longer be counted on as money in the bank.

WHEN SHOULD A COMPANY SPONSOR AN EXISTING EVENT?

Many companies do not have available the financial, human or creative resources to create a special event from scratch. Buying into a successful, existing event is a great opportunity. Sometimes a company just cannot create the new event it wants in order to reach a targeted audience because the event already exists or because there are rights controlling the use of names, images and even performers. Here are some questions to consider when deciding whether to create a new special event or sponsor an existing event:

- Is the sponsor price affordable and within budget limitations?
- Will the event reach the targeted audience?
- Is there any other way to reach this audience?
- Is the sponsor fee cost-effective for the audience on a cost-per-consumer basis?
- If the project is successful, are there long-range opportunities and a guarantee for future involvement?
- Are there opportunities as a partial sponsor or supplier?

Here is how Burson-Marsteller describes an ideal sponsorship of a special event:

1. Begin with an audit.
2. Include thorough, ongoing research and analysis.
3. Base sponsorship on sound marketing objectives and strategies.
4. Time the sponsorship to break through all other special-event clutter over the full term of the sponsorship.
5. Use unique, cost-effective, creative tactics.
6. Capitalize on full benefits of the sponsorship.
7. Reach all corporate audiences.

GENERAL SALES AND MARKETING QUESTIONS TO ASK

Since the 1980s, Burson-Marsteller has counseled a number of clients who have been sponsors of the Olympic Games. While the following are questions the company poses to its clients before finalizing Olympic sponsorship, the questions would apply before any decision is made on any special event.

Introductory Questions

1. How do you define your business?
2. How do customers/prospects perceive you?
   - domestically
   - internationally
   - by product/service/geographic market
3. How do you want to be perceived by each specific customer group?
   - near term (two to five years)
   - long term
4. What are your key equities/liabilities in terms of customer perception?
5. What are your overall sales and market share projections?

6. What are the business reasons for your Olympic involvement?
   - increase volume
   - gain new accounts
   - showcase new products/services/capabilities
   - other

7. What other factors entered into your decision to become an Olympic sponsor?
   - give added value to your products/services
   - special interest in promoting international good will through sports
   - defensive move to shut out competition from gaining sponsorship

8. What general benefits do you expect from your Olympic tie-in? Of these, which are priorities and why?

9. What market segments do you want to target?
   - major international accounts
   - small international accounts
   - U.S.-Australia or Australia-U.S. shipper (for the Olympic Games in 2000 in Sydney; otherwise to continent or country of the games)
   - specific business categories
   - other

10. What geographic regions do you want to target?
    - Far East
    - Canada
    - United States
    - Europe
    - other

11. To what audiences do you want to merchandise your Olympic sponsorship?
    - consumers/customers
    - trade and business partners
    - internal
    - media
    - special interest groups

12. Of these audiences, which take priority and why?

13. What messages do you want to communicate to each audience?
    - reliable service
    - broad service network
    - good service at reasonable prices
    - fewer restrictions
    - good tracking information
    - good investment
    - great place to work
    - growing force in international communications

14. Will you have an on-site sales presence in Atlanta (1996), Nagano (1998) or Sydney (2000)? If yes, where? How will it be staffed? What regu-

lar and/or special products/services will be offered? How will these be promoted and publicized?

15. What operations/facilities/equipment do you currently have in these cities?

16. How do you plan to modify/upgrade these for the games?

Re: Competition

17. What is your market share?
    - domestically
    - internationally
    - by product/service

18. What trends or changes are impacting share now? What might impact share in the future?

19. How are you presently positioned against competitors? How might you attempt to change/improve this positioning in coming years?

20. Whom do you regard as your chief competition? Why, specifically are you concerned about them?

21. What plans, if any, might your chief competitor or others have to dilute the competitive value of your Olympic sponsorship?

22. Do they currently sponsor or plan to sponsor any of the national Olympic committees or national or international governing bodies of sport?

23. How might they merchandise these "side-door" sponsorships?

24. What should you do to pre-empt these competitive challenges?

Re: Advertising/Promotion/Public Relations Packaging

25. Do you sponsor other sporting events? If so, which and why?

26. How have you merchandised these sponsorships? Have these tie-ins been successful? How have they failed?

27. Will you position you company as the "official...," as a "proud sponsor...," or other?

28. Have you developed a composite logo? How and where will this be used? On your shipping envelopes, packages? On company vehicles? On uniforms?

29. Are you familiar with the rules governing the use of the Olympic rings, name, logo and trademarks? Are your advertising agencies?

30. Have you developed any initial advertising plans?

31. What are your objectives/strategies?

32. What are your media and research objectives, plans?

33. What creative is in the works?

34. What promotions are under consideration? How will advertising and publicity support these?

35. What identification/signage will you have near the Olympic facilities? Have you secured this signage yet?

36. Have you designed an Olympic pin? How can you make your Olympic pins distinctive/unusual in order to communicate your image?

37. How many pins should you create?

38. How will you fulfill the thousands of consumer requests for pins you will receive from collectors?

39. Will you merchandise your Olympic sponsorship after the games conclude? If so, how?

Re: Tickets

40. How many tickets will you receive?

41. When will you receive them?

42. How will you keep them secure?

43. Who will manage the inventory? Who will register all requests, and who will have decision-making authority to choose between conflicting requests?

44. How will you handle employee or customer requests for tickets? What/who are your priorities?

45. How and when will you distribute your Olympic tickets?

46. If you plan to give Olympic tickets away, how will you meet IRS requirements regarding reporting these as gifts?

Re: Entertainment

47. How many people do you expect to entertain in the city of the games?

48. Who will these people be?

49. What quality of accommodations, meals, and so forth are appropriate?

50. How will you transport these people from airport to accommodations, from accommodations to events?

51. How many vehicles will you need?

52. What types of vehicles make sense, given the scheduling parameters and traffic patterns/predictions?

53. What will these cost? Who offers them? When must you order these to minimize cost while retaining flexibility to allow for changes?

54. Have you made plane reservations for your guests?

55. Do you have hotel reservations?

56. How many on-site staff are needed to handle all guest logistics?

57. How will these staffers communicate during the games?

58. What special entertainment (dinners, receptions) are planned?

59. Do you have special security requirements for VIP guests or corporate executives? Should we notify local/international law enforcement agencies?
60. Will you document your Olympic program? How?
61. Will you entertain media during events? Which? Where and how?
62. What potential crises or problems does your sponsorship pose?
63. Which are realistic? How do you deal with these?

Re: Evaluation

64. How do you plan to evaluate the success of your sponsorship?
    - consumer awareness
    - sales volume
    - customer comments/feedback
65. How frequently should you evaluate these measures?
66. What is the best or most cost-effective methodology?

BEFORE YOU SIGN THE CONTRACT

Before signing any contract to sponsor any special event, be sure everything you want is spelled out. This would include your rights for marketing public relations and promotion, licensing, merchandising, use of logos and trademarks. Also make certain that you receive all agreed upon and appropriate tickets (both free and those that can be purchased) and available hotel accommodations. Most organizers and marketers of special events will have a general information and sales brochure with a detailed menu of what the sponsor receives for "x" dollars of payment.

Warning: Be sure there is an understanding regarding involvement of the competition both in the event and in being able to buy commercial time in the television broadcast of the event.

PROMOTE YOUR INVOLVEMENT

The reason a fee was paid to become a sponsor of a particular event was to create a public awareness of a company's product or service or to build a marketing program around the special event. Just paying the rights fee and walking away doesn't do the job. This is where marketing public relations is important, because the event provides countless opportunities to gain important media exposure. All too often a company will become involved with the Olympic Games and not launch a campaign until 18 to 24 months prior to the competition, when in fact, the rights have been paid for a four-year period.

MEDIA OPERATIONS WHEN HOSTING AN EVENT

Bob Condron, associate director of public information and media relations for the U.S. Olympic Committee in Colorado Springs, believe there are basics one must follow to make the media operation work, whether the event is the Olympic Games or a local dart throwing championship (Condron 1993).

Condron notes that anyone responsible for media operations at an event will have to battle the promoter, organizer and others for seats and space at the event. The host sees the space given the media and photo as lost income. Television may see the media space as cluttering up the picture. Security officers see such areas as only creating another security problem. He says that adequate space is necessary and can be obtained with a little planning and by convincing others that the media are a necessary part of any large event. Following are some of his recommendations:

Print Media

A Place to Sit. Provide ample work space, access to a telephone, power and a seat that provides a good view of the competition or event. It should be reserved for media only. Unless it is a rock concert or some form of entertainment, it needs to be relatively quiet, non-boisterous and secured. It should be in a credentialed area and policed to ensure that only authorized personnel can enter. Be sure that the venue crew does not plan to turn off all lights and power and rip out all the telephone lines 10 minutes after the event.

A Place to Work. This can be a press row or press box or in a separate area near the press seating but away from fans and any disruptive factor. The media workroom should be a secure area for coats, terminals, cameras and other possessions. It needs to be separate from any hospitality area. Access to refreshments is nice, but don't mix revelers and workers. If an informal interview room is used, it needs to be separate from the work room.

Interview Area. In events attended by a large number of media, it is advantageous to have a formal interview area. This can be a big room, a tent or a specially constructed piped and draped area away from noise and fans. A sound system is needed for large media turnouts. A mult box for radio and television personnel is needed at large functions.

Theater seating for the media and an area for television cameras need to be planned in advance. Do not let television camera operators come in and dictate where they will set up—especially in front of the writers. Do this in advance and stick to the plan.

The photo area could be in front of the head table in a marked-off area.

Condron believes that a better option is to provide a riser in the back of the room with power and a mult box for audio. This camera platform could be level with the head table platform so that the cameras are shooting over the heads of the seated press. An 18- to 24-inch riser is a good height to clear any heads in the audience and provide television cameras with a good shot to the head table. The distance to the head table can not be more than 30 to 40 feet. This may cause the layout of the room to be horizontal rather than vertical so that television is close enough for a decent shot. A carpeted platform keeps the mike noise to a minimum.

Team Sports. For events a dressing room may be opened to all reporters regardless of gender. Plan ahead and involve all parties ahead of any competitions so that whatever the interview policies are, they are communicated in advance to the media, athletes, coaches and security.

Hospitality Area. This is a fringe area that doesn't help the writers write a better story or the broadcasters do a better broadcast, but it usually is appreciated by the media. It can be simple and a nice bonus.

Phones. To many of the media, phones are mandatory. A media director can have the media install their own phones or can have a number of phones installed to use on a first-come, first-served basis. Straight-line phones are cheapest and charge-a-call phones more expensive. This can be a big expense, but it is a necessary expense for media coverage and for a large part of the overall media services.

Photographers

A Place to Shoot. Give the photographers a designated photo area located where they will see the action and can cover the event. It should be in a place where they have uninterrupted line of sight to the action and secure enough so photographers can get where they need to be without having to compete with others for space. Provide photographers with visible identification such as bright colored armbands or even bibs.

Lighting. Lighting is critical to good photography. Bring in several local photographers before the event and measure the lighting intensity. When photographers check in for credentials, give them a fact sheet with details to allow them time to plan their film and lighting needs. In some events specific positions may be assigned to certain photographers.

Photo Host. Consider having a coordinator who works specifically as the point person for photographers and oversees this part of the media operation.

Storage Area. Because of the array of equipment needed by a photographer, all of it cannot be carried everywhere at all times. A secured storage area is needed for lenses, film, tripods, coats, sweaters and other items. This should be clearly designated "for photographers only."

Guidelines. The fact sheet for photographers also should spell out all ground rules as to where they can and cannot go, services available and what they can expect.

Broadcasters

Rights-Holding Crews. The rights-holding broadcast crew, especially a television network that has paid the producer or organizer a fee for the right to broadcast the event, generally gets what it wants—within reason. A key for the media coordinator is to make sure that their desires don't become a disaster area to the remainder of the media. Get the television plan in writing. Meet with the crew and find out where the camera spots will be, where the talent will be, what the interview needs are, what access their credential has and what kinds of access restrictions are imposed on other media. Condron reminds us that everything the rights-holding crew wants is not necessarily carved in granite, and they need to abide by some commonsense rules and work with the media coordinator and others. Just because the event is televised does not mean that television can change the event.

Non-Rights-Holding Crews. Unless prohibited from covering the event by any network agreement, these crews are afforded the same privileges as the other media covering the event.

Radio Play-by-Play. If the media coordinator hosts many events in a year, it may be more economical in the long run to install phones for the year and bill a proportional share to each broadcast crew that uses the phone rather than install new lines for each event.

Other Areas

Left Hooks. Condron defines a *left hook* as something that you don't see coming and it floors you before you know it. He says left hooks are to be feared, and one needs to plan for them and think about them. One example is a television camera set up in front of the press row that wasn't discovered until walking in the arena three hours before the start of the event. Another is television holding up the start of an event for 15 minutes for a live shot while the other reporters miss deadlines and television news slots.

Condron cites other left hook experiences he has encountered including part-time security personnel clearing all the photographers out of an area that was marked "photo area only"; the VIP hospitality room set up in the media work area; an attendant in the media parking lot allowing the Mormon Tabernacle Choir to use up all limited media parking spaces; the media will-call window closing one minute after the beginning of a conference championship game; the telephones not fitting computer terminals; and all the members of Mrs. Smith's fifth grade being allowed to stand in the photo area at the football game.

Here are his recommendation for avoiding left hooks: Have the operation so well planned and tied down that *nobody* can screw it up. Go over plans with television production crews, security personnel, venue operations, drug testing, event management, coaches, managers, athletes, ticket takers, clean-up crews, stat crews, play-by-play typists and your own family.

Press Staff Duties. If ample talent is available, put someone in charge of each area: photo area, interview room, work room, press row, and so on. The media coordinator should not be assigned an area but be free to float.

Parking. At every large event there needs to be an area set up for media parking. It can be a combination of VIP-media or a separate area that can be entered with a special credential. A key here is to get a parking lot attendant who has good common sense and knows all types of credentials that allow the holder to park in the lot. There will be times a member of the media doesn't have a pass for some reason.

Let 'em Know Up Front. Before the action starts, let the media know what is available to them and what services they can expect to receive. Prepare a "Media Guidelines and Services" sheet and distribute it at the check-in point, where they will be seated, in the media workrooms or in photo areas. Spell out everything they will need to know with names, phone numbers, faxing service and even airport shuttles.

Credentials. At most events a media credential is needed for access to media areas. Send out an advisory well in advance and let the media know how to apply for credentials. A media coordinator can send out a credential application to organizations in the area or can accept requests by way of letter from the organizations. It usually is best not to mail the credentials, but to have the media pick them up at a certain location in advance. If credentials are mailed, they seem to have a way of getting lost, ending up in the hands of the sales department and their neighbors, or just disappearing altogether. They can be delivered, along with parking passes, or picked up at a central office or location.

Will-call Window. If credentials are not mailed out or picked up in advance, have a system in place where the press can pick up credentials at the event. This usually is at a special ticket or will-call window. Try to have a special media will-call window, separate from the general public. Have the area well marked and always staffed. A communications system should be in place so that the will-call office can immediately contact the media coordinator if there is a problem. Always have extra credentials on hand at the office to distribute.

First Person Theory of Press Relations. Condron believes that many events have been judged by the initial meeting between a member of the media and the first person met from media operations. He suggests having a point person every member of the media meets first who makes the media feel at home and will resolve any problem.

Advisory Group. For larger events it sometimes is advisable to put together an advisory group that reviews the plan in advance before tickets are sold and no space is available. This helps bring about a feeling of mutual cooperation.

Flexibility. Somewhere down the line, one of the many people who deal with the media will have to make a decision that was not covered in any of the pregame meetings. That decision may affect the way that journalist will view the organizers of the event forever. For example, if a member of the media is standing in the rain outside the will-call window, is the ticket taker going to say, "Would you care to come in out of the rain and stand in here while we try to get you your credential?" Or is that person going to say, "Your name isn't on the list," and continue to be disinterested and of no help? Either way, the media person will remember.

Details. Do not leave anything to chance. Make sure every person dealing with the media knows his or her job. Plan, practice and bring backups for everything.

Don't Scrimp on Staff. Personnel and staff are items that can't be trimmed. If there is a budget problem, make the cuts from somewhere else in the budget.

Volunteers. Know how to work with volunteers. Condron has some excellent points to remember about volunteers: "They come in all sizes, shapes, colors, religions and backgrounds, and they're all unique. They have names and families, each has done something meaningful and they all share an abiding interest in helping. "Know their names. 'Hey, you!' doesn't cut it. Find out what they do or have done. Maybe they can be helpful in ways you haven't imagined."

He cites the case of one group of volunteers at a recent U.S. Olympic Festival that included the public relations director of one of the world's largest oil companies, a high school journalism teacher, an advertising agency owner, four retired newspaper writers, three homemakers, and a tae kwon do instructor. Each had something unique and special to contribute. The journalism teacher even recruited 30 of the top journalism students in the city and organized them to help with the media operations for the festival's 37 venues.

He cites an example of how not to treat a volunteer. "Hey buddy, take this trash out," shouted the 22-year-old press assistant to the middle-aged man who had volunteered his time to work the event. Turns out the man was a 55-year-old professor who taught students biochemistry at the university and who was part of a team that won the Nobel Prize for a breakthrough in genetic research. The Ph.D. was a volunteer who signed up at the local office to assist with the U.S. Olympic Festival and was assigned to the media room. Now he was carrying a trash can filled with stale breakfast rolls and coffee grounds and being yelled at by an insensitive youngster.

MEDIA HOST'S OUTLINE

Craig Miller, assistant executive director for media and public relations for USA Basketball in Colorado Springs, developed the following outline, which includes most, if not all, areas to address when hosting or setting up a press work room and seating at an event (Miller 1993):

- I. Credentialing
  - A. Credential Application Form
    - 1. Length of stay
    - 2. Phone needs
    - 3. Fax needs
    - 4. Hotel needs
    - 5. Car rental needs
  - B. Credential Approval Process
  - C. Hotel Reservation Form
    - 1. Arrival and departure dates
    - 2. Type of room
    - 3. Credit card guarantee
  - D. Telephone Line Rental Form
  - E. Credentials Codes and Access
    - 1. Type of credential (photo, logo, fill-in, etc.)
    - 2. Credential codes
      - a. Media (print, TV, radio, photo)
      - b. Team members
      - c. Organizing committees
      - d. Federations
      - e. Technical (referees, technical committee, etc.)
      - f. Service/concessionaire
      - g. VIPs
- II. Media Hotel
  - A. National Governing Body (or event promoter/organizer) Work Room
    - 1. Operating hours

2. Staffing
3. Work room needs
   a. Room setup (chairs, tables, etc.)
   b. Copy machine
   c. Computers/typewriters
   d. Phones
   e. Fax

B. Media Credential Issuing Room
1. Operating Hours
2. Staffing
3. Room needs
   a. Room setup (chairs, tables, etc.)
   b. Photo credential systems
   c. Computers/typewriters
   d. Phones
   e. Fax
4. Signage

C. Media Work Room
1. Operating hours
2. Staffing
3. Room setup (chairs, tables, etc.)
4. Work room needs
   a. Outside phone lines
   b. Hotel phones
   c. Power
   d. Bulletin board
   e. Distribution tables/trays
   f. Video feeds (event, interview area, etc.)
5. Signage

D. Press Hospitality Room
1. Operating hours
2. Staffing
3. Room setup (chairs, tables, etc.)
4. Beverages/food
5. Signage

E. Press Transportation
1. Shuttle service from media hotels to event
2. Service schedule
   a. Times
   b. Intervals
   c. Drop-off and pickup sites
3. Staffing
4. Signage

III. Event Site

A. Press Gate Entrance
1. Hours
2. Staffing (one person with walkie-talkie)

3. Signage
   a. Entrance signage
   b. Media work room
   c. Interview area

B. National Governing Body (or organizer) Work Room
1. Hours
2. Staffing
3. Needs
   a. Copy machine
   b. Computers/typewriters
   c. Fax
   d. Phones
   e. Video feed

C. Event Media Seating Areas
1. Staffing
   a. PR staff
   b. Security
2. Seating charts
   a. Fixed
   b. Changing
3. Needs
   a. Setup
   b. Power
   c. Phone lines
   d. Monitors for statistics/replays
4. Signage

D. Press Work Room
1. Operating hours
2. Staffing
3. Needs
   a. Setup (chairs, tables, banners, etc.)
   b. Typewriters
4. Power
5. Phones (charge-a-call type for media)
6. Fax area
   a. Fax machines
   b. Fax operators
   c. Faxing fees fixed
7. Distribution area
   a. Staffing (one coordinator)
   b. Setup (tables, trays, boxes, etc.)
8. Copy area
   a. Staffing (one coordinator, technician, operators)
   b. Copiers
   c. Supplies (paper, toner)
9. Video/audio feeds of games/interviews
10. Signage

E. Media Interview Room

1. Staffing
    a. Moderator
    b. Coordinators for interviews
    c. Remote microphones for media questions
    d. Quote takers and typists
    e. Security
2. Needs
    a. Setup (risers, chairs, banners)
    b. Public address system for front area
    c. Translation system (languages needed?)
    d. Audio patchbox
    e. Video patchbox
    f. Video platform/power
3. Signage

F. Media Interview Mix Room
1. Staffing
    a. Moderator/coordinator
    b. Quote takers
    c. Security
2. Needs
    a. Setup (chairs, risers, etc.)
    b. PA system
    c. Audio patchboxes
3. Signage

G. Media Hospitality Area
1. Staffing
2. Needs
    a. Setup (chairs, table, etc.)
    b. Schedule
    c. Menu
3. Video/audio feed of event/interviews
4. Signage

H. Press Parking
1. Staffing
    a. Attendant
    b. Security
2. Needs
    a. Press parking passes
    b. Lot list
3. Press shuttle transportation
    a. Designated drop-off and pickup areas
    b. Schedule
4. Signage

IV. Press Services

A. Pre-event: attracting media

B. Event program
1. Rosters
2. Relevant copy

3. Event schedule
4. Event background
5. Athlete information
6. Features
7. National governing body (or promoter, organizer) feature
8. International federation feature
9. Host city feature
10. Sponsorship

C. Event Services
1. Daily notes
2. Event statistics
3. Event standings, results, whatever

D. Post-event
1. Event results
2. Event capsule summaries
3. Post-event quotes

V. Event Ad-Libs: Don't worry. Be happy.

EVENT SECURITY

Event security should report to the public relations coordinator or director, not vice versa. Be sure the organizing committee, the producer and the event director understand this and explain this to the head of security. Establish a close working relationship with the head of security early on, keep him or her involved in all planning, and ask for the security chief's suggestions and cooperation, but any final decision must be that of the public relations professional.

WHAT TO DO WHEN THE WHITE HOUSE CALLS

Having the president of the United States, the vice president of the United States or important members of the administration, such as an ambassador or cabinet member, in attendance often will ensure media coverage for a special event. The visit also will create disruption, disruption and more disruption.

Most often the public relations staff of the elected and appointed political leaders look for good photo opportunities. Photo opportunities are especially sought out during election-year campaigns by all candidates. Sometimes an invitation will be extended for a group or team to come to Washington, D.C., for a celebration on the South Lawn or in the Rose Garden.

The sponsors and organizers of the event must ask how important it is for the coverage and to have a person this important attending the event. The question must be asked: "Is the tradeoff and media exposure worth the hassle?"

When the president of the United States agrees to come to an event, then the White House advance staff and the Secret Service will come in and completely take over the venue. Throw out all plans. Be prepared for anything to change and to change at the last minute.

For the safety of the country's chief executive, it is reasonable to have the venue inspected in advance by dogs and trained personnel and to have everyone attending the event walk through metal detectors. However, the Secret Service often demand that all attendees be in the venue two hours before the president arrives.

The advance team may ask for specific and expensive changes to be made in the venue—changes or alterations that are not in an approved budget. The Secret Service may do likewise at the last minute or even change what had been agreed upon with the advance team.

John Martin Meek of HMI, Inc., in Washington, D.C., says limits can be placed on demands, especially where money is concerned. If the money is not in the budget, then there must be compromises. There are other cases in which this is not possible. He cites the case of an event where the program already had been printed and at the last minute the White House decided the president would attend. Overnight the programs had to be reprinted (Meek 1993).

Meek notes as an unreasonable demand the request for very expensive construction for staging that only will result in a better photo op. This is where the host must stand ground and not agree to everything being demanded.

GOING TO THE WHITE HOUSE

This also can be an event, and people should be prepared for long waits and glitches. Again, because of security, people will have to be in line outside one of the White House gates two hours before the event.

In 1988 during the annual meeting in Washington, D.C., of the U.S. Olympic Committee, then Vice President Bush was to honor the male and female Athlete of the Year in a ceremony in the theater of the Old Executive Office Building. Several days in advance of the event, a list of names, social security numbers, dates of birth and places of birth of all people expected to attend was given the White House staff so there would be no delay in clearing everyone for entry.

Regardless how well plans are made in advance, a name always gets lost somewhere in the system. One time it happened to be Michael Janofsky of *The New York Times* and the uniformed Secret Service refused to allow him entry with other sportswriters. The Secret Service were given the original list of those attending to compare with their list. They had been given all the information necessary on Janofsky. A request was made by a senior member of the vice president's staff to allow access, but this request was denied by the Secret Service. This may seem unreasonable, but those involved with a special event must realize that the Secret Service personnel have but one mission: to protect the President at all cost. Media relations are never considered.

TIPS ON DEALING WITH THE WHITE HOUSE

1. Check out the person who first calls you. Get the correct spelling on his or her name, title, the name of the office in which the person works and the name of the head of this office or department.

2. Get telephone numbers and fax numbers. Ask the person for his or her home telephone number so you can call in the event there is a last-minute problem.

3. Check out anyone who is part of the advance team. Often people will claim they are "from the White House" when in fact they are not full-time employees or are volunteers who may be assigned just to a project or a campaign.

4. Remember that advance people and White House staffers will promise *anything* to get the job done. Try to argue with them *after the fact* if things did not turn out the way you expected.

5. Get everything agreed upon in writing, in writing, in writing.

6. Often the person making initial contact will not be in a position of authority and cannot make commitments until clearing them with a superior. Find out who that person is and deal with the decision maker. Get in the loop and have a dialogue with that individual.

7. Spell out what is wanted regarding videotape and photographs. Ask to bring your own photographer and camera crew if the event is at the White House, because you may be there with an event and not get the archival coverage you expected or were promised.

8. If you have an event in a hotel or other venue that is rented and there are suppliers, inform them in writing that only you can authorize any additional expenditure. One advance team ordered an additional $30,000 of lighting for a room the evening before the event to be attended by the president and told the hotel sales personnel that the cost had been approved and would be paid for by the sponsor. The sponsor found out about the cost, which was not in the budget, at the end of the event and long after the White House team had left.

9. Know the team leaders of Secret Service and establish a dialogue so the Secret Service members know the key people with the event and can clear VIPs through certain areas and make last-minute adjustments. At an event in Los Angeles, one person coordinating with one part of the Secret Service neglected to provide a revised and updated list of guests to all concerned, which resulted in members of the Los Angeles City Council and County Board of

Supervisors, along with other VIPs, being temporarily denied access to an event to which they had been invited.

10. Confirm and reconfirm everything discussed.
11. Be prepared to make all kinds of unreasonable changes and accommodations.
12. Be prepared to throw all advance planning out the window.
13. Plan for budget cost overruns.
14. Most of all, remember you can say "no!"

REFERENCES

Condron, Bob. 1993. "Media Operations When Hosting an Event." *Public Relations Handbook.* Colorado Springs: U.S. Olympic Committee, pp. 29-36.

Meek, John Martin. 1993. Interview. Washington, D.C.: HMI Inc.

Miller, Craig. 1993. "A Media Host's Checklist." *Public Relations Handbook.* Colorado Springs: U.S. Olympic Committee, pp. 37-40.

13

SPORTS MARKETING

Just as *synergism* was the buzzword for the 1970s, *sports marketing* became the "in" term of the 1980s. Sport is a powerful and effective medium of communications. Sport is universal—it overcomes language barriers; bridges ethnic, sex and age gaps; and reaches people in every corner of the world. Sport is education, it is politics; in some countries it sometimes borders on religion.

Interest in sports, sporting events, leisure-time recreation and corporate identification with sports increased tremendously in the mid-1970s. Leading marketers and companies recognized the power and effectiveness of using sports to reach audiences. The Super Bowl was in its infancy. Few people in the United States had heard of the World Cup or had any interest in soccer. There was an explosion in sports consulting and related business opportunities. Industry newsletters and publications emerged and national business magazines devoted space on a regular basis to what was going on in sports consulting and marketing.

The Olympics did not reach new levels for marketing until the 1984 games in Los Angeles. There are several reasons this happened:

1. Companies recognized the extent to which sports pervades domestic and international lifestyles and decided to use sports initiatives to better publicize and market products and services and to enhance corporate images.

2. Television advertising costs escalated dramatically, making sponsorship of sports events an alternative and sometimes a better use of the advertising, promotional and public relations dollar.

3. The plethora of sports programming on network, cable and pay television made the ability to reach consumers through television advertising more difficult as network audiences declined and sports became even more fragmented with cable and syndication.

SPORTS MARKETING OPPORTUNITIES

Until the 1980s most of the sponsorship dollars for sports events came from cigarette and alcohol companies. In 1984 only 1,200 North American companies sponsored events, according to a report by the International Events Group. This increased to more than 4,000 in 1990. In terms of dollars, sporting event sponsorship amounted to $400 million in 1984, $1.35 billion in 1987 and $2.5 billion in 1990 (Ukman and Ukman 1994).

There are numerous ways a company can become involved in sports marketing. A few of these include:

Sponsoring an Existing Event or Program. Many companies sponsor golf and tennis tournaments on a national or local basis. Others have become sponsors of the U.S. Olympic Committee for a range of $1 to $5 million or of the Olympic Games through the International Olympic Committee for a price of $10 to $30 million. Coca-Cola, which first became an Olympic sponsor in 1928, is the world's largest Olympic sponsor and is involved with virtually every national Olympic committee. Sponsorships can range from $500 for a basic event to $50 million for the World Cup, the soccer event that will reach almost the entire population of the world. At the grass-roots level, you see a hardware store or supermarket sponsoring a Little League baseball team.

Creating a New Event to Showcase the Company. Virginia Slims did this with its tennis tournament when cigarette advertising was being banned on television. Other sponsors work directly with a sports organization to establish a new event.

Becoming an Official Supplier of a Team or Event. This is easily done by providing company products or services to the team or to the event. While this is a common practice for apparel and shoes, Xerox also has built a close relationship with sports by providing equipment and personnel to run and maintain its equipment during major events. For years Swiss Timing was the official timer for all Olympic and world-class sports events until Seiko decided it wanted a piece of this market. The official timer's name was always shown on television during competition. Soon companies began bidding for the right to be the official timer, not only providing the equipment and personnel, but even paying a lucrative rights fee to provide the service. This is just another way to gain exposure and recognition for a product or service.

Radio or Television Advertising Associated with an Event or Team. This should never be used alone but only integrated into a more comprehensive campaign. Too often a sponsor or its agency believes it can accomplish its objectives just by purchasing commercial time to tell its story. By combining media buys with various elements of sports marketing, the company can hit a home run with its efforts.

Site Signage. Here the company's name and product are identified in the stadium or arena. Paid signs and banners include everything from scoreboards to the "official" tables at courtside for basketball games to a company's logo on the 50-yard line of a football game, such as The Mobil Cotton Bowl Classic. Sports event site signage is one of the few outlets for cigarette advertising that still allows it television exposure. During NBC's 93-minute telecast of the 1989 Marlboro Grand Prix there were 4,997 images of the Marlboro signs, 519 of the Marlboro billboards and 249 of the Marlboro car. The brand name was visible 46 of the 93 minutes, or 49 percent of the telecast.

Promotional Signage. This takes signage one step farther, with the company's name, product or service identified as part of the competition itself. You see professional golfers with identification on their shirts and caps. The manufacturer of the racquet is readily identified by tennis players. Those in automobile racing wear sponsor patches on their helmets and competition clothing. Racecars are covered with sponsor decals and today names of companies and products are even on the sails and hulls of boats in competitive sailing. Even a boxer with Everlast on his trunks, wearing Reebok shoes and a robe that says Coca-Cola, is a sports marketing vehicle. In 1970, Sunkist became the first company to put its logo on the official competitor numbers worn in a major track and field event it sponsored. This has now become a standard practice.

On-site or In-store Promotions. This is another effort associated with the event or with the team. Promotions can be self-liquidating premiums, contests or purchase discounts.

Public Relations and Publicity. For years this was the most overlooked opportunity in the sports marketplace. Public relations and publicity incorporates many of the available tools, from the use of spokespersons for personal appearances or media tours to creating special publications, film or video presentations to publicity associating the company name, product or service with a team or event. This is the sports marketing strategy that can provide significant impact with maximum cost-effectiveness.

Merchandising. This incorporates a company or product name with an event on a T-shirt, mug or other promotional material. For many years, shoes made by the Converse Rubber Company were easily identified by a star. The company that truly recognized the importance of its trademark and logo on equipment was adidas, first with the three stripes and then with the trefoil. Seeing the success of adidas, many other companies followed suit (Economist 1992).

Licensing. This gives the right to someone to produce or sell merchandise with a product, company, team or event name on various types of promotional materials as outlined in the previous paragraph.

Use of Originally Scored Music. For years there was an immediate association of an upbeat marching score with Gillette and its sponsorship of professional boxing.

Special Publications. One of the most famous is the bubble gum card made famous by Topp's. Other companies have effectively used how-to, instructional publications and posters to further create an awareness and identity.

For the investment to provide results, several of these elements must be incorporated into a strategically planned and structured program. All too often, companies have paid for the sponsorship rights believing that sponsorship alone would achieve the marketing objectives.

According to Harold Burson, chair of Burson-Marsteller, the Los Angeles Olympic Games taught corporations that sponsoring an event is not enough and that sponsorships are not self-promoting: "It used to be just write the check and put the logo on your products. Now sponsors write the check and merchandise the hell out of it (Burson 1993)." Visa International did just this for the 1988 Olympic Games in Seoul, Korea, when it earmarked half of its entire public relations, marketing and advertising budget to promote its Olympic sponsorship for more than 18 months leading up to the games.

Any effort, whether for a specific sports event or for a continuing sports marketing program, needs to be integrated to the point where one element supplements and reinforces the others. In the past, sponsors all too often have overlooked integrating a marketing public relations campaign with their sponsorship.

CAMPAIGN OBJECTIVES

What do you want to achieve using sports marketing? Just as with any other marketing effort, the goals and objectives should be established before a decision is made to use sports marketing. The two must work together. Here are some considerations:

Introduction of New Products or Brands. During the mid-1970s, racquetball was emerging as a sport. AMF Voit was the single major producer of racquetball balls and therefore any increase in participation in the sport would automatically result in an increase in the sale of balls. With the market penetration AMF Voit already enjoyed, all it had to do was to get more people to begin playing the sport. The company launched a diverse and comprehensive marketing communications effort to reach people of all ages and sexes. Publicity featured young couples playing racquetball as an inexpensive date. An exercise poster and wall chart were sent to clubs to encourage warming up before playing in order to prevent injury. A panel of racquetball professionals was formed to further enhance Voit's role as a leader in the sport. At the same time, Voit directed an effort to builders and developers to spell out the financial opportunities of owning and operating racquetball courts. If more people wanted to play, there had to be more facilities. Not only did AMF Voit profit from the growth of racquetball, every company associated with the sport also benefited.

Reposition Old Products, Brands and Image. At the time Tone soap was the second leading facial soap, Armour-Dial looked for ways it could increase sales. One of Tone's principal ingredients was cocoa butter. Research showed that people associated cocoa butter with good skin care and used it to protect skin against sun, wind and the elements. Through its public relations firm, ICPR, Armour-Dial launched a comprehensive sports marketing effort that included publicity, special publications, tennis professional Vic Braden as a representative, a syndicated television series of tennis tips, a video for tennis clubs and organizations and a promotional tie-in with the World Team Tennis League, and resulted in increased sales of Tone soap. Once considered just a facial soap for women, Tone began to be used as a shower soap by men and women alike after tennis, golf, skiing, sailing or other similar outdoor activities. As the effort became even more successful, Armour-Dial's advertising agency, which opposed this direction for marketing the soap, was told by its client to prepare a television commercial based on tennis to encourage use of Tone as more than just a facial soap. The ad agency would not reveal if the commercial was successful.

Reinforce Existing Products, Brands and Image. Marketing alcoholic beverages can be difficult because of advertising restrictions and limitations. Don Smith Consultants created a successful campaign for Seagram's 7-Crown brand that got tremendous recognition, not only for Seagram's corporate but for the product itself. Smith worked with the National Football League, Major League Baseball, National Basketball Association, National Hockey League, Professional Golfers Association and Lady Professional Golfers Association to annually select the outstanding professionals in each sport by means of a computer-based evaluation system that measured performance under pressure. The program was extended to involve the professionals at sales meetings and industry conferences, and the publicity in newspapers and magazines and on radio and television was greater for the company than any other effort it had ever undertaken (Smith 1994).

Shortly after being purchased by an Australian company, Rainer Brewing Company of Seattle committed to a three-year sponsorship of the U.S. windsurfing speed slalom championship, the most prestigious windsurfing event in the world for both amateur and professional windsurfers, to demonstrate its continued commitment to the Pacific Northwest region. The event gave Rainer an opportunity to sponsor a major event in its backyard—in the Columbia River Gorge—and also lay claim to a new sport that was not identified with any particular corporate sponsor. The challenge for The Rockey Company, the Seattle public relations firm handling the campaign, was to pull together a major, first-time effective sponsorship in only three months. Press materials reached media from Vlaeburg, South Africa, to Bingen, Washington. Media coverage included two segments on network television, a full-page, color spread in *USA Today* and coverage by journalists from 12 countries. There was extensive coverage from area media including a first-ever, hour-long Pro-Am television special produced in conjunction with a Seattle-based network television affiliate (Rockey 1994).

Develop New Markets. During the 1988 Olympic Games in Seoul, Korea, Federal Express signed on as a worldwide sponsor so it could create an awareness as well as open new international markets. Federal Express expected that through its contacts with the marketing representatives of the International Olympic Committee and the Seoul Olympic Organizing Committee, it could enter the Korean market with its air express service. It also anticipated returns in other foreign countries by being a worldwide sponsor of the Olympics.

Develop New Services. For years 3M Company sponsored the celebrity-studded Bing Crosby Pebble Beach Pro-Am Golf Tournament, also called the "Crosby Clambake." This is one of the few PGA-sanctioned golf tournaments in which celebrities play in actual competition with the professionals. As one of the financial supporters of the event and a television sponsor as well, 3M used the event as an occasion to entertain its important customers and talk about new products and services. The tournament now is sponsored by AT&T, whose name has been used in the title since the 1977 death of Bing Crosby. AT&T also uses this as a special hospitality event for its key customers in business services.

Achieve Market Segmentation. Manning, Selvage & Lee effectively used sports marketing to reach specific market segments for two of its clients. The Thorneburg Hosiery Company retained tennis great Martina Navratilova to endorse its Thor-Lo PADDS athletic hosiery and to do radio interviews in cities where she was appearing in a tournament. A promotion also was arranged with the radio station for a contest giving away the special socks. The agency also created a "Senior Walk" program that touted the benefits of wearing the Thor-Lo line of athletic hosiery to senior citizens. Working with senior citizen centers and local podiatrists in California, Florida and Texas, seniors wore the socks during a supervised group outdoor program and were lectured by a podiatrist on the benefits of good foot health (Manning et al. 1993).

The Upjohn Company, manufacturers of Micronase medication for diabetics, used sports to generate consumer awareness about diabetes. Oakland A's and New York Yankee pitching star Jim "Catfish" Hunter, a diabetic, was retained for a 15-city media tour to tell the Upjohn story that was directed at more than five million Americans who have undiagnosed Type II diabetes. A Diabetic Hall of Fame Award named for the pitcher was presented to an individual who changed his or her life for the better after being diagnosed as having diabetes.

Promote Product and Brand Differentiation. Mohawk Carpet division of Mohasco Corporation wanted to make an impact to its trade customers, and cycling was selected as a sport in which the company could have high visibility with a limited budget. In 1980, the world's richest single-event bicycle race was created with a $100,000 purse. Because women are important retail customers, a women's race was part of the event. Pete Kalison, head of Mohawk's advertising and public relations, teamed up with the author to make it happen. Kalison is a veteran of sports marketing who was an associate producer for Howard Cosell at ABC, who introduced Astroturf for Monsanto Chemical and who for a time was an executive with the New York Yankees.

Approval and sanctioning for the Mohawk bicycle race were done through the U.S. Cycling Federation and its international governing body. A race advisory committee was formed that included representatives from the leadership of the cycling federation. Atlantic City was selected as the site for the race, with participation and support from Resorts International. The vice president of marketing for Resorts was Michael Marks, also one of the early veterans of sports marketing whose career had included executive positions at The Spectrum in Philadelphia, The Forum in Los Angeles and Madison Square Garden in New York. He knew the value and impact of promotion and television. The race began and ended on the world-famous boardwalk in front of the Resorts hotel and casino.

The event was announced a year in advance with a New York press conference. Sheila Young Ochowicz and Sue Novara Reber, two U.S. world champion cyclists were retained by Mohawk for personal appearances. A bicycle with a digital readout speedometer was set up at the press conference, and the media representatives were given a chance to beat the speed of the two world champions. The two women appeared in uniform at all major trade shows throughout the year and attracted record crowds to the Mohawk showroom and exhibit. They also made media appearances in the cities of the trade events, talking not only about cycling competition but also about bicycling safety for people of all ages. Prizes, including Olympic apparel, were awarded to those who came closest to the speed of the world sprint champions. A logo was created and Tiffany was retained to design the trophy. Publicity appeared in the sports pages and in the carpet and home furnishings industry and bicycling industry trade publications. A kiosk was designed for retail showrooms promoting the race and cycling in general. A contest was held for both retail and trade winners to attend the big race in Atlantic City and be guests of Resorts International.

Arrangements were made with Mizlou Television to syndicate a one-hour program on the race, 40 minutes devoted to the men's race and 20 minutes to the women's race. There was advance coordination with all the cycling teams to maximize publicity for the event, especially with the 7-Eleven team, which featured five-time Olympic speed-skating gold medalist Eric Heiden. It was the first time as much television time was ever devoted to the sport of cycling and a first-ever in the United States for coverage of women's cycling. The total campaign achieved all sales and marketing objectives for Mohawk Carpet.

Accomplish Image Enhancement. In 1984, Burson-Marsteller used Olympic sponsorship to change increasingly negative consumer views of an entire industry. The firm's research showed that the public viewed candy as an indulgent junk food. For M&M/Mars the strategy was not to fight this perception, but to join the health conscious by associating its M&M candies and Mars bars with the ultimate example of health and fitness, the Olympic Games. The Los Angeles Olympic Organizing Committee was approached with the idea of M&M/Mars being not the official candy but, rather, the official snack food of the Olympic Games. M&Ms and Mars bars were distributed throughout the Olympic Village and in the media rooms and staff feeding areas at all venues throughout Los Angeles. As part of a consumer retail promotion, 20-ounce commemorative Olympic jars filled with M&Ms for sale were supported by six-foot-high traveling glass jars filled with candy. The giant jars were taken to high-traffic areas in the top 20 U.S. markets. Consumers had a chance to guess the number of candies in the jar, and the 10 who came closest to the actual number won all-expense-paid trips to Los Angeles. The comprehensive two-year marketing communications program resulted in a dramatic sales increase of the brands as well as a positive shift in consumer attitudes about the role of candy in the diet (Burson 1993).

Reinforce Community Relations. One of the most successful sports marketing programs ever undertaken was the Ford "Punt, Pass and Kick" contest that began at the community level and ended with competition at the NFL conference championships. Many companies have tried unsuccessfully to imitate the Ford program by trying to adapt it to other sports. None has achieved the success that Ford did by involving virtually every Ford dealer in the United States.

The Southland Corporation went a different route to involve its 7-Eleven people at the community level between 1982 and 1985. As part of Southland's Olympic sponsorship, Don Smith Consultants and the author collaborated to create the Southland Olympia Award. This program recognized those athletes who best displayed the spirit of Olympism, not only in athletics, but in leadership and scholarship as well. It was sanctioned by the U.S. Olympic Committee, and any amateur athlete at any level of competition was eligible. A prestigious selection committee was formed of Olympians Rafer Johnson, Cathy Rigby, Sheila Young Ochowicz, Eric Heiden and Bob Mathias. The program was announced and entry forms sent to every public, private and parochial high school, college and university, athletic conference, sports federation and newspaper, magazine, radio and television station in the country. Nominations were solicited from all sources.

At its peak, the Olympia Award program reached three million young Americans. The award itself was a recreation of a Panathaenic amphora given to outstanding Greek athletes in 526 B.C. This museum-quality replica was immediately identified with 7-Eleven and Southland. Recipients of the honor included world champions and Olympic medalists as well as extraordinary high school and college athletes. The award ceremonies were special events that ranged from a luncheon or reception to a halftime presentation at a major college football game with some 75,000 people applauding the honored athlete. In almost every case, a local 7-Eleven representative was part of the event.

During the period of this sponsorship, more than 200 athletes were honored with the Southland Olympia Award. Every presentation received extensive local and regional media coverage. The award became not only one of the most sought-after by athletes, but also the most identifiable marketing effort ever undertaken by Southland. Presentations were made to annual meetings of the College Sports Information Directors Association as well as the executive directors of all the sports federation representatives of the U.S. Olympic Committee. Southland and 7-Eleven had virtually become synonymous with the Olympic movement and amateur sports. The good will generated with the various Olympic sports federations, collegiate conferences and high school organizations was tremendous. For several years after new management of Southland discontinued the program, the company continued to receive nominations of deserving candidates.

Increase Name Recognition and Identity Internationally. Iveco, an Italian manufacturer of light- and medium-duty trucks, used Burson-Marsteller to build awareness of the Iveco name and its link with commercial vehicles. Although the company was owned by Fiat and had a 95-year heritage in the business, the new name was not well known even in Europe and virtually unknown in the United States. Yet the company wanted a global program that would reach across national and regional boundaries. The target truck-buying audience of white-collar males was researched, and sports was targeted as one way of reaching this market. In the mid-1980s Iveco sponsored 57 sports events in 15 countries during the three-year campaign period so its name and its vehicles would be displayed in high-impact media around the world. The major sports events selected to sponsor were:

- World Cup football (soccer), from qualifying rounds in 120 countries to the 24-nation finals in Spain in 1982
- Davis Cup tennis, from qualifiers in 36 countries to the finals in the United States and France
- IAAF World Track & Field Championships, which featured athletes and teams from more than 60 nations
- World Championship Boxing, with a package of 12 bouts in the United States

The sports marketing campaign included media and press relations, publicity, design and production of site signage, vehicle logistics, research and special advertising in print and on television and publicity. It was a total multimedia and multinational communications program. The efforts reached 264 million boxing fans, 500 million football (soccer) enthusiasts, 200 million tennis fans and 350 million followers of track and field. The pre-program research among truck-buying influentials indicated that 85 percent would watch one or more of the sports chosen, and the postgame research revealed that 79 percent of the European audience recognized Iveco as a manufacturer of trucks, up from a base of 32 percent. In the United States, Iveco's recognition jumped from 3 percent to 32 percent.

Develop Relationships With Governments, Especially in Foreign Nations. Many countries throughout the world have a minister of sport, a cabinet-level position with the same rank and reporting channels to the president as, for example, in the United States, the secretary of education, secretary of state or secretary of the treasury. There is no comparable office in the United States.

Coca-Cola probably has been more effective in endearing itself to the highest levels of government in countries throughout the world than any other company and it has most effectively used sports as its vehicle to do this. Don Keough, the former president and retired chair of Coca-Cola, once said, "We can be written out of business by the stroke of a pen in some 160 countries where we now do business. Through sports marketing we can maintain a dialogue and relationship with the leaders of a country that few other opportunities give us." In the early 1970s, Coca-Cola retained Bill Toomey, the 1968 Olympic decathlon gold medalist, to develop a demonstration sports marketing project for the company in Brazil. Working with experts in sports medicine, biomechanics and testing, Toomey designed a five-event competition that would test an individual's speed, quickness, endurance, strength and agility, results of which would identify sports and events in which the athlete could be expected to best perform. The events were selected so the competition and testing could be done at the most remote of facilities. No special equipment was needed except for a stopwatch and tape measure. Toomey's efforts helped identify five outstanding athletes who became Olympians for Brazil. Coca-Cola personnel were involved at the local level as well as the highest levels of the Brazilian government. Tremendous good will was achieved by the company. While the program could easily have been adapted to other markets, such as the United States, it met with resistance by marketing and public relations executives who had a "not invented here" syndrome.

THE EVENT AND TELEVISION

If you are sponsoring an event with your name as part of the title and also have site signage, you want the maximum number of people to see the event. You want to make certain the event is televised by a major network or one of the sports cable networks. When you are considering sponsoring an existing event or creating your own, be sure to also consider packaging the event for television. Assurance that the event will be on television also allows the sponsor or packager to sell site signage and involve more sponsors and suppliers.

The event can be sold outright to a network or sold on a syndicated or bartered basis to commercial or cable outlets. Don't overlook opportunities for the event to be televised in foreign countries, especially in those markets where you want product exposure. Depending on the sport, sometimes foreign rights fees can exceed those of the United States.

In some cases you may be responsible for providing the production of the event. In such cases it is important to have an originating station that you can work with to provide the production and, if the event is live, a satellite feed.

When you negotiate the sale of the event to a network, be sure to discuss the promotional spots and support the network will provide to build the television audience. Someone not experienced in television packaging all too often may sell the rights without considering ancillary benefits.

Build the Television Audience

Getting the event on television is only the first step. If you have name identification, site signage or commercials as part of the program, you want the maximum number of people to see the program. This means building the audience.

There are companies that provide this expert service. The networks will do some promotion, but if you want to protect your own interests, you need to make an extra effort.

The covers of the weekly television sections in newspapers don't just happen. You need to develop a creative idea for the cover and then have several variations so the graphics can be provided on an exclusive basis in certain markets. Plan ahead to be sure you meet the editorial deadlines for this section which sometimes can be four to six weeks in advance of publication.

Work with some of the stars of the event to do telephone interviews with leading television writers of newspapers in major metropolitan markets. There are also sports writers who write about television on the sports pages. Be sure to contact both. Develop a special publicity and marketing campaign to build the television audience.

SCOPE OF SPONSORSHIP

There are various levels of sport a company can look to for sponsorship or involvement. The cost of participation and sponsorship also varies greatly and is generally proportionate to the audience delivered, the same as an advertising rate for a media buy.

Professional. This area would include any professional league or conference including the National Football League, Major League Baseball, National Basketball Association, National Hockey League or associations that represent the players to professional organizations that oversee sports including golf, tennis, boxing, surfing, beach volleyball and other professional games.

Collegiate. There are numerous possibilities to work sponsorship and participation arrangements with colleges and universities as well as junior colleges and community colleges in many sports. Opportunities also exist at the conference levels (Southwest Conference, Big 10, Atlantic Coast Conference) and national levels (NCAA, NAIA and JUCO).

Recreational. This is the true grass-roots level of sport and involves noncompetitive sports that could include jogging, cycling, tennis, swimming and other forms of unorganized fitness and exercise. One central organization that can help direct a sponsor to a sport is the President's Council on Physical Fitness and Sports.

Amateur. This level can range from Pop Warner football and Little League baseball to involvement with the U.S. Olympic Committee, any of the Olympic sports federations, the Olympic Festival and State Games.

International. When you are looking for a global connection, there are organizations that sponsor world cups and world championships in almost every conceivable sport. Major events include the Olympic Games, World Cup and Davis Cup.

THE ORGANIZATION OF INTERNATIONAL SPORT

Sport is organized internationally in three main areas: (1) the international sports federations, (2) the national Olympic committees and (3) the International Olympic Committee itself. To better understand the structure of international sport, reading several specific books is recommend. To best understand the history of the Olympic Games, read the revised edition of *An Approved History of the Olympic Games* by Bill Henry and Patricia Henry Yeomans and *La Fabuleuse Histoire des Jeux Olympiques* by Guy Lagorce and Robert Pariente. To best understand the politics of international sport, check out *The Lords of the Rings* by Vyv Simson and Andrew Jennings.

International Olympic Committee/Comite International Olympique. This is one of the toughest clubs in the world in which to become a member. English and French are the official languages of the IOC/CIO. The public misperceives that every country that has an Olympic team is a member, this is not true. While there are 194 countries that have Olympic organizations and teams, only 73 nations are represented on the International Olympic Committee. Headquartered in Lausanne, Switzerland, this august body has 89 individuals (some countries have two representatives).

The group and its president decide who belongs and who does not belong. While a country may submit names of candidates and recommend a preference for a person to represent the country, the final decision regarding membership is by the committee itself. The national Olympic committee of a country does not determine who represents the country on the IOC. Members of the IOC are its representatives in their respective countries and not delegates of their countries within the IOC. Another misperception is that countries bid for the right to hold the Olympic Games. The Olympic charter requires that cities must bid. Cities request this permission through their own national Olympic committees. In the United States, there is competition for the right to submit a candidacy to the International Olympic Committee. For example, the 1932 and 1984 Games were awarded to the city of Los Angeles and the 1996 Games to the city of Atlanta, and not to the United States. The organizing committees for the XVIII Winter Games in 1998 in Nagano, Japan, and the games of the XXVII Olympiad to be held in 2000 in Sydney, Australia, report to the IOC/CIO. However, the international sports federations are responsible for approving the venues and technical arrangements and for actual conduct of the competition (Wendl 1994).

General Association of International Sports Federations/Association Générale des Federations Internationales de Sports. Also referred to as GAISF or AGFIS, this organization represents the 85 recognized international sports federations that are the official governing bodies of that sport. For example, the U.S. Gymnastics Federation and the Canadian Gymnastics Federation would be members. The international federation is the organization that establishes the rules and conducts the sport at the Olympic Games as well as its world championship and world cup events. The Olympic sports have subcommittees for summer and winter sports. The Association of the International Winter Sports Federations is based in Thunersee, Switzerland, and is involved with those winter sports that will be in the Olympics. Its counterpart is the Association des Federations Internationales Olympiques d'Ete or the Association of Summer Olympic International Federations, based in Rome, Italy.

GAISF/AGFIS is headquartered in Monaco, Monte Carlo. English and French are its official languages. While all Olympic federations are members of GAISF/AGFIS, other interesting federations include the Federation Internationale Motocycliste, based in Maarn, The Netherlands, for various motorcyle race events; International Orienteering Federation, based in Wallisellen, Switzerland; Federation Internationale de Polo, based in Buenos Aries, Argentina; Federation Internationale de Sauvetage Aquatique, in Flensburg, Germany, for lifesaving; and even the International Federation of Sleddog Sports based in Pocatello, Idaho, which staged sleddog racing exhibitions at the 1994 Winter Olympics in Lillehammer, Norway. The Organizing Committee of the 5th World Games, to be held in Port Elizabeth, South Africa, in July 1997, reports to GAISF/AGFIS as its sanctioning body. The World Games includes such sports not held in the Olympics as tug of war, casting, waterskiing and sports acrobatics (Meuret 1994).

There also is an Association International Contre la Violence Dans Le Sport, which works to prevent violence in sport, and the Comite International Pour Le Fair Play. Other members or associate members include associations representing the sports press, military sports, Catholic sports and Macceabean Games.

Association of National Olympic Committees/Association des Comites Nationaux Olympiques. The United States Olympic Committee and 193 other national Olympic committees are members of this organization, which is headquartered in Paris, France.

Throughout the world there are various regional organizations representing national Olympic committees. The U.S. Olympic Committee also is a member of the Organizacion Deportiva Panamericana, the official body responsible for the Pan American Games every fourth year, in the year before the summer Olympic Games. There also are the Olympic Council of Asia, Oceania National Olympic Committees, Association des Comites Nationaux Olympiques d'Afrique and Association des Comites Nationaux Olympiques d'Europe, among others, that are responsible for regional competitions similar to the Pan American Games. The Olympic Council of Asia, for example, is responsible for sanctioning and overseeing the Asian Games.

BEWARE OF MANAGEMENT CHANGES

Some of the best comprehensive sports marketing programs have been changed, altered or discontinued primarily because of a change in management and a "not invented here" complex. If a program has been successful, top management should take a close look or get a second opinion from an outside consultant before shelving any program.

Programs all have a finite life span. Some just run out of gas; others are victims of new marketing objectives, or new decision makers in key positions. It is important to stay abreast of corporate marketing goals, trends in the business and consumer patterns. Consultant Don Smith believes that a good sports marketer is aware of these nuances and can anticipate situations before they develop. This enables the sports marketer to change the sports sponsorship or program so that it continues to be an effective marketing strategy. It doesn't always work, but many sponsorships can be salvaged by maintaining this flexibility and anticipation. That is the challenge of the business today.

PROGRAM DEVELOPMENT CHECKLIST

Here are some basic steps to follow in implementing a sports marketing program:

- Orient, research and discuss all available data to identify problems, objectives and opportunities.
- Identify and select target publics to which the program will be directed.
- Develop creative concepts for the program that will maximize the thrust that best meets the established goals.
- Recommend techniques and mechanics that are most adaptable to implement the creative concepts.
- Organize a team, based on disciplines and experience, most able to execute the program.
- Establish a time or phase calendar for program implementation.
- Maintain a continuous liaison with all involved to monitor results and

modify or restructure elements of the program, if necessary.

WHAT TO LOOK FOR IN A SPORTS MARKETING TEAM

Using sports marketing skillfully and effectively requires a high degree of specialization. Until the sports marketing boom, for many years there was less than a score of highly skilled professionals who had been effectively practicing sports marketing in the United States and worldwide. The work and service they performed did not yet have the label of *sports marketing*. Suddenly sports marketing was a field everyone wanted to enter. Worst of all, many Sunday afternoon couch-potato quarterbacks and ex-jocks thought it was an easy way to make money.

Some of the early pioneers of sports marketing included the author, Don Smith, Mike Harrigan, Patrick Nally, Horst Dassler and Bill Toomey.

The author was fortunate to begin his career as a college sports information director and used this knowledge to combine corporate sponsorship with sports promotion. Early in his career a client was the AP Parts Company of Toledo, which had sponsored the car that two years in a row had won the Indianapolis 500. At that time the event was not televised, and widespread exposure for the sponsorship was limited to newspaper coverage. The car was the favorite to win the auto race for an unprecedented third time. Sports cartoonists were popular during this time, so well in advance of the race, arrangements were made with three of the best—Murray Olderman of NEA, Tom Paprocki's "by Pap" of Associated Press and Alan Maver of King Features—to do syndicated cartoons about the car and its driver. Feature stories and columns were developed with sportswriters at major metropolitan newspapers. Arrangements were even made with "The Ed Sullivan Show" to have the race car flown specially to New York to be on the Sunday night program, provided it won. The driver did his job and won the No. 1 pole position for the race. Unfortunately, when the announcer proclaimed, "Gentlemen, start your engines," the engine on the car froze and it had to be pushed off the track into the pits. The campaign and publicity ended suddenly.

Don Smith began his career as a sportswriter, then joined the New York Giants professional football team and went on to chair the public relations committee of the NFL and head public relations efforts for the first dozen Super Bowls. He is one of the most respected professionals in the business today and has headed his own firm that provides counseling and service in broad areas of professional and Olympic sports. Recently he has served as president of the New York Sports Commission. He has authored a score of books, including one about the origin of sport. He and the author worked together for five years serving The Southland Corporation for the 7-Eleven Olympic marketing program, co-producing the famous nationwide tour of the 1984 U.S.

Olympic medal winners that included a ticker tape parade in New York City.

Although not an attorney, no one knows the legal and technical structure of amateur and Olympic sports in the United States better than Michael T. Harrigan. In the July 8, 1974, issue of *Sports Illustrated*, then Vice President Gerald Ford wrote: "The Administration has under advisement a plan—Mr. Mike Harrigan's to create 'a President's Commission on Olympic Sports.' " After Ford became president, in June 1975 he asked the late Gerry Zornow, chair of the board of Eastman Kodak, to chair the commission and Mike Harrigan (1994) to direct it.

The commission's work and report, which was issued in January 1977, remain a watershed in American Olympic sports history. It was the most comprehensive work ever of its kind and because of it, the Amateur Sports Act of 1978 became law. Among other things, this law solved the 50-year dispute between the Amateur Athletic Union (AAU) and National Collegiate Athletic Association (NCAA). Harrigan was responsible for the broad and specific strategy of the act and one of the very few responsible for writing the law.

The commission and public law were the sole catalysts that transformed the U.S. Olympic Committee and the various governing bodies of sport in this country from do-nothing travel agencies into organizations concerned more fully with identifying, recruiting, developing, training and funding athletes of all skill levels. For the first time the law guaranteed provisions that protected the right of an athlete to compete and developed a method for resolving conflicts and disputes outside of the legal system.

In 1977, Harrigan co-founded Trigon Sports International, Inc., which is now based in Falls Church, Virginia. His firm does Olympic sports planning, development, fund raising and marketing; government relations for sports organizations and a wide range of consulting including interpretive work on the Amateur Sports Act. He also has helped Olympic bid cities succeed in their bids and many other related areas.

Patrick Nally, a British public relations and advertising executive, teamed up with adidas' Horst Dassler to form West-Nally, which took sports marketing to new levels in the 1970s. By representing the major international sports federations, the firm could control all world cup and world championship events and thereby all sources of revenue including sponsorship rights, television rights sales, site signage and licensing and merchandising. In 1975 West-Nally teamed with the author and his ICPR firm to form ICPR/West-Nally, which produced some 35 major world cup and world championship events in 16 different sports, including the World Cup (soccer). A new concept for selling football was created called Intersoccer 4, which became the format used today by the International Olympic Committee for its TOP (The Olympic Program). West-Nally became one of the first full turnkey sports marketing companies and had offices throughout Europe, Latin America, Asia and the United States.

Olympic decathlon gold medalist Bill Toomey was one of the more creative marketers in developing new ideas and concepts for sponsorship. His company became a part of ICPR in 1975 and then was part of the ICPR/West-Nally partnership. Toomey, now an executive with the U.S. Olympic Training Center in San Diego, was the creator of the Golden Mile and many other well-known events.

Ask About the Qualifications of Your Team

Look at these qualifications and ask questions about the people who will be part of the team. For example:

- Multidisciplined in more than one area of sports marketing with an understanding of and experience in advertising, marketing, public relations, television packaging, event management, promotion and the media
- Multicultural and multilingual
- Experienced and understanding of sport to know the costs associated with various events and the people who manage the sport as well as the exploitation possibilities of a sport
- Knowledgeable politically to know the decision makers and leaders in the sport in which you are going to be involved
- If international, a knowledge of the culture and language of the sport and the country or countries that will be involved or where the event will originate
- Creative and performance-motivated with proven results
- Has management capability in running an event, creating an event and promoting an event
- Experienced in negotiating sponsor's rights and fees in sponsoring an event
- Experienced in packaging an event for television and in negotiating rights and sales of the program both domestically and internationally
- Familiar with what is needed to originate a program for television with a base station
- Knowledgeable in building a television audience
- Experience in development and fund raising

REFERENCES

Burson, Harold. 1993. Interview. New York: Burson-Marsteller.

The Economist. 1992. "The Sports Business." July 25.

Harrigan, Michael T. 1994. Interview. Fairfax, Va: Trigon Sports.

Henry, Bill, and Patricia Henry. 1981. *An Approved History of the Olympic Games.* Special edition. Original edition 1948. Los Angeles: Olympic Organizing Committee.

Lagorce, Guy, and Robert Pariente. 1982. *La Fabuleuse Histoire des Jeux Olympiques.* Paris: Éditions O.D.I.L.

Manning, Selvage & Lee. 1993. Information and promotional materials. New York.

Meuret, Jean-Louis. 1994. Correspondence with author. Monte Carlo, Monaco: General Association of International Sports Federations. February.

Rockey, Jay. 1994. Interviews and correspondence with author. Seattle: Rockey Public Relations. April-May.

Simson, Vyv, and Andrew Jennings. 1991. *The Lords of the Rings.* New York; Simon and Schuster.

Smith, Don. 1994. Interview and correspondence with author. New York: Don Smith Consultants.

Ukman, Jon, and Lesa Ukman. 1994. Interviews, correspondence with author, and informational material. International Events Group. March-May.

Wendl. Karen. 1994. Correspondence with author. Lausanne, Switzerland: International Olympic Committee. January 31.

14

HOW TO TARGET SPECIAL MARKETS

America is changing. The demographic composition of tomorrow's consumer of products and services is changing. The population is moving from the Northeastern and Midwestern geographic areas of the country to the South and the West.

The work force is changing. By the year 2000 more than two-thirds of the new entrants into the U.S. work force will be women and members of ethnic minorities. Males already are less than 50 percent of the population in each racial and ethnic group (U.S. Dept. of Labor 1993). If the Environmental Protection Agency listed such a category, it wouldn't be too many years before it considered the U.S.-born, white male an endangered species.

More than 32 million people, five years of age or older, speak a foreign language at home, compared to 23 million in 1980. Spanish is the preferred language by 17.3 million (*Hispanic Link* 1993). The top-rated, most-listened-to radio stations in Los Angeles, Miami and San Antonio are Spanish-language radio stations (Adelson 1994).

African American consumers spend an estimated $250 billion a year. Spanish-speaking people spend almost $180 billion a year. Salsa has now surpassed ketchup as the number one condiment in the United States. The production of tortillas in the United States exceeds that in Mexico (Oaxaca 1994).

The changes that already have taken place with the greatest immigration into the United States since the late 1890s and turn of the century have placed new demands on marketing public relations professionals for creative techniques to reach special market segments. The demands for special considerations will be even greater in the next century.

According to Dr. Steve H. Murdock, professor of sociology and head of the department of rural sociology at Texas A&M University, the United States is now the third largest nation in the world in terms of population and likely will continue to be so through the year 2020. However, its population growth will continue to decline. Murdock cites China, with nearly 1.2 billion people, and India, with 870 million, ahead of the United States, with 252 million. The former Soviet Union had ranked as the third largest nation before its breakup (Murdock 1993).

In his book *An America Challenged* (1993) Murdock charts the following projected U. S. population growth after the 1990 U. S. census:

1990	248,709,873
2000	274,815,465
2010	298,109,073
2020	322,601,703
2030	344,951,379
2040	364,349,040
2050	382,674,080

Dr. Murdock notes that immigration to this country is characterized by increasing diversity: "Although Europeans dominated immigration to the U.S. for much of the nation's history, immigration to the U.S. is now dominated by immigrants from Latin America and Asia."

Other important trends and events he cites (Murdock 1993) include:

> California, Florida and Texas accounted for more than 54 percent of all population growth from 1980 to 1990.
>
> Minority populations are growing more rapidly than the white, or Anglo, population and are increasing as a proportion of the total population.
>
> Households will be smaller, with more persons remaining single or becoming single again after marrying once.

Dr. Murdock, who also is the chief demographer for the state of Texas, cautions that measuring race and ethnicity is difficult:. "The U.S. Bureau of the Census has generally measured the concepts of race and ethnicity by respondents self-identifying themselves on questionnaires on two separate items. For example, in the 1990 Decentennial Census, persons were asked one question in which they were to identify themselves in terms of the racial categories of White; Black; American Indian, Eskimo or Aleut; Asian and Pacific Islander; or whether they were members of some other racial group. In a separate question, they were asked whether they were of Spanish/Hispanic Origin and, if they indicated that they were of Hispanic Origin, they were asked to indicate of which Hispanic group they were a member. As a result of the use of two separate questions, many census reports show data divided by racial groups and then a separate tabulation of data by Hispanic Origin. Even when racial/ethnic data are reported together, Hispanic is often shown with a note that 'Hispanics may be of any race.' Many data users want to add values for Hispanics to the racial categories but in so doing Hispanics are counted twice since they are already included in the counts by racial group (Murdock 1993)."

Even the term *minority* can be misleading. In Los Angeles, with a tremendous influx of immigrants, there really may be no majority group, per se. In some cities what might be considered an ethnic minority is actually a demographic majority.

DIFFERENCES AND SIMILARITIES

Porter/Novelli Public Relations (1994) defines eight different characteristics that distinguish some groups from others and seven outstanding similarities that tie cultures together.

The Differences

1. The group is more important than the individual. Traditional white American culture favors the rights of the individual over the rights of all, but in the African American, Asian American and Hispanic communities, the rights of the group are more important than those of the individual.

2. The extended family, including grandparents, is important in positions of authority and respect in African American, Asian American and Hispanic cultures. In the Caucasian community this setup has given way to a smaller, nuclear family.

3. Religion and the church are an essential part of African American and Hispanic cultures but have lost dominance in many parts of the white community.

4. Food is a characteristic that distinguishes ethnic groups, especially among whites—German Americans, Italian Americans and Polish Americans, for example.

5. Sociologists say African Americans, Asian Americans and Hispanics may have a greater ability than Caucasians to communicate through symbols, gestures and nonverbal communication.

6. People of color who live in culturally diverse environs are more likely to be culturally literate and flexible than are Caucasians who live in predominantly or exclusively all-white communities.

7. While English is the language of the United States and the language of business, there are many languages in the nation's tapestry, from foreign languages to teenspeak.

8. Communities of color are far more likely to group around ethnic iden-

tity while Caucasian communities may group around causes.

The Similarities

1. The concept of family is universal among cultures.
2. Lifestages are commonalities among teenagers, college students, older persons and people of the same background.
3. Sport transcends all cultures.
4. Food is often the first exposure many people have to other cultures and enables people to share their heritage.
5. Music is another medium that crosses cultural barriers.
6. The concept of the American Dream, defined by family, faith and home ownership, is a shared ideal.
7. The anecdote and storytelling are common and persuasive forms of communication shared by all cultures.

LEARN FROM MISTAKES

When a special market must be reached in order to accomplish the objective of the marketing public relations program, it is important to involve a professional who is knowledgeable and experienced in the language, culture and nuances of that audience.

General Motors made a classic error when it introduced its popular Chevrolet Nova in Mexico without changing the name. It learned too late that Nova translated into Spanish, *no va*, literally means "it won't go." And the Mexican consumer responded by not buying a car that "won't go."

Other literal Spanish translations created problems for U.S.-headquartered companies. Braniff Airlines' efforts to promote the comfort of its new all-leather seats translated into asking its passengers to "fly nude." Since the Spanish word for beer, *cerveza*, has a feminine ending, Budweiser's "King of Beers" became the "Queen of Beers," not something a macho Mexican male would even think about drinking. Coors had even more problems when its "Turn It Loose" slogan translated into "Suffer from Diarrhea." And when Perdue Farms said "It takes a tough man to make a tender chicken," it came out to the Spanish-speaking consumer: "It takes a sexually stimulated man to make a chicken affectionate."

Fay Fleming (1994), vice president of marketing for Provident Counseling, St. Louis, lists what she believes are the 10 most common mistakes in minority marketing:

1. Ignoring a billion-dollar potential market.
2. Not developing an internal organizational structure to handle minority marketing.

3. Sponsoring promotional events only at the event.
4. Not working closely with the local sales force.
5. Using focus groups and basing long-term strategic decisions solely on insights.
6. Spending a disproportionately low amount of money compared to the value of the minority market.
7. Having the general market advertising agency handle the minority market.
8. Treating the minority market with a public affairs mentality.
9. Underestimating the value of the minority consumer.
10. Limiting the scope of a minority marketing effort.

FOUR COMMON MYTHS

"My personal philosophy is that marketing to ethnic minorities is really just an extension of effective marketing," says Lou Nieto, director of ethnic marketing for Kraft USA in Glenview, Ill. "We do not treat an ethnic market any differently than we would treat any other marketing group. If there is a need to segment a market by ethnicity, be sure you become totally knowledgeable about the target market." Nieto (1994) outlines four myths that create problems for people trying to reach Hispanic and African American consumers.

Myth No. 1

To market effectively to Hispanics, some people say three versions of every message must be developed so it is customized for the Cuban Americans, Puerto Rican Americans and Mexican Americans. While each group has obvious differences in the way Spanish is spoken and there are clearly different colloquial phrases and vocabulary words, a common language can be used to reach them all. This is no different than what marketers have been doing to reach people in the United States with different dialects of English from Boston to Atlanta and Texas to California.

Myth No. 2

There is a misperception that Hispanics are brand loyal, and once you get them as customers, they will remain loyal to a brand for a lifetime. Research has shown that the dynamics that work for the general public will work for Hispanics, that Hispanics have a propensity to switch brands just like any other consumer and Hispanics have no more or less loyalty to a brand than the average population does.

Myth No. 3

Marketers should not be fooled into believing if they target the top 10 or top 20 television programs, they will reach African American audiences. What African Americans watch on television varies greatly from the average U.S. television audience. For example, Table 14.1 shows the top 20 television shows for 1991 in African American households and overall U.S. households.

Only one show with predominantly African American cast, the "Bill Cosby Show," which no longer is on prime-time network television, ranked in the top 20 for total U.S. television households (at 15). Among African American television households, only "Cheers," "NFL Monday Night Football" and "60 Minutes" of top-10-ranked shows for the United States overall even made the top 20 rankings.

Table 14.1. Top 20 television shows for African American households and for overall U.S households, 1991

Television Program	African American Rank	Total U.S. Rank
A Different World	1	13
Fresh Prince of Bel Air	2	22
Bill Cosby Show	3	15
In Living Color	4	48
ROC	5	73
Blossom	6	40
Family Matters	7	29
Married With Children	8	34
Royal Family	9	63
In the Heat of the Night	10	31
Cheers	11	4
Step by Step	12	26
Knots Landing	13	38
NFL Monday Night Football	14	8
True Colors	15	61
Teech	16	64
Law and Order	17	34
Parker Lewis	18	105
Monday Night Movie	19	21
60 Minutes	20	1
Roseanne	25	2
Murphy Brown	56	3
Designing Women	50	5
Home Improvement	27	6
Full House	21	7
Coach	51	8
Major Dad	97	10
Unsolved Mysteries	33	11
Murder She Wrote	42	12
Evening Shade	107	14
Northern Exposure	82	16
CBS Sunday Night Movie	32	17
Empty Nest	42	18
America's Funniest Home Videos	114	19
Wings	28	19

Source: Porter/Novelli Omnicon PR Network, *Re-weaving the Tapestry of America,* 1994.

Myth No. 4

The fourth myth is that by using a black actor in an advertisement, the message will effectively reach the African American consumer. The concern must be whether or not the person being targeted is being reached personally, not what color the actor is. If the situation being shown is not relevant to the lifestyle of the targeted individual, then the message will be tuned out and lost.

TARGETING AFRICAN AMERICANS

African Americans today make up about 12 percent of the U.S. population, and their numbers are expected to rise steadily into the next century. They are estimated to constitute about 15 percent of the total population in 2050. Table 14.2 charts this growth.

Stereotypes, misperceptions and myths are more prevalent in special marketing and ethnic or minority marketing that in almost any other field. The definitive work regarding African Americans as portrayed in advertising and public relations is *Aunt Jemima, Uncle Ben and Rastus: Blacks In Advertising, Yesterday, Today and Tomorrow* (1994) by Marilyn Kern-Foxworth, associate professor of journalism and public relations at Texas A&M University. The late Alex Haley wrote the foreword for her book which says it all: "Blacks in America have not been portrayed justly and fairly in advertising.... [T]he images...perpetuated by public relations have not averaged very favorably. It is important for us to realize what effects such depictions have had on Black people's self-respect, self-esteem, self-concept and self-identity. We can't deny the importance of advertising and public relations in our lives as they are definitely a reality of human existence." (Kern-Foxworth 1994)

How many people know that there are more whites (61 percent) depen-

Table 14.2. Population growth of African Americans in the United States

Year	Total	Percent of U.S. Population
1970	22,550,000	11.1
1980	26,482,000	11.7
1990	29,986,000	12.1
2000	33,834,463	12.3
2010	38,200,689	12.8
2020	42,910,788	13.3
2030	47,551,578	13.8
2040	52,284,693	14.4
2050	57,315,588	15.0

Source: Steven Murdock, *An America Challenged.*

dent on welfare than there are people of color? Or that Blacks proportionally spend just as much shopping annually as do their white counterparts? Studies show that 55 percent of college-educated, high-income Blacks chose ethnic as opposed to national identity and 36 percent say that both are important.

According to Kern-Foxworth, one of the most popular black personalities was Aunt Jemima, who became an integral part of the American culture by the turn of the 20th century. Aunt Jemima also ushered in the beginning of the convenience foods era with a prepackaged pancake mix that today represents more than $300 million in sales for Quaker Oats Company and is the nation's most popular pancake mix. Kern-Foxworth notes that Nancy Green, born a slave in 1934 in Montgomery County, Kentucky, made her debut as Aunt Jemima at the 1893 World's Columbian Exposition in Chicago greeting fair visitors, singing songs, telling stories of the Old South and cooking and serving more than one million pancakes by the time the fair had ended. Since then, Aunt Jemima has been involved in special events, public appearances and media interviews to promote the sale of the pancake mix.

> The stereotypes associated with the Aunt Jemima image are considered negative by most Blacks—a happy slave, devoted servant, natural born cook, happy-go-lucky, grinning and childlike. Her physical attributes were totally opposite of how white America traditionally defined beauty—dark-skinned, extremely broad features and extremely overweight. The traditional red bandanna headwear was symbolic of slavery. The red bandanna was replaced in 1968 by a checkered red headband. In 1989, Quaker Oats introduced a new Aunt Jemima with a more contemporary look with soft, grey-streaked hairdo, pearl earrings and a white lace collar. The red checkered headband was gone. Because the company was so skillful in integrating the symbol of Aunt Jemima into American culture, it has had a profound impact on the image that Blacks have of themselves and of the image whites have of Blacks. (Kern-Foxworth 1994)

Black History Month—A Special Event

Dr. Kern-Foxworth (1994) notes that one of the most comprehensive public relations campaigns undertaken by a group of people was to establish Black History Month, now celebrated in February. It was first observed as a week in 1926 and expanded to a month in 1976. "Over the years, corporations have viewed Black History Month as an occasion to strengthen their marketing and public relations strategies directed toward the African American consumer market." Following are examples of how some major corporations targeted black consumers:

- Coca-Cola sponsored a "Share the Dream" Scholarship Sweepstakes using the vision of Dr. Martin Luther King, Jr. Two $25,000 grand prize scholarships and eight $10,000 first prize scholarships were awarded.

• Kraft offered a free booklet based on the theme "Creativity . . . the Heritage of African American Cooking." The booklet contained traditional and modern recipes used by African Americans in the United States and noted that the heritage of African American cooking is an expression of family tradition.

• Amtrak profiles a leading Black with a public service ad during the month. Inventor Garret A. Morgan was profiled with inspirational copy citing how he didn't see color as an obstacle; his invention of the gas mask saved thousands of lives during World War I. The text concluded that "he may have invented the traffic signal, but he never saw a red light."

• Budweiser began a tradition of offering poster reprints portraying "The Great Kings & Queens of Africa" accompanied by a history of each.

• McDonald's initiated a Black History Makers of Tomorrow program for African American teens. The theme was "McDonald's Believes Making Black History Is Not Just a Thing of the Past." The company also has made available a coloring book series during Black History Month, *McDonald's Salute to Black Inventors* which features African American inventors who made significant contributions in areas of communications, safety, work ease, food and transportation.

• Philip Morris Companies, Inc. produced a radio documentary series for Black History Month that went to more than 400 radio stations. Three half-hour programs during the month were heard by an estimated 15 million people and resulted in a dozen awards for the producers. Themes and titles of the programs in recent years have been about music with "The Blues: Triumph of a Unique American Art Form"; a focus on role models with "Black Achievers: Prescriptions for Progress"; and "Thurgood Marshall and the Struggle to End Legal Segregation." Philip Morris also published for public distribution a comprehensive *Guide to Black Organizations* with complete information on African American leadership organizations, colleges and universities and political organizations (Gomez 1994).

Reaching African Americans

Getting the story delivered to African Americans in the United States does not present a practitioner with a need for many of the disciplines needed to communicate to Hispanics or Asian Americans. It requires a thorough knowledge of the culture and media, but English, and not a foreign language, is used for the communications vehicle. There are no segmented subcultures or cross-cultures.

Special distribution services have current and detailed lists of African American media and journalists (see Chapter 4). Special publications and special events are among the basic marketing public relations tools that provide effective means of communicating to African Americans.

American Urban Radio Networks in Pittsburgh, Pennsylvania, now produces a number of shows that it says reaches 91 percent of Black America.

They run 2½-minute and 5-minute news shows on the hour and a number of feature shows during the week on a variety of radio stations throughout the country (*Partyline* 1994).

TARGETING ASIAN AMERICANS

Asian Americans, who today account for nearly 5 percent of the U.S. population, grew 108 percent between 1980 and 1990 and will grow to more than 17 million people by 2010, according to figures from *Re-Weaving the Tapestry of America* (Porter/Novelli 1994).

Data from the U.S. Bureau of the Census breaks the Asian American population into six major groups. In 1990 the breakdown was as follows:

Chinese	22 percent
Filipino	21 percent
Japanese	19 percent
Asian Indian	10 percent
Korean	9.5 percent
Other	18.5 percent

However, Lynne Choy Uyeda, president of Lynne Choy Uyeda and Associates of Los Angeles and also founding president of the Asian American Advertising and Public Relations Alliance, believes the Asian American market is even more fragmented. She divides her primary target markets as follows (Choy Uyeda 1994):

- Chinese
- Japanese
- Korean
- Vietnamese
- Pacific Islander Group
  - Filipino
  - Native Hawaiian
  - Samoan
  - Tongan
- Southeast Asian
  - Cambodian
  - Hmong
  - Indonesian
  - Laotian
  - Malay
  - Thai

While the Census Bureau statistics list 10 percent of the Asian American population as being Asian Indian, Choy Uyeda considers this group borderline in the overall category.

She notes that many people do not know that among Vietnamese, Thai and others from Southeast Asia, there are many ethnic Chinese. To market to the Asian American market the practitioner must understand cross-cultures. "The Chinese immigrated to many places in Southeast Asia and not only retained their language, culture, religion and identity, but embraced the language, culture and tradition of their new homeland. Some have been Vietnamese and Thai for generations, but still hold on to their basic culture. Now they are adding a new culture and tradition in the United States." (Choy Uyeda 1994) To reach these cross-culture groups, she says several approaches are needed including targeting the media that reach, for example, the Vietnamese as well as the Chinese.

Problems happen when someone does not understand the language or culture. A classic error occurred when Pepsi-Cola wanted to reach Asian Americans and literally translated into Chinese its slogan, "Join the Pepsi Generation." The message came out "Drink Pepsi and Join Your Dead Ancestors." Choy Uyeda says this was insulting, insensitive and blasphemous to Asian Americans whose culture reveres and worships ancestors.

To reach Asian consumer markets in the United States, Choy Uyeda (1994) offers 10 tips:

1. Develop personal relationships.
2. Know the leaders, the players and the power structure of the community and be sure they know you.
3. Walk the streets of your target audience; get into their shoes and get into their skins.
4. Know and understand the community organizations that have credibility, leverage and influence. Get involved with the opinion leaders.
5. Know the dos and don'ts of business and culture etiquette.
6. Know how to go to the source.
7. Out of respect for the language and culture, translate and typeset all news releases in the language of the media to which the story is being sent.
8. Work with a public relations practitioner who has experience in the mainstream and understands the fundamentals of the business and the culture. For example, be cautious of using an Asian American who has started a firm, hung out a shingle and has had no training or experience with mainstream public relations, who is being hired just because of Asian ancestry.
9. Avoid stereotypes of karate-chopping; bowing men; and women in Asian attire who are serving men.
10. Encourage situations that portray Asians as part of mainstream society without focusing on their "Asianness."

Choy Uyeda says there are fewer than 40 important media that effectively reach the Asian population in the United States, and some newspapers and magazines are published overseas. Her office translates every story into the language of the media outlet and then has the news release typeset. "Many of the print media outlets are mom-and-pop operations and they just don't have the time or staff to do translations," Choy Uyeda adds. "Most important is that the editors appreciate what we do. In the Asian culture respect is very important. By our doing this, it shows respect and the editors are more inclined to print our stories 'as is,' unedited.

"It is expensive but you must forget the expense if you want to target this specific market. You can't go halfway. Business Wire now has an Asian circuit to distribute our releases by fax on our letterhead. And as with any mainstream media, the practitioner must know the media, the format and the type of stories they are looking for." (Choy Uyeda 1994)

For the California Department of Health Services, Choy Uyeda's firm undertook a major antismoking campaign. In the Asian community, smoking is a part of the male culture learned in their country of origin and prevalent among male immigrants to the United States. In order to drive home the message to this target audience, Choy Uyeda's strategy was to play on the importance of family in the Asian culture. The slogan was "For the Sake of Your Children, Quit Smoking," with a strong message about how harmful secondhand smoke was to children and the entire family. Talking to the male smoker about health care would not have worked, she said, but saying that smoking around children is like pointing a gun at them and pulling the trigger made an accepted appeal to the men as head of the family. News and feature stories, op-eds and opinion pieces were written and editorials developed working with the newspapers and magazines throughout California. The news releases were customized for each segment of the Asian community, with numbers specifically for and pertinent to Filipinos, Koreans, Chinese and other groups and subgroups.

Research has determined that there was an 89 percent awareness of the antitobacco campaign among Asians in California and a 29 percent reduction rate of tobacco use in California since the campaign was launched in 1990.

Special Events

In 1979 Congress proclaimed Asian/Pacific American Heritage Week, which was expanded to the month of May in 1990 by a presidential proclamation. The period provides opportunities for companies to become involved in sponsoring important local and community events.

TARGETING HISPANICS OR LATINOS

As a percentage of the total U.S. population, the Hispanic or Latino segment nearly doubled between 1970 and 1990—from 4.6 percent to 9.0 percent—and is expected to skyrocket to more than 21 percent by 2050 (Table 14.3). Along with this population explosion comes the opportunity to garner

Table 14.3. Population growth of Hispanics in the United States

Year	Total	Percent of U.S. Population
1970	9,294,509	4.6
1980	14,603,683	6.5
1990	22,354,059	9.0
2000	30,602,142	11.1
2010	39,311,562	13.2
2020	48,951,768	15.2
2030	59,197,188	17.2
2040	69,827,229	19.2
2050	80,675,012	21.1

Source: Steven Murdock, *An America Challenged.*

an increasingly important market. Table 14.4 shows the Hispanic populations in 10 key markets.

The 1990 U.S. Census breaks out the Hispanic population in the United States as follows:

Mexican American	60 percent
Puerto Rican	12 percent
Cuban	5 percent
"Other" Latinos	12 percent

Hispanic and *Latino* are words that many people use interchangeably to describe this rapidly growing ethnic market, though there is a definite preference in some cases. For example, *The Los Angeles Times* will not use the word *Hispanic* and will use only *Latino*; with other media executives the reverse is true. A leading magazine reaching this important market is named *Hispanic.* Even an important industry trade association is known as the National Association of Hispanic Journalists. The word *Hispanic* relates to the people, speech or culture of Spain, deriving from *Hispania,* meaning "from Spain." Yet many Hispanics in the United States boast of their Indian descent, minimize their Spanish ancestry and identify themselves both physically and spiritually in hemispheric meso-American terms. Some people believe *Latino* is

Table 14.4. Hispanic populations in 10 key markets, 1992

Market	Hispanic Population
1. Los Angeles	4,779,118
2. New York	2,777,951
3. Miami	1,061,846
4. San Francisco	970,403
5. Chicago	893,422
6. Houston	772,295
7. San Antonio	620,290
8. Dallas	518,917
9. San Diego	510,781
10. El Paso	411,619

Source: Steven Murdock, *An America Challenged.*

more proper. It is a derivative of Latin and areas where Romance languages are spoken, including Cuba, Mexico, Puerto Rico, the Caribbean, Central and South America, and also France, Italy, Spain and much of Europe. There is as diverse opinion on the use of *Hispanic* or *Latino* as the people with whom you talk. For simplicity, this book uses primarily *Hispanic.*

Before targeting messages to or about this consumer and demographic market, be sure to know if there is any preference between *Hispanic* and *Latino* with the media to whom the story is being channeled. Public relations professionals also must be careful how the word *America* is used. Mexicans and Central Americans consider themselves *Americans* and refer to those living in the United States as *Norteamericanos,* or North Americans. The word *America* should not be used to generically describe the United States when Spanish-speaking audiences are a target market.

According to the 1990 U.S. Census, 17,339,172 people five years of age or older speak Spanish at home. Table 14.5 shows the states with the greatest concentration.

Reaching the Spanish-Speaking Market

There are more than 300 Spanish and bilingual radio and television stations and more than 350 Spanish and bilingual newspapers and magazines in

Table 14.5. States with greatest concentration of people who speak Spanish at home, 1990

State	Number
1. California	5,475,367
2. Texas	3,442,418
3. New York	1,848,349
4. Florida	1,447,233
5. Illinois	728,121
6. New Jersey	621,347
7. Arizona	478,157
8. New Mexico	388,123
9. Massachusetts	228,374
10. Pennsylvania	213,024
11. Colorado	203,877
12. Connecticut	167,007
13. Virginia	152,655
14. Washington	143,594
15. Maryland	122,851
16. North Carolina	106,963
17. Indiana	90,146
18. Nevada	85,474
19. Oregon	83,072
20. Louisiana	72,173
21. Oklahoma	64,511
22. Kansas	62,056
23. Utah	51,945
24. Idaho	37,078
25. Rhode Island	35,469

Source: 1990 U.S. Census.

the United States. Special distribution services that keep up-to-date mailing lists can provide translation and mailing services to the Spanish-language media, as can Business Wire and PR Newswire.

According to Arbitron, the national radio rating service, Spanish-speaking radio stations are the highest-rated stations in Los Angeles, Miami and San Antonio. KLAX in Los Angeles has an audience of 89,500 listeners during an average quarter-hour time period.

Univision, Telemundo and Galavision are national television networks. Radio Bilinguay is a new Spanish-language programming service for public broadcasting stations. "Latino USA" is a weekly, 30-minute radio program that is produced in English for PBS radio stations. Its format is intended to heighten national awareness of the entire Latino community (El Noticiario Nacional 1993).

CBS Americas, formerly the CBS Hispanic Radio Network, and United Press International now provide newscasts in Spanish on an hourly basis to listeners in both the United States and Latin America. Called Noticias CBS Americas, this news service presents all international news, with an emphasis on topics of particular interest to the Spanish-speaking audience.

In 1986, thc *Miami Herald* launched *El Nuevo Heraldo*, a Spanish-language supplement to its newspaper. It is now considered the most successful and influential Spanish-language edition in the country. Since then, other mainstream newspapers have started other weekly supplements. These special editions are not in the full circulation run of the press, but are distributed in targeted circulation areas that have high concentrations of Hispanics. Some of the successful editions include:

La Raza Domingo (Chicago Sun-Times)
Exito (Chicago Tribune)
*Las Noticias (*Denver *Rocky Mountain News)*
La Estrella (Fort Worth Star-Telegram)
El Sol (Idaho Falls Post Register)
Noticias en Español (Laredo Morning Times)
Nuestro Tiempo (Los Angeles Times)
El Nuevo Tiempo (Santa Barbara News-Press)

Edward Rincon, president of Rincon & Associates, in Dallas, says there are three types of Hispanics in the United States—the "traditional Hispanic," who is Spanish-dominated; the "transitional Hispanic," who speaks and uses both English and Spanish; and the "acculturated Hispanic," who depends mostly on English.

Whether you are trying to get the message delivered to and received by Hispanics or Latinos, it is important to be sure the communications effort is professionally done. In 1976, the author was a founding partner of ICPR public relations in Los Angeles, then the second-largest public relations firm in the western United States, and responsible for forming a Hispanic marketing division. It was headed by Fernando Oaxaca who was fluent in the language and grew up in the culture in El Paso. Oaxaca, a past president of the Hispanic Broadcasters Association and former co-chair of the Republican National Hispanic Assembly, has since founded and heads Coronado Communications in Los Angeles. Since ICPR's bold move, almost every major public relations and advertising agency has established a department that specializes in providing marketing public relations services for Hispanics.

"The growth of the Hispanic market, combined with rising Latino consumer purchasing power, started the Hispanic public relations pendulum swinging away from Anglo-owned and toward Hispanic-owned agencies," says Octavio Nuiry, president of the Hispanic Public Relations Association and manager of public relations for AD Rendón and Asociados, a full-service advertising, public relations and sales promotion agency formed in 1984 in Irvine, California. "For generations the rule of thumb dictated that U.S. corporations would hire *los gringos* to plan and execute their Hispanic communications programs. If Latino public relations professionals were ever retained, they were hired to do seasonal project work, usually a cultural event like *Cinco de Mayo* (May 5) festival or a *Septiembre Dies y Seis* (Mexico Independence Day) parade. When the project ended, that was it, *hasta luego*!" (Nuiry 1994)

Nuiry says at AD Rendón, even though he is fluent in the language, they use professional translators. "We believe it is important to generalize as much as possible with the language and avoid specific idioms or cultural land mines." He also believes it is important to know the media personally, and he regularly attends conventions of Hispanic publishers, journalists and broadcasters.

Understanding the nuances of the community is most important. The author was involved in holding a press conference for the Hispanic sports media in Los Angeles to announce the hemisphere regional competition for soccer's World Youth Cup, at the time the largest soccer event that had been held in the United States. One of the major sponsors insisted that the press conference be held at 10:30 in the morning. The "experts" in our firm's Hispanic marketing division recommended 5:30 p.m. because most of the Spanish-speaking sportswriters and sportscasters had other full-time day jobs and only worked part time in the media. A morning press conference during the working hours for their jobs would have meant "no shows." The sponsor contact demanded that the press conference be held in the morning because that was the only time an important company executive could be in Los Angeles. After the firm confirmed it in writing and outlined the risk the sponsor would have to assume, the sponsor changed its mind and a late-afternoon press conference was held. It was a success. Even if it inconvenienced his travel plans, the corporate executive was impressed.

Special Events

Sponsoring local special events is another important way of reaching into and becoming involved with the community. Different cultures within the overall Hispanic community have different holidays. Two important holidays that are celebrated by Mexican Americans are *Cinco de Mayo* (May 5), marking Mexico's victory over an invading French force in 1862, and *Septiembre Dies y Sies* (September 16), Mexican Independence Day. Puerto Rican Day is celebrated on various days in June. Most Hispanics celebrate Columbus Day (October 12) even though the general public considers it an Italian American holiday. Many national and regional corporations sponsor activities at events on major holidays.

A Kodak special event was held at Miami's Festival of the Americas at Tropical Park to provide a picture-taking opportunity celebrating Hispanic performing arts. People attending the festival had an opportunity to have their photos taken with their favorite soap opera stars from the Telemundo network. Kodak also provides financial support for the California Museum of Latino History, said to be one of the largest repositories of Hispanic-American documents and artifacts in the United States. (*PRJ* 1991)

Hispanics have a high incidence of diabetes. Upjohn Company worked with the American Diabetes Association and had physicians screen more than 3,000 people for the disease in Los Angeles in a single day (*PRJ* 1991).

JCPenney works with the Hispanic Designers, Inc., a non-profit organization dedicated to recognizing Hispanic talent and cultural contributions to the design industry, to sponsor an annual "Model Search." The event is held during Hispanic Heritage Month (September 15 to October 15), and 28 contestants are invited to participate in the finals. The program involves Hispanic shoppers and store managers and creates exposure for the company in the Hispanic and fashion industry communities. The contestants all must be between 18 and 25 years old, be non-professional models and be of Hispanic descent. Male and female winners and runners-up receive scholarships, wardrobes, luggage, cosmetics and a chance to appear in JCPenney's Hispanic advertising and promotion campaigns (*PRJ* 1991).

Special Publications

Some companies tap into Hispanic markets through a variety of special publications. For example, in 1979, JCPenney published its first Spanish-language catalog.

Even earlier, in 1976, shortly after establishing its Hispanic marketing division, ICPR helped Whirlpool Corporation capture the major appliance market from General Electric in the Hispanic community. The first step was a bilingual warranty followed by instruction panels in Spanish on the major appliances. Since the industry was moving to snap-in panels it was no problem to make this accommodation. Inventory requirements were only for the panels. The program was backed up with a strong local publicity campaign supporting the retailers in their community.

Philip Morris Companies, Inc. published two books aimed at the Hispanic market. One was *Hispanic Presence: Historical Beginnings*, a book edited by Frank de Varona that commemorates Hispanic contributions to the United States and was published in 1993 in cooperation with the National Hispanic Quincentennial Commission. According to Philip Morris's Francis Gomez, "The book is about role models many young people and even older people are unaware of. It fills in gaps in American history about little known achievements by Spaniards, Puerto Ricans, Cubans, Mexican Americans and others of Hispanic heritage who enriched our nation in many fields." Philip Morris joined with the Congressional Hispanic Caucus Institute to publish the *National Directory of Hispanic Organizations*, a fact book about Hispanic organizations, Congressional representatives, census information and accounts about important leaders who contributed to the exploration and settlement of the United States.

What Do Hispanic Editors Want?

From a 1993 survey of 400 Hispanic newspaper editors, News USA of Alexandria, Virginia, found the following to be the 10 most requested subjects:

1. Education	74.4 percent
2. Legal issues	62 percent
3. (tie) Environment	61 percent
Entertainment	61 percent
5. (tie) Health	59 percent
Business	59 percent
Medicine	59 percent
8. Editorial commentaries	56 percent
9. Child care	55 percent
10. Consumer items	53 percent

According to *PR Reporter* (1992), a survey conducted by Derus Media Service of 315 Spanish, Spanish/English and English Hispanic publications listed the following as priority topics of interest:

1. (tie) Food	70 percent
Health	70 percent
3. Consumer tips	60 percent
4. Entertainment	57 percent

5. Education 52 percent
6. Travel 43 percent

Other topics mentioned included sports, beauty, culture, business, agriculture, automotive, law enforcement and firefighter news, sewing, interior design and gardening.

Both surveys found that almost all use camera-ready copy and between 51 and 54 percent prefer this format.

Research Is Important

Before Kraft USA introduced a new product to the Hispanic market, it wanted to be sure that it had properly named and positioned the product. After a review of its mayonnaise product line, it realized that most products in Latin America are made with lime juice rather than lemon juice. It developed a mayonnaise made with lime juice and through market testing found that it was preferred by Hispanics to the regular line of Kraft mayonnaise products made with lemon juice. The word for *lime* varies among the Latino cultures in the United States, so it was important to use a generic name for the new product that no one could misinterpret—Kraft Mayonesa con Jugo de Limon Verde, literally, "Kraft mayonnaise with the juice of a green lime" (Nieto 1994).

The multimedia campaign included radio and television advertising, local event sponsorship, publicity releases in all media, product stories with recipes directed to food editors and home economists, sampling in retail stores, couponing in stores and direct-mail couponing.

According to Lou Nieto at Kraft USA, the most important step was doing the research before the product introduction so the consumer knew exactly what it was.

TARGETING NATIVE AMERICANS

According to the 1990 Census, there were nearly 2 million Native Americans in the United States, up from 248,000 in 1980, and in terms of percentage, the fastest growing of all minority groups. By federal law, an individual must be at least one-fourth Indian by ancestry, and each of 542 recognized tribes has its own qualifications.

According to the 1990 Census, the greatest concentrations of people classified as Native American, Eskimo or Aleut are in the following states:

1. Oklahoma 246,631
2. Arizona 190,091
3. California 184,065

4. New Mexico	128,068
5. Alaska	84,594
6. North Carolina	78,390
7. Washington	76,397
8. Texas	52,803
9. Michigan	52,571
10. New York	50,540
11. South Dakota	49,648

According to *USA Today* (1994), the leading Native American tribes are:

1. Cherokee	308,132
2. Navajo	219,198
3. Chippewa	103,826
4. Sioux	103,255
5. Choctaw	82,299

A tribe is a sovereign government on its land, with powers to hold elections, tax, limit land use, set criminal and civil penalties and control trade. As a sovereign government, many tribes are turning to gambling casinos, legal on Indian land, as a means of producing revenues.

Because of the small numbers overall compared with other ethnic groups, Native Americans are one of the most difficult groups to reach. It is extremely important to understand the rich Indian culture and tradition and the importance of "trust responsibility." The tribal leaders are the primary means of communicating to Native Americans, most of whom live on reservations. Some of the special distribution services, however, do have lists and recommendations on ways to reach this highly specialized audience (USA Today 1994).

TARGETING WOMEN

It is one of life's great ironies that women are considered a "minority" when, in fact, they make up more than half the population and are expected to do so well into the future (Table 14.6). But because the United States is a patriarchal society, the majority of decision makers and power holders (especially in the political arena) are men. Thus, men's concerns are placed in the mainstream while women's concerns are broken out and treated as a specialized market.

Based on the forecast shown in Table 14.6, manufacturers of products and suppliers of services for women can feel comfortable that their target market should continue to be consistent as marketing plans are developed to maintain long-term sales.

Table 14.6. Population growth of women in the United States

Year	Total	Percent of U.S. Number
1990	127,470,455	51.3
2000	140,477,322	51.1
2010	152,097,297	51.0
2020	164,293,730	50.9
2030	175,692,519	50.9
2040	185,905,538	51.0
2050	195,403,359	51.1

Source: Steven Murdock, *An America Challenged.*

Almost all the basic marketing public relations techniques can be used to target a campaign or program to women. All the special distribution services have basic mailing lists. Probably the most important consideration in a program directed to women is to be sensitive to the issues women generally support. Health care is a traditional women's concern, and creating an awareness for early detection of breast cancer narrows the focus further to women in particular.

Using Sports to Reach Women

The Women's Sports Foundation was an organization that offered one company an opportunity to reach new customers. A key objective for Within Multivitamins, which were designed especially for women by the addition of extra iron and calcium, was to associate the product with active, healthy lifestyles and appeal to the target consumer. Edelman Public Relations Worldwide developed a multifaceted program that offered women advice on sports and health under the Within name. A series of conferences on health and nutrition for the athletic women were held on college campuses throughout the country. Presentations featured sports physiologists, sports nutritionists, coaches and Olympic athletes. Using the expert prolocutor for newspaper, radio and television interviews in each conference city, publicity was secured for the Within/Women's Sports Foundation event and mentioned the Within health and nutrition message.

In 1991, the original and most prestigious women's running event lost its title sponsor. Known as the L'eggs Mini-Marathon for 13 years, it became simply the Women's Mini-Marathon. The event had traditionally attracted thousands of women including elite runners from all over the world. After researching the event and its history and talking with the New York Road Runners Club, the event coordinator, Edelman Public Relations Worldwide, recommended to its client, Whitehall Laboratories, makers of Advil, that it become the race's title and sole sponsor.

With only a month to go before the race, the firm immediately alerted key media of the change in the title sponsor, so on race day it would be known as the Advil Mini-Marathon. World-class runners were contacted to ensure their participation in the race. Dr. Peter Bruno, sports medicine specialist, was retained and scheduled for media interviews in the two weeks leading up to the race to discuss how runners prepare for the event. A press conference was held two days prior to the race to introduce the celebrity runners and again stress the Advil sponsorship.

Site signage was strategically placed throughout the race course, including water stations, so it would be visible on television coverage by "ABC's Wide World of Sports." Additionally, hats and bags prominently featuring the Advil logo, as well as the traditional race T-shirts, were distributed to the runners prior to the race. Following the race, a press conference was held for the top three finishers. After only one month of planning, the Advil Mini-Marathon had generated more than 200 million impressions (Hayes 1994).

TARGETING OLDER AMERICANS

In looking to target older Americans, Texas A&M's Steve Murdock advises the practitioner to segment this group further, into middle-age and elderly groups: "The aging of the population will be substantial over time, but will occur most rapidly after the baby-boomers have reached elderly ages" (Murdock 1993).

According to Murdock, the percentage of population 65 years of age or older will rise as follows:

1990	12.6 percent
2000	12.7 percent
2010	13.3 percent
2030	20.2 percent
2050	32.6 percent

> It is only after 2011 when baby-boomers begin to enter the elderly ages (those born in 1946 would be 65 years of age in 2011) that the proportion of the population that is elderly increases dramatically. Between now and 2011 it is more correct to refer to the U.S. population as a middle-aged population than as an elderly population.
>
> This is a major consumer market segment. People earn most of their income and their salaries are highest when they are between 45 and 55 years old. Baby-boomers also are characterized as being extremely competitive and many are relatively affluent. They must be seen as an important segment of the market (Murdock 1993).

How to Reach Older Audiences

Based on the information of demographer Murdock, all older people are not alike. Too often practitioners will segment people by age and put this entire market in an "over-50" or "over-55" category when there are very important segments within the overall market. Those in their 50s will have completely different interests than those who are in their 70s and 80s. One single organization that knows the most about older Americans is the Washington, D.C.-based American Association of Retired Persons, or AARP. It has published information and guides to help marketers reach this special audience, including a training program, "Serving Older Customers," and a set of guidelines to encourage positive communications to people 50 years or older, "How to Advertise to Maturity." Regardless of age, any professional involved in reaching people over 50 should subscribe to the AARP's *Modern Maturity* magazine.

James R. Holland, director of communications for the American Association of Retired Persons, lists these guidelines as appropriate for any communications program to an over-50 audience (*PRJ* 1991):

1. Don't make a long story short. Older people like to have plenty of product information on which to make a decision.
2. Take at least 15 years off your target groups. People tend to feel younger than their chronological age.
3. Don't put all older people on a diet. Most eat the same foods as anyone else, and many have been cooking nutritious food for years.
4. Keep a sense of humor. More time to relax means more time to smile.
5. Don't take the romance out of life. There may be more time for it.
6. Help older people plan for their future. Life is continuing, not rushing toward its close.

"Communicators should portray older adults as part of the mainstream of society, and not as separate and isolated," says Holland. "Show them alive, engaged, achieving and producing, not as suffering in pain, enduring loneliness, and out of touch with today's world. Older people have a broad range of interests, incomes and lifestyles. Clear communication and identifying their individual needs are the keys to successful interaction with customers of any age."

Frank Conaway, founder and president of Primelife, a marketing communications company based in Orange, California, that specializes in programs for the 50-year-old-and-over market, cites some interesting statistics: (*PRJ* 1991)

- Seniors account for 80 percent of all commercial vacation travel, particularly first-class air travel and luxury sea cruises. They spend 30 percent more than their younger counterparts while traveling.
- By the time the baby boomers retire, the life-care and health-care business will be a $75 billion industry. However, health-care problems should not be exploited when addressing this market.

- The automobile industry sells 48 percent of all luxury cars to people over 55.
- Nearly 80 percent of all savings dollars are owned by and 68 percent of all money market accounts are controlled by people 55 years or older.
- Many mature adults who are retired look for organizations to serve as volunteers.
- People age 50 to 64 are generous donors, giving charitable organizations an average of 3 percent of their income. People 65 and older give 2.7 percent of their income to charitable causes.

The special distribution services also have extensive mailing lists and breakouts to reach this very important and economically- and politically-powerful audience.

CHECKLIST FOR TARGETING SPECIAL AUDIENCES

For any marketing public relations effort directed to a special market, either be sure the practitioner directing and implementing the program meets a standard for experience, or retain a professional who does know the market. In particular, one should:

- Know and speak the language, know the idioms and the slang.
- Know and understand the culture.
- Understand the issues that are important to the group.
- Know and understand the subcultures and the cross-cultures.
- Know the media, what they want and in what format they want to receive the information.
- Have established relationships with national and community leaders.
- Have established relationships with the national organizations.
- Be experienced in both mainstream and special market public relations.
- Know how to recognize strategies that could (and did) backfire, such as developing special programs that target women and African Americans for sales of cigarettes or using special promotions of alcohol products, such as malt liquor, to African Americans.

REFERENCES

Adelson, Andrea. 1994. "Spanish-Language Radio Leads" in *New York Times.* January 24.

Choy Uyeda, Lynne. 1994. Interview. Los Angeles: Lynne Choy Uyeda and Associates.

El Noticiario Nacional. 1993. Texas Association of Chicanos in Higher Education. July.

Flemming, Fay. 1994. Interview and correspondence with author. St. Louis, Mo.: Provident Counseling. March-April.

Gomez, Francis D. 1994. Interview. New York. Philip Morris Companies, Inc.

Hayes, Wendy. 1994. Interview and correspondence with author. New York: Daniel J. Edelman, Inc.

Hispanic Link Weekly Report. May 3, 1993. Citing U.S. Census Bureau report of April 27, 1993.

Kern-Foxworth, Marilyn. 1994. *Aunt Jemima, Uncle Ben and Rastus: Blacks in Advertising, Yesterday, Today and Tomorrow.* Westport, Conn.: Greenwood Press.

Murdock, Steven H. 1993. *An America Challenged.* Boulder Colo.: Westview Press.

Nieto, Lou. 1994. Interview. Glenview, Ill.: Kraft USA. April.

Nuiry, Octavio. 1994. Interview and correspondence with author. Irvine, Calif.: AD Rendón and Asociados. March-April.

Oaxaca, Fernando. 1994. Interview. Los Angeles Coronado Communications.

Partyline. 1994. No. 1760. February 7.

PR Reporter. 1992. April 13, p.4.

Public Relations Journal. 1991. February, pp.12-13, 30; May pp. 14-15, 20-21.

Porter/Novelli Omnicon PR Network. 1994. *Re-weaving the Tapestry of America.* Washington, D.C.

USA Today. 1994. April 28, pp. 6A, 7A.

U.S. Department of Labor. 1993. Washington, D.C. Office of Federal Contract Compliance reports.

15

HOW TO REACH INTERNATIONAL AUDIENCES

Getting a message communicated to an international audience is one of the most challenging of all marketing public relations tasks. Not only must the practitioner overcome cultural and, in most cases, language differences, but also a different style and way of doing business. Add to this a geographic distance.

The decade of the 1990s brought with it the importance of understanding a global economy. For many companies this also meant a more competitive international marketplace. The role of marketing public relations became even more important in positioning a company or organization and its products and services to potential customers in many new and different countries.

Having someone in a country who is a citizen, who speaks the language, who knows the culture and who knows the media is the most practical and effective way of reaching a target audience in a country. However, not all companies or organizations can afford to locate a public relations office in a particular country. Nor does a budget or a campaign always warrant retaining a professional practitioner in a foreign country.

Resources in the United States can be effectively used to deliver a message in a faraway land. Chapter 3 listed various directories available with names of international media as foreign editorial representatives and bureaus located in this country. Paid services outlined in Chapter 4, such as PR Newswire, place the publicity release on the national news wire of that country: Tass in the former Soviet Union, Kyodo News Service in Japan, Agence

France Presse in France and Reuters in all of Latin America. The firm will even provide translation services if necessary (Steinberg 1994).

TransContinental TV, a subsidiary of Worldwide TV News Corporation, distributes sponsored programming and even video news releases internationally through its Targeted Television Distribution Service. Worldwide TV News is owned in part by Capital Cities/ABC and provides international feeds several times a day (O'Dwyer 1994). Telemundo has a 24-hour television news service broadcast to Latin America and Spain. In the United States it is available only on cable.

Another outlet rapidly becoming universally accepted is CNN's International Network. The program is in English and available on cable television throughout Europe and in many other countries. Radio is an important communications vehicle in emerging countries; BBC radio is dominant in most of Africa.

One should not overlook participation with federal agencies, such as the U.S. Information Agency, which has its Worldnet television network and Voice of America. Worldnet, the largest television network in the world, has downlinks to every U.S. embassy in the world.

There are two universal ways of reaching an audience anywhere in the world. One is through sport. The other is through music. They both are universal languages. Sport is so very obvious, with the increasing number of Olympic sponsors and companies that select sports special events as a way of building awareness. No single company has done a better job of using sports to reach customers worldwide than has Coca-Cola.

THE OLD "AMERICAN SELL" JUST WON'T WORK

International audiences are much less susceptible to American-style public relations and marketing efforts, according to John Mosher, managing director of Ibex International in Washington, D.C. Mosher directed a number of international programs, including Sports America and Arts America, for the U.S. Information Agency, where he was a director during the Reagan administration. He later served as vice president of international programs for Special Olympics. "Americans have to accept that audiences in other parts of the world have rigid structures and don't change their ways quickly unless you can start the avalanche of a national fad," he says. Mosher cites as examples of fads the worldwide hula-hoop craze and how golf virtually took over in Japan. "Foreign markets are already formed into certain groups that do not invite penetration. You have to establish your legitimacy with one or another group. In many countries, this further involves winning their trust in a real sense (Mosher 1994)."

Mosher notes that in Austria, even more than in the United States, many important decisions are reached at social events such as cocktail parties: "In Salzburg, the former Soviet Consulate, which under normal circumstances would have had a staff of only two to three people, had more than 40 people. Since Austria was neutral, it was an important drop-off point for Soviet spy information coming out of Germany only three kilometers away. The United States had a one man consulate in Salzburg. When Jimmy Carter was president he closed the consulate, the United States lost its last representation at Salzburg social events which would always be attended by two to three Soviets. The Austrians could only protest discreetly because of the neutrality law under which the country was reunited." Mosher knows Austria well because he lived in Salzburg, where he had an international consulting business, for 20 years. He is fluent in German and other European languages. Mosher (1994) observes:

> The Salzburg festival, with many receptions, dinners and other events besides concerts, brought together all of the leading German industrialists. With the end of the Cold War, the role of Salzburg changed and recently the consulate, which was reopened by the Reagan Administration, has again been closed down as an economy move.
>
> At a time when the U.S. must position itself in an increasingly competitive global economy, American representation around the world is very thin in many countries now because of these cutbacks. Salzburg is only one example of what has happened around the world.

REACHING AUDIENCES THROUGH DIPLOMATS

Embassies and consulate offices can be very effective and helpful in reaching audiences in foreign countries. The embassies are in the best position to identify audiences and even create events. According to Mosher, the trick is to get them interested in the event in a way that helps them in their own public diplomacy goals with the locals. "They like 'target of opportunity' speakers who are coming to the country at no expense to our government or staff time," he says. "But of course they do not want to expend energy identifying an audience for fly fishing seminars or suntanning sessions, unless American-made products can be exported through the promotion (1994)."

The author has worked with people in numerous embassies and consulates around the world for media contact, introductions and advice on marketing a product in a particular country as well as for invitations and mailing lists. The U.S. foreign service, both in Washington and abroad, is a tremendous and inexpensive resource and does not charge a fee.

KNOW THE LOCAL CULTURE

Mosher (1994) makes the following observations about U.S. practitioners' dealings with foreign sources:

> With most foreigners, with exceptions sometimes of the British, the business conversation has been well prepared on both sides beforehand. There is no business conversation during an event. Americans never learn this. The deal may or may not be concluded by one sentence just before the parties separate. Foreigners usually don't want long conversation about the details most Americans love to thrash out endlessly. Someone else will take care of that.
>
> The frontal assault most Americans so dearly love usually offends foreign audiences. Their first interest is to find out how real or genuine the American really is and does that person or his or her company have any sincere interest in the people of that country, their nation, their culture, their specific problems or what is good for them. Many Americans I have encountered overseas seem to think this aspect can be taken care of with a few nice phrases. Not at all.
>
> Japan is a special case because it is a nation as a single family [Mosher once lived in Japan and is fluent in the Japanese language as well.] In fact, Japanese ward offices have family records going back forever. Until very recently, all Japanese citizens were somehow related to one another and if they were not, they didn't count in the proceedings. In order for a single Japanese to make a business decision, he must, in effect, consult with the entire family, before coming back with a meaningful, concrete reply.
>
> Even then he would prefer a vague reply. It is impolite to be concrete. Japanese is a vague language. There is no singular or plural, for example. Tenses are often omitted. People speak using word roots. On the other hand, there are about 468 different words for "you," depending on the precise relationship between the two parties, who is older, wiser, related to whom, from what region, and so on. Relationships are precise, but statements are left flexible and subject to endless interpretation.

ADAPTING TO LOCAL LAWS AND CUSTOMS

Following are case examples of companies that conducted successful international campaigns in marketing public relations.

Arthur Andersen's Publications and Seminars

Arthur Andersen & Company is the 12th largest private U.S. company, with worldwide revenues in excess of $6 billion and 67,000 people located in 324 offices in 72 countries. It must adapt its marketing strategy to different countries. Some still do not permit advertising. Others continue to ban direct solicitation of clients. In France there are various classes of auditors, with individual professional institutes for each. Tax is separate from audit and so is management consulting. In Italy, audit and tax professionals cannot practice together.

This difference among nations was a tremendous challenge facing H. Zane Robbins as he developed ways to communicate the Arthur Andersen story on a global basis. "We had an interesting situation: inexperienced marketers (the partners) trying to sell an intangible service (the audit) to unknowledgeable buyers (company chief financial officers)," says Robbins. (1994) "It was a professional marketer's dream...or nightmare.

"In the early 1980s, during one of the first meetings of our marketing group, someone said: 'I know how to market consumer goods and industrial products, but how do you market professional services?' In checking Chicago bookstores, none had any books on marketing professional services. Since there simply weren't any, we wrote our own."

Robbins started with research to find out what people in the United States knew about Andersen and the so-called Big Eight firms. Another research study attempted to collect views held by corporate financial officers, college accounting faculty and audit committee personnel. The results confirmed the firm's views that factors used to judge technical competence include many interpersonal skills.

As the marketing program was being developed, Robbins said his group took the seven conventional steps in selling and laid that against the purchasing process used by buyers of professional services to develop the following:

Sales Cycle	Purchasing Cycle
1. Identify prospects	1. —
2. Get the prospect's attention	2. Gain awareness of suppliers
3. Create interest in the service	3./4. Qualify acceptable service providers
4. Stimulate desire for service/firm	
5. Convince the prospect	5. Select service provider
6. Close the sale	6. Hire the firm of choice
7. Provide after-sale service	7. Retain the firm

"To accounting firm partners this was a revolutionary concept," said Robbins. "Our first challenge was to gain acceptance of the plan within the partnership before we could do any effective marketing to clients and prospects. Professional partnerships are very different from corporations. Every partner is an owner and Arthur Andersen had 2,500 in 72 countries (1994)."

The next step was to develop the marketing tools. The company had developed publications written by partners and managers but lightly edited by relatively inexperienced journalism graduates. Experienced communications experts were hired, and instead of converting partners' manuscripts into print, the drafts were used as source material and the copy recast to appeal to reader interest. Graphics were improved for the publications.

Special interest seminars such as dealing with government health-care regulations, executive financial planning and inventory management had been another traditional activity of accounting firms. Robbins took full advantage of this vehicle of communication to further strengthen the marketing program and worked with the partners to develop more interesting topics and build attendance by corporate decision makers.

The seminars became an opportunity to publicize the firm's activities. Advance news releases and postmeeting summaries were sent to key media. Interviews were arranged for key partners with appropriate business publications and newspapers. In some cases, opinion research was conducted to create a basis for the seminar presentations and for publicity on the results of the research.

The overall marketing efforts created a sound basis for broad-based publicity that reached all segments of individual industries and often spilled onto the business pages of newspapers across the country. The partnership also uses other conventional tools of marketing communications including video, a variety of special events and even some advertising.

"In any marketing program it is important to measure the results against your goals," says Robbins. "We measure our results in two ways—by surveying attitudes in the marketplace and by counting the cash. Up to now, we have done well by both measures. Over the last five years, our worldwide revenues have increased by 113 percent, we have regained our position as the world's largest professional service firm and our profits have continued to increase in spite of depressed economic conditions across the world and intensive price competition in the marketplace."

United Parcel Service Multinational Program

As United Parcel Service prepared to implement major international service expansion in 1988, it sought public relations support from Edelman Public Relations Worldwide that would introduce the company to new markets where it was unknown. Also, as a privately held company, it was a classic "no comment" business and rarely had practiced proactive public relations (Hayes 1994).

Press conferences were held in New York, London and Hong Kong to announce the first phase of its global expansion to 41 countries. Subsequent activity in the area of international expansion included a series of acquisition announcements and additional announcements of new routes and services to more than 175 countries.

An international journalist familiarization trip brought 15 reporters from Europe and Asia for a tour of UPS's Louisville air and ground facilities and a presentation by the company's CEO. A second trip was coordinated a year later. Edelman offices throughout the world developed market-specific programs that included sponsoring the Hong Kong Little League and counseling local management on local issues, which included a hub operation and development outside London.

In Europe a major pan-European campaign was developed to raise the UPS profile to businesspeople. Following research of possible prospects, a survey formed a regular monitor of business opinion in Europe and an information source for the media and the academic, business and government communities.

The opinion survey sought the opinions of 1,500 senior directors from Europe's top 15,000 companies. The first survey focused on business trends such as the Maastricht Treaty, economic growth potential in the single European market and future world trading patterns. The second survey covered matters such as the changes likely to occur in the wake of the single market and trade between Europe and the Far East.

The results of each survey were published in an executive summary document in six languages. This was the central communications tool for all elements of the program.

Target audiences were the European business community and the media in each country, including national daily newspapers and broadcast media as well as business, management, financial, economic, transport and distribution publications. Secondary audiences in Europe were influencers of business such as government officials, politicians, business schools and professional bodies such as chambers of commerce. In the United States, Canada and Asia-Pacific regions, the campaign targeted similar groups.

The bulk of the work was in Belgium, France, Germany, Italy, the Netherlands, Spain and the United Kingdom. Edelman produced an action guidelines manual for all UPS district managers and public relations contacts in each country participating in the project.

The results of the first survey were announced at simultaneous media events linked by satellite in London, Paris, Madrid, Milan, Brussels and Dusseldorf. The live audience at each event watched a satellite downlink from Brussels, where representatives from Harris Research and UPS explained the results of the survey. European Community (EC) commissioner Christiane Schrivener commented on its significance to the EC. At each venue, a local UPS representative discussed the national significance of the results. Each national representative was joined by a third-party commentator from the academic, economic or business community of that country. All representatives were media trained and their speeches prepared in advance (Hayes 1994).

Specialized press kits were prepared for each country and distributed to journalists from a wide range of business, trade and broadcast media. Each press kit contained the executive summary, a pan-European press release, a nationally focused release, a country backgrounder, a UPS country fact sheet, a UPS Europe fact sheet and a biography of the UPS representative with photograph. All key media not attending the events were contacted by telephone, and specially targeted releases were developed to suit the interests of the different media in different countries.

Copies of the executive summaries of the surveys were distributed to individuals in western European national governments, the European Community and the U.S. government. Media coverage from national daily newspapers and broadcasts reached over 80 million people in Europe and a direct-mail campaign exceeded a 12 percent return.

An International Friendship Card

In 1992, American Greetings embarked on an American Greetings to the World initiative that brought together people throughout the world. A giant greeting card was designed and traveled throughout the United States and to Russia. The tour was launched with a White House ceremony and ended at the International Balloon Fiesta in Albuquerque. As the card was toured across the United States, sponsored by retailers, it was inscribed with more than one million messages symbolic of world peace and friendship. While the card toured, the American Greeting to the World Pen-Friend Network continued to flourish, and the company flew a Virginia girl to Amsterdam to be with her Dutch pen pal (Hayes 1994).

Edelman Public Relations Worldwide handled the campaign and secured retailer sponsors and festival appearances in 14 major U.S. cities. More than 50 million consumers were reached through regional and local market publicity. The card consistently received local television and radio coverage as well as major newspaper stories. More than one million Americans signed and approximately five million viewed the card. An additional 26 paper scrolls measuring five miles were completed. The company's Pen-Friend Network added 25,000 names to total 600,000 actual correspondents.

CHECKLIST FOR INTERNATIONAL PROGRAMS AND PROJECTS

- Know the language.
- Know the culture.
- Know the media and what they want.
- Know the best way to deliver the story to the media.
- If you don't know the aforementioned points, retain someone who does to do the job.
- Contact the English-language media in the foreign country.
- Contact foreign media representatives in the United States.

RESOURCES

Telemundo
2300 W. 8th St.
Hialeah, FL 33010
Phone (305) 884-9611, fax (305) 884-9610
(Sergio Lopez-Miro, communications manager for news and public affairs)

TransContinental TV
1995 Broadway
New York, NY 10023
Phone (212) 721-0597

REFERENCES

Hayes, Wendy. 1994. Background information materials. New York: Edelman Public Relations Worldwide. April 22.

Jack O'Dwyer's Newsletter, New York, J. R. O'Dwyer Co.

Mosher, John. 1994. Interview and May 16 letter to author. Washington, D.C.: Ibex International, Inc.

Robbins, H. Zane. 1994. "Development of a Worldwide Communications Strategy." Chicago: Arthur Anderson & Co. April.

Steinberg, David, vice chairman PR Newswire. 1994. Letter to author. March 28.

16

HOW TO CREATE A SPEAKERS' BUREAU AND USE SPOKESPERSONS

The use of an organized speakers' bureau and third-party, or surrogate, speakers, celebrities and expert spokespersons is an effective way to expand the reach and impact of a program. The most important consideration is to have control over what the speaker says publicly about a product, service, cause or issue. In a campaign or program, there must be continuity and uniformity in the message being communicated.

Within every company, organization and institution, official spokespersons should be identified who can speak officially regarding policies or actions. These will be the individuals who should be used for media interviews and the most important public programs. Prepare both a priority list of officers and executives ranked in the order of who should respond first and a subject list of who should respond to or address certain issues. The two lists may or may not be identical but certainly would be similar and overlap some of the names.

Speakers' bureaus give national organizations with various geographic operations an opportunity to really reach out for grass-roots support. Speakers at this level need national office support with prepared speeches and audiovisual materials.

Surrogates, or third-party representatives, will be individuals who are not employees of a company or organization but who support what the company or organization is advocating. They are particularly helpful on cause or issues campaigns. They also need support with prepared speeches and materials. Some surrogates will be well known and outstanding in their area of knowledge or experience.

A celebrity or expert spokesperson will be one who is generally paid to deliver a product message because of his or her image as an athlete or entertainer or by having reputation and achievement within a discipline. This person will be someone who can be scheduled for media interviews and who will turn out an audience at a public event.

HOW TO SUPPORT YOUR SPEAKERS

Even the most articulate of speakers needs training. Before important speeches, the spokesperson should be rehearsed and trained. The speaker will need supporting materials not only to be professional, but to ensure that everyone speaking publicly for the company or organization is telling the same story. This is why it is important to prepare a speaker's kit or speaker's manual for use by any individual in this role.

For convenience, the information can be as simple as in a folder with pockets, or a three-ring binder with dividers. The number being produced will drive the cost and ultimately the available budget.

Following are recommended elements of a package for speakers, surrogates and representatives:

- Instructions on how best to use the materials in the kit and especially, where policy is concerned, that the speaker not deviate from the prepared remarks.
- One or more speeches on a single, important subject, of different lengths such as 10 minutes, 20 minutes and 30 minutes.
- A series of speeches on a second or additional subjects.
- An outline of what type of speech to use before what type of audience. The speaker should feel comfortable in being able to deliver a speech on a subject about which she or he is familiar and not be embarrassed by being asked a question that could not be answered.
- A backgrounder of brief answers to frequently asked and anticipated questions regarding the company, organization or institution and its products, services or issues.
- Anecdotes related to the subject, which could be used when the individual is making an informal presentation and has an opportunity to get the message told.
- Helpful tips and dos and don'ts when making a speech, when appearing on radio or television, during a media interview and during a press conference.
- Phone and fax numbers and address of the person speakers should contact at the national office who is responsible for directing the program.
- If audiovisual materials such as a 16mm film, 35mm slides, overhead transparencies or a videotape are part of any of the presentations, there should be a page describing the film, slides or tape as well as instructions on projec-

tion equipment needs and how a room should be set up to accommodate the program. In some cases the speakers will be provided with copies of the audio-visual program, and in other cases they will be sent the program on an as-needed basis. This should be explained in the speakers' kit.

• Computer disks of the speeches and other information that are IBM compatible and Macintosh compatible on whatever type of disk the speaker prefers. This will allow the speaker to print out the speech in a preferred format and font size.

• In large speakers' bureau programs where it is not feasible for central scheduling from a national office, speakers may be responsible for their own scheduling within their geographic regions. In such cases there should be how-to tips on scheduling an appearance.

• Reporting forms and self-addressed, stamped envelopes should be included for the speaker to return to the national coordinator. This will be a record of the day and date of the speech, the event or organization addressed, the number of people attending, which speech was used, results, a critique, and so forth.

• Each speaker should have personalized biographies and photographs to give to a program chair or the media. Some national coordinators generally will take care of this for the speaker, but personally having extra copies is a good idea. In large programs it may be more feasible for the speaker to take this responsibility.

Speaker Information in Directories Used by Media

One way to provide the media with immediate access to your speakers and representatives is to buy a listing in *The Yearbook of Experts, Authorities & Spokespersons.* This book is published annually in the spring and is an inexpensive and cost-effective way to let the media know about a source for interviews. More than 8,000 copies of this publication are distributed annually to newspaper editors; program directors of national radio, television and cable outlets; decision makers at local television and radio stations; magazine editors; wire services and news bureaus; libraries; syndicated columnists and foreign journalists; broadcast societies and press clubs. Information is indexed for the media by topic, by geographic location, and alphabetically by name of the organization or the speaker. Some companies list multiple topics for their speakers. More than 10,000 topics are cross-referenced to the listings. For information on the yearbook contact Mitchell P. Davis, editor of *Broadcast Interview Source,* 2233 Wisconsin Ave. N.W., Suite 540, Washington, DC 20007-4104, phone (202) 333-4904 or (800) 955-0311, fax (202) 342-5411. The yearbook costs $47.50.

Opportunities at Conventions and Conferences

National and regional conventions and conferences are excellent sources for speaker placements. The person or office responsible for national coordination of the speakers should prepare a perpetual calendar listing all important conventions and conferences. Since most of the annual conventions start making commitments for speakers at the next convention virtually the day after the previous one ends, it is important to plan months ahead for scheduling.

The calendar should list the dates and place of the meeting, the phone and fax number and address of the individual responsible for scheduling speakers and moderators, the lead time required for scheduling of speakers, the theme of the convention and topics defined for certain panels. This information should be updated periodically as meetings are held and new events are added and appropriately noted.

The trade magazines covering the industry or subject material of interest should be screened for announcements of meetings. The event directors of associations and organizations responsible for producing the meetings also should be contacted for dates and contact information. Be familiar with the theme of the convention, and identify specific panels to match the expertise of the spokesperson with the needs of the convention program chair.

Important national conventions attract important national and regional media. If a public relations representative is not present at the meeting with the spokesperson, then the individual responsible for media relations for the convention should be contacted with materials supporting the spokesperson. Every major convention speech should include one or more newsworthy items. A publicity release should be prepared based on these points from the speech. Copies of this release should be available in the convention's press room, along with the full text of the speech and a one- or two-page executive summary with key sound bite points, plus the speaker's biography and photograph.

Local Opportunities

The national program coordinator and each member of a speaker's bureau should look for speaking appearance opportunities on a local and regional level. Every local, state and regional chapter of a national organization is always looking for entertaining and educational programs and good speakers, whether it is a community service club such as Kiwanis, Rotary, Lions or Soroptomist or a business or professional organization such as the local chamber of commerce, bar association, Society for Human Resource Management or National Association of Manufacturers.

Just as the master calendar was developed for national office speakers, a list of local, state and regional organizations should be developed with the name, address and phone and fax number of the president and the program chair. A letter should be prepared and sent to these organizations mentioning the availability of a speaker and suggesting a program. The program should be one of interest for the organization, and the credentials and experience of the speaker should be outlined as well as the subject that would be discussed.

High schools can be an important outlet if youth are part of or involved with the target audience. A list can be developed by calling the schools directly for the name of the principal. The effort also can be coordinated through the superintendent of schools, but this would include only the public, and not the parochial or private, schools. As was done in seeking speaking appearances before organizations, the letter sent to the principals should suggest a speaker and the subject, which must be of interest and value for a school to call an assembly of its students.

With both an organization and a school, no media opportunity should be overlooked. Is there news worthy to distribute a publicity release? If the spokesperson is a celebrity, then the media should be alerted for a possible interview. Often an athlete, under contract to be a spokesperson for a national company, will make appearances at high schools to talk to students about the dangers of drugs. This can be a photo opportunity as well as a sound bite on local radio or television.

As national spokespersons are scheduled on nationwide tours, consideration should be given in each market for a possible media event with an organization or school. When he was chair of the President's Council on Physical Fitness & Sports, Arnold Schwarzenegger did this very effectively by scheduling meetings in various states with governors and committees on physical education in the schools. Coinciding with the meetings, he scheduled an appearance at a school to be involved with the children.

HOW TO GET THE MOST FROM YOUR CELEBRITY

Athletes and entertainers can be productive vehicles through which a product, service or issue message can be delivered. In most cases the media will turn out just for them. Many celebrities already volunteer for charities and organizations that support causes of their interest.

If you decide to use a celebrity, be sure you get one who will help accomplish your marketing communications objectives and believes in what the company or organization is selling. You want to select someone who will bring stature to the product or service and who will identify with the target audience. For a program with widespread public appeal, you will want someone who is publicly recognized. Market research will help ensure that all these considerations are met.

When possible, try to get in direct contact with the celebrity for a decision if you are asking for participation in a non-profit organization. Agents are not interested in seeing their clients give away their time because agents do not receive any commission for work when the celebrity is not paid. Most public relations representatives or Hollywood press agents believe they are doing a service for their clients by saying "no" to most requests. In fact, some automatically turn down all requests, without even asking their clients. In some of these cases, the celebrity client could be personally interested in supporting the effort. Find a contact and pursue the celebrity through personal contact.

When considering an athlete or entertainer as a spokesperson or representative for a commercial, for-profit product or service, then work with the celebrity's agent, attorney or public relations representative. However, if you do have direct personal contact, it will expedite the matter because you can get a quick "yes" or "no" response that otherwise may take weeks.

Have everyone involved in the total marketing communications and advertising campaign determine any needs of the celebrity so that a complete package can be described. Before there was a cohesive marketing communications effort, those responsible for advertising would make a deal with a celebrity without asking anyone else. A price would be agreed upon. Then public relations would want to use the celebrity for media or trade personal appearances, to be quoted in publicity releases, to be cited in a publication, to appear in a video feature, or any number of other possible uses, only to find out that the price quoted by the celebrity's agent was not affordable within the parameters of the budget or the celebrity just did not want to become more involved in the program.

Before making any deal, outline all anticipated needs, especially the days and locations of meetings or a tour, and seek one price for the complete package. The sum of the elements is always cheaper than buying each part of a program on an individual basis. Most of all, make it workable because it is something all parties want to have happen.

Do not have a complicated contract, but a letter agreement that is as simple as possible. If it becomes too complicated it will become a matter that only attorneys can resolve. Include morals and drug clauses that will protect the company from any incident it would consider embarrassing or that would discredit the celebrity's image as a speaker for the company. For example, if the celebrity is involved by wearing certain fashions, it might be important to consider putting a weight clause in the contract. Outline the parameters for expenses so there are no surprises on the cost of hotel suites, limousines, incidentals or traveling companions.

One major company almost lost a credible and outstanding spokesperson because a letter agreement was two months overdue and was "still under consideration" by its corporate legal department. The letter agreement was a simple pro forma one that the public relations advisor had drafted himself and used frequently on behalf of various clients working with a number of celebrities. In each case, the client's legal counsel had approved the agreement. The situation was explained to the client, who insisted on a meeting immediately with the attorney to answer why this matter was taking so long. The young attorney, only a couple of years out of law school, was adamant that "these things take time...this is a very important document...it could have serious ramifications for the company...and is certainly not something I would just immediately approve, without further research." The attorney's time charges also were being billed against the marketing communications budget.

The public relations counsel intervened, saying to the young attorney, "I really can't understand why this is taking so long. This is a pro forma letter." Begging the issue further, the public relations counselor went on, "You certainly read and studied *Kingsfield on Contracts*[1] in your law school, didn't you?" When the attorney replied, "Of course, I did," the response was "Well, that is a recommended pro forma marketing communications letter agreement to use with celebrities right out of Professor Kingsfield's book! There should be no reason at all for any delay." Flustered, the attorney left, promising the marketing director to look into it immediately. The public relations counselor told his client about "Professor Kingsfield." The next call made was by the marketing director to the corporate executive vice president explaining what had happened, how the attorney had stalled and how the spokesperson would be lost if the agreement could not be executed immediately. Before the day was over, the agreement was faxed to the celebrity.

HOW TO WRITE THE SPEECH

Great writers may be born, not made, but almost anyone can learn to write a good, understandable speech. It takes clear thinking, knowledge of the subject matter, hard work and creativity.

A speech must be written for the ear and not the eye. The listener will hear the words only once and not have an opportunity to go back, as with a written word, to be sure she or he understands the message being communicated.

The subject you select should be part of the overall copy platform and one that will help accomplish objectives of the marketing communications campaign. Tailor it to your audience and know the mix of age and sex, educational background, attitudes and prejudices and professional disciplines.

The speech should have an opening, a middle and an ending built around the copy theme and subject selected. Know the time allotted for the speech and write to that length. Do not overwrite, and be sure it matches the delivery of the speaker. Most speakers will deliver a speech at a rate of about 140 words a minute; however, some may talk more slowly. For a longer speech, the speed of delivery could make the difference of several minutes. This is why rehearsals and practice are so critical to a successful presentation.

Arrange the points to be made in the speech in a definite, intentional or-

1. Kingsfield refers to the legendary Professor Kingsfield, played by the late John Houseman, on the popular television series "The Paper Chase." His specialty course was contracts.

der. A chronological or time order often is easy to follow when outlining the steps in a process. Space order is useful when describing such things as computerization. Begin at one end of what is being described and move directly to the other end without jumping around. A cause-to-effect order, or vice versa, would be suitable when discussing regulations. A problem-to-solution order could involve a number of causes or issues.

In the Beginning. First get the attention and arouse the interest of the audience. Do this with something personal and anecdotal, by asking a powerful or rhetorical question, by making a dramatic statement or quotation, by giving a shocking fact or figure, or by performing some action that will attract attention to the subject matter.

The speaker also can refer to something historical, by painting a wonderful word picture with sensory images and bringing the audience into the picture with the speaker, by using a song title or line in a popular commercial, or with lines of poetry. From the beginning, start to focus on the central theme; sometimes it may be more harmful than helpful to tell a joke to get attention.

Let the audience know that you know who they are and that you plan to address their needs. The beginning, like the ending of a talk, should do its job without being dragged out. In some cases, when the audience already knows the background and is interested, it is best to begin with a statement around the theme and go right into the body of the talk without unnecessary introduction.

The Main Body. This part of the speech should be well organized and the material clearly outlined so that the theme, or message to be communicated, is reinforced or proved, is clear, is made memorable and is developed by supporting materials to the point that the audience will be impressed.

Statistics can be one element of a powerful presentation. Use only figures that are valuable in establishing your point and that are easily understood by the audience. Point out the significance of your figures and the relationship between the statistics and the point they support to your audience. But don't go overboard with the number-crunching or your audience will start to tune out. Keep statistics brief for maximum punch.

Sensory images are good to use in a speech to get the audience to visualize on a thought and become part of your overall picture. These images could include food; family; sports, entertainment and fun; common fears, or something else that would be familiar to both the audience and the speaker.

Analogies, comparisons and contrasts are useful, especially when you can make an unfamiliar point more meaningful by relating it to something the audience already knows.

Define technical terms and words used in a specialized sense. Use terms that listeners will understand. If an idea is somewhat complicated, state it more than once, using different words or a different approach to be sure the audience understands the message being communicated.

Avoid Gobbledygook. Shortly after former Rep. Edward J. Derwinski of Illinois became Secretary of Veterans Affairs in the Bush administration, he brought in Air Force Lt. Col. James S. O'Rourke, a Cambridge-trained English professor, to streamline writing and communications. He noted that bureaucrats overuse words such as *optimum* and *utilize* and suggested that better substitutes would be simply *best* and *use.*

O'Rourke also pointed out some classic gobbledygook which included:

- "Sea-air interface climatic disturbances" for *waves*
- "Electronically adjusted, color-coded vehicular-flow control mechanism" for *traffic light*
- "Individual aerial deceleration mechanism" for *parachute*
- "Combat emplacement evacuator" for *shovel*

Always use words the audience will understand, otherwise the message may be lost. Technical words and phrases should be saved for a technical audience. However, if there are no substitutes, use them but give the audience the definition.

Quotations from authorities can be effective in supporting the theme. The authority quoted must be known to the audience or an important authority in the field. The authority should be unbiased on the issue and the person's testimony current.

Closing. Hammer home the message. Give the listeners a warning and let them know that you are ready to conclude the speech. Many of the items that were good to open a speech also are good to effectively conclude a speech. Summarize or restate the main points of the talk. Also close with a dramatic story, example, anecdote, question, challenge or quotation, or recommend a course of action.

Leave the audience members with the main theme and message foremost in their minds. The conclusion should wrap up the entire speech, not just the last point, and should not include any new points. It should be strong and persuasive and positively state what you want from the audience.

Here are some general tips to help one be a better speaker:

- Have the speech well organized.
- Use short sentences.
- Use language that is natural, personal, concise and concrete.
- Use your speaking and not your written vocabulary.
- Keep the words simple and short.
- Avoid tongue-twisters or words that would be difficult to pronounce.

- The speech should be more informal than the written style.
- Frequent use of "you" and "we" is desirable.
- Don't try to convey too many ideas. Leave the audience with one or two key points.
- Embellish the speech with figures of speech.
- Define the vocabulary and jargon of the audience and know which catchphrases might get their attention.
- Use words familiar to and easily understood by the audience.
- Use concrete words rather than abstract words.
- Illustrate points with examples from personal experience.
- Don't be afraid to repeat the main points. It just reinforces them.
- Cite sources and have documentation available.
- Use quotes and data from recognized experts.
- Avoid mixing multiple types of data, such as percentages, numbers and dollars, all in the same sentence.
- Generally, round off large numbers unless you have to give an absolute, specific figure.
- Statistics and figures have more impact if presented visually with slides.
- The closing should be definite and conclusive, not vague, uncertain or dragged out.
- Type the speech using a large, easy-to-read type and in all-capital letters.
- Do not split a sentence or thought. Start the paragraph on the next page.
- Type the script with wide top, bottom, left and right margins.

HOW TO DELIVER THE SPEECH

The best researched, written and prepared speech can be a disaster if the delivery and presentation are not a success. The three factors that determine how effectively a speech will be presented are the speaker's voice, body and eyes.

When beginning the speech, let the audience know you are in charge. Speak with confidence and authority so the listener knows that you know your subject and what you are talking about.

How the audience sees you is very important. Words can be discounted in favor of body language when your voice is saying one thing and your body is saying another.

Voice. Effective voice control is one of the most important factors in holding the attention of an audience and in displaying confidence and poise. Vary the speed and tempo of the delivery as well as the volume and pitch to hold the audience's interest and attention. To make certain points, "color" key words or phrases with both pitch and rhythm of delivery. The average speaker utters about 140 words a minute, but to emphasize a point should slow down to about 100 words a minute. To provide a change of pace for a quick transition, speed up to as much as 175 words a minute. Here are some tips for better voice control:

- Speak up and make yourself heard to the person in the back of the room.
- Do not compete with outside or distracting noises. It is all right to pause for a moment while the noise goes away.
- Before you begin talking, if you are very nervous, take a deep breath and then yawn or laugh to help relieve tension.
- Speak clearly and correctly pronounce each word.
- Vary the speed for voice control. Pause for effect.
- Speak in your normal voice. A variety of tones or pitches is important to prevent a monotone delivery.
- Modulate your voice for emphasis by speaking louder or more softly.
- Never speak faster than the audience can listen.

Body Language. Your body should be relaxed, with natural gestures, facial expressions and posture. Good posture gives the audience an impression of force, purpose and directness. Stand tall, with your weight evenly distributed on both feet. Movements should be meaningful.

A smile, frown, raised eyebrow, yawn or sneer all convey information to the audience. Facial expressions continually change during a talk and are constantly monitored by the listener. Some researchers believe that facial expressions are a better indicator to an audience of the meaning behind the message than are the speaker's words.

Use of hands is important. For example, the powerful symbol of a fist is universal. Let your hands become an integral part of your speech. Keep your hands away from your face and avoid scratching yourself or handling your glasses. Some additional tips:

- Don't hide behind the podium. Stand beside it, walk around it and use your body and hands.
- Don't lean on a podium or lectern unless you want to do it for effect by moving toward the audience to make a point.
- Avoid the monotony of hands in pockets or behind the back.
- Don't fuss with clothes or use annoying gestures.
- Stand erect and control any nervous habits.
- Keep your hands off the microphone. Be careful how your hands move on the podium or lectern in the event the sounds are amplified by the microphone and public address system.
- Avoid aimless wandering on the platform and aimless hand movements.
- Never smoke or chew gum.

Eye Contact. Always maintain eye contact with the audience. It is a direct and powerful form of non-verbal communication and can elicit a feeling of trust. Divide the audience into quadrants and look at the audience. Look at the different quadrants as you speak to involve the total audience. When you see nodding heads, closed eyes or glazed stares, you know you are not getting through to your audience.

Psychologists say that downward glances are generally associated with modesty and eyes rolled upward are associated with fatigue. Sometimes eyes moved to the side when a question is asked reveals that a person does not want to truthfully answer the question. A few more tips:

- As you scan the audience, single out different individuals and talk to them while maintaining eye contact.
- Try to establish a series of short eye contacts with as many members of the audience as possible.
- Let your eyes be animated and show happiness, sorrow, surprise and excitement.
- Never look away when a question is being asked.

Rehearse the Presentation

Even the best speakers rehearse their presentations. Schedule a training session and be sure the speech gets the message across. Have professionals be sure your voice, body and eyes and are all effectively working for you.

Have professionals videotape and critique the speech. Go over words and phrases, the pace and tempo of delivery, how key words are colored and whether you are effectively using your hands. Be sure you are familiar with the material so that the right words come naturally and spontaneously.

If you don't use professional help, practice yourself by imagining the audience in a room at your office or home and speak to that audience as you would during the actual presentation. If you cannot videotape your delivery, then tape-record it, play it back and critique it yourself. If possible, also try to check out the auditorium, hall or room where you will be speaking in advance to get a comfortable feeling for your environment before you are on center stage.

HOW TO USE VISUAL AIDS

Of our five senses—sight, hearing, touch, smell and taste—the simultaneous combination of sight and hearing can be a most effective means of communication. Don't believe that one picture is worth a thousand words. The argument you will hear in return is to read the Gettysburg Address, The Lord's Prayer, The Ten Commandments, the Preamble to the Constitution or a sonnet by Shakespeare. During World War II's Battle of the Bulge, General McAuliffe made his point with just one word: "Nuts." However, when properly used, good graphic or visual aids will enhance the presentation. Remember, the audience only hears your spoken words one time, but they can be reinforced by being seen on a screen.

Visual aids can range from a chalkboard or easel with paper to 35mm slides, overhead projector slides, or a film or videotape. The larger the room and the greater the distance between the projector and the screen, the stronger the bulb needed. If the projection bulb is not of a proper strength, the image on the screen will be too dark.

Generally you will have the controls for a slide projector at the podium or lectern. The overhead projector slides you will control or will have an assistant controlling for you. A film or videotape will need to be started on a cue from you.

Placement and size of the screen is important. In most situations, the bottom of the screen should be at least four feet off the floor so the audience has an unobstructed view of the entire screen. For optimum viewing, the accepted standards for audience placement in relation to the screen are:

- Distance to the closest viewer: two times the width of the screen.
- Distance to the farthest viewer: six times the width of the screen.
- Widest angles of view: 22 degrees from the centerline of projection for a beaded screen; up to 50 degrees from the centerline of projection for a lenticular screen; and a matte-finish screen allows the widest angle of viewing for the front rows but is not recommended for long-distance viewing. Extremely wide horizontal angles of vision should be avoided. The screen should be at a right angle to the projector to eliminate keystoning, a distortion of the image in which the enlarged picture is out of proportion. Keystoning is a common problem with overhead projectors and often cannot be eliminated.

Here are some more tips to keep in mind when using visual aids:

- Visual aids must be large enough to be easily seen or read from the farthest point in the audience.
- Slides and charts should be simple and uncluttered, with a minimum of detail.
- Keep all aids out of sight until you are ready to use them.
- If you use 35mm slides, be sure to use dark slides wherever there is a pause and at the beginning and end of the presentation so there is no white screen.
- Try not to turn your back on the audience.
- If you have to write on a board or easel, do not talk until you turn and face the audience, even if you have a microphone with you.

- Never stand between a visual aid and the audience.
- Never use a visual aid in front of an audience until you have rehearsed with it.
- Tell the projectionist what your cues will be so that he or she knows when to turn on a projector or film or videotape.
- Have an extra copy of your speech to give to the projectionist.
- Never turn off all the lights. Leave some lights on in part of the room for those in the audience who want to take notes.
- Use a pointer that will project a mark on the screen if you need to emphasize aspects of your visual aids. The new laser pointers, while expensive, are quite effective.
- Get the projected aids off the screen as soon as you are through with them, otherwise they become a distraction.

17

HOW TO BUILD COALITION SUPPORT

Webster's says the word *coalition* comes from the French word *coalescere*, and defines it is as:

> 1. a: the act of coalescing: UNION; b: a body formed by the coalescing of orig. distinct elements: COMBINATION; 2. a temporary alliance of distinct parties, persons or states for joint action.

In public relations a coalition is a support group that can be organized because it believes in a product, service, issue or candidate. If the coalition is properly organized and motivated, it can be an integral and effective part of any campaign.

While coalition groups are more popularly used in political campaigns and to support issues, product manufacturers and professional and trade associations have organized coalition support when product sales or services are threatened or are close to being impacted by any form of regulation.

One of the most obvious efforts to build coalition support for a cause or issue is that by the National Rifle Association. It has organized not only its members, but coalition groups to fight any form of gun control. Each group—manufacturers, wholesalers, dealers, collectors or sportshooters—has its own reason for support of the cause. Likewise, the tobacco industry has organized smokers' rights groups, farmers, company employees and others to protect its interests. Fan clubs of celebrities and Hollywood stars are a simplified example of a coalition group.

A POLITICAL CAMPAIGN STRUCTURE

The most comprehensive use of coalition support in a campaign will most likely be in a political campaign. Few product manufacturers or service providers would have as diverse a constituent group to organize into a coalition.

In a political campaign, the candidates seek to get support and a vote from every possible individual. Generally, coalition groups are organized based on demographics. Groups of people, even with contrary views and at opposite ends of the demographic scale, can be found to support the same candidate; for example, youth and senior citizens or labor unions and management. Other coalitions include:

- Accountants
- Athletes
- Attorneys
- College students
- Drug control groups
- Educators
- Entertainers
- Ethnic groups
  - African American
  - Asian American,
  - Hispanic/Latino
  - Native American
  - Pacific Islander
  - Cuban Americans
  - Greek Americans
  - Italian Americans
  - Latvian Americans
  - Irish Americans
  - Any other ethnic group that wants to be organized
- Geographic
- Home builders
- Judges and judicial members
- Military, both active and retired
- Realtors
- Women

The list could go on and on with a group from almost every profession, discipline or interest.

SELECT A COALITION THAT WORKS FOR YOU

Before organizing a coalition you need to do the following:

1. Define what it is you want the coalition to do.
2. Define who the coalition will be.
3. Define the number of possible coalition groups.
4. Ask if such a group or groups can be organized. Is there a way to reach the people to organize them?
5. If organized, is there leadership in the coalition and each group that can be counted on to deliver?
6. Will the coalition be believable to the media? To the general public? Is there any chance of a negative reaction because of the coalition group that is organized?
7. Is it possible to get a recognizable individual (such as a celebrity) to be chair of the coalition?

HOW TO USE THE COALITION

One of the early steps in the process is knowing how to use the coalition. There are a number of things you can ask of the coalition once it is formed:

- To help with any volunteer effort that is needed, from organizing an event to handing out literature or showing up at a public meeting or rally
- To write letters to the editor
- To write letters to politicians
- To write op-eds or opinion pieces (Here you want to be careful and only use someone with either a recognizable name or an appropriate title.)
- To hold meetings and public forums to discuss issues and create a media event or opportunity
- To make public speeches, if the chair of the coalition or any member has a name that would be well known to the media or the public (Also schedule them for radio and television talk shows and for media interviews.)

COMMUNICATE WITH THE COALITION

It is essential to keep the coalition informed. Any coalition member who has agreed to help and even lend his or her name, as well as even possibly contribute to the cause financially, should be kept completely informed and up-to-date on the issue. This can be done with a periodic letter from the chair of the coalition. Consider the use of a newsletter if it really serves a purpose and can be accommodated within the budget. Be sure to also send each coalition member a fact sheet or some printed form with the pros and cons and answers to any questions that may be asked. Coalition members, to be effective, must have the party-line answer to any question.

Some coalitions offer opportunities to provide information on a self-liquidating basis because the members will pay a nominal charge. In the case of a product, the coalition also can be an opportunity for couponing or even responding to random samples and research.

A CASE FOR A COALITION

Take the situation of a leading boat manufacturer that has a major manufacturing operation in the West. Sales have been falling over a five-year period in spite of a strong consumer demand for boats. The reason is that there are no slips, marinas or harbors where a new owner can dock the boat. Add to this market research that shows the company could increase its sales at least 10 percent a year for the next five years.

On one hand there are strong environmental concerns over any new construction or development. The boat manufacturer is faced with a dilemma of closing its West Coast operation and centralizing everything in the East. This would add an additional cost to the product because of the expense of shipping the boat across the country.

One way to fight back is to organize other boat manufacturers and form an organization or coalition that in effect would be a trade association. Next support is needed from people who do not have a direct financial interest in the manufacture and sale of the boats. These can include current boat owners who may want to trade up but cannot do so because larger slips are not available. The potential boat owners who will purchase either a new boat or a used one, creating a move-up, buy-up situation, can be reached through dealers and brokers. Add to this all the manufacturers and suppliers of products and services for the boating industry as well as lodging, foodservice and financial service industries who become a part of any marina.

The boat manufacturers also can look for support from other recreational organizations and ancillary groups such as the Coast Guard Auxiliary, Sea Scouts and others. And there will be natural support from the employees who face the threat of losing their jobs, and from their families, friends and relatives.

Once organized, this consortium of coalitions could be a most effective and powerful group to go out and convincingly tell the story of the need for new boat docks. In most cases, marinas have been an extremely profitable investment and steady cash flow for most local governments. The case needs to be stated economically and environmentally as well as the importance of providing the public access to natural resources.

A similar situation could be outlined in almost every part of the country where someone has wanted to build a new recreational property, whether for skiing, golf, tennis or whatever reason. Some people are opposed to any development and while very much a minority, they are a well organized, vocal minority that knows how to use the media to influence the decision-making elected and appointed politicians.

TURNING ADVERSARIES INTO ADVOCATES

For over two decades, environmental groups urged consumers to boycott tuna products because widely used fishing techniques were harmful to dolphins. And as the world's largest tuna processor, StarKist bore the brunt of the bad publicity. Public concern with the issue gained momentum over time, and by the late 1980s, a small but growing number of consumers and institutions stopped purchasing tuna altogether. Legislation requiring canners to label tuna products was introduced in Congress.

By 1989, it was clear that decisive action was necessary to turn the issue around. Edelman Public Relations Worldwide counseled StarKist on the effects possible initiatives would have on consumers, environmental activists and Washington lawmakers. The Edelman firm recommended that StarKist pursue an aggressive, "Dolphin Safe" campaign. Once the new policy was created, however, the millions of consumers with existing strong opinions about StarKist still needed to be informed of the change. Edelman's media relations, environmental policy and consumer marketing expertise combined to create an event with dramatic impact (Hayes 1994).

Months of planning were conducted in absolute secrecy. But in order to give the new policy maximum credibility and maximum news value, key environmentalists and lawmakers were contacted 36 hours before the announcement press conference. Literally overnight, longtime critics were converted into active supporters.

On April 12, 1990, more than 100 media representatives gathered to hear the announcement and listen to nationally recognized environmental activists and a senior U.S. senator present glowing tributes to the new StarKist policies. That evening, Peter Jennings opened his national ABC broadcast with the story. CBS and NBC also featured the story prominently. The StarKist declaration appeared on the front pages of *The Washington Post, The New York Times, The Los Angeles Times, USA Today,* the *New York Post* and many other important daily newspapers across the country. A StarKist executive and a Greenpeace official discussed the issue live on "CBS This Morning." *Time, Newsweek, U.S. News & World Report* and food industry trade magazines all carried the news. Video B-roll and written material were incorporated into virtually all the media coverage of the event.

As a result of careful planning and execution, StarKist has emerged as a corporate environmental leader, and it continues to work with the Edelman firm to build the groundbreaking announcement press conference into a long-term marketing advantage.

THE PROFIT MOTIVE

In some cases a coalition group may be organized because one manufacturer has a proprietary or exclusive item or option on a product, but it may be priced higher because of that exclusivity. Here the manufacturer may build coalition support to enact regulations or legislation that would require all manufacturers to provide the same option.

For example, certain manufacturers of safety helmets for motorcyclists and bicyclists can point to the number of lives saved and how many people escape serious injury because they were wearing helmets. Coalition support was raised from a number of interest groups, including non-profit organizations involved with head injuries or medical care.

The bottom line is: Would that same manufacturer have supported legislation that would require all motorcyclists and bicyclists to wear safety helmets if the product it manufactured was a widget and not a safety helmet? Perhaps not.

REFERENCE

Hayes, Wendy, 1994. Background information materials. New York: Edelman Public Relations Worldwide. April 22.

18

HOW TO MEASURE RESULTS

There are any number of ways to measure results of a marketing public relations campaign. One is to look at the success of the media effort in terms of media exposure: the clippings and mentions on radio and television. Another is to do a qualitative analysis of how effective the media exposure was in reaching and motivating the targeted audience. Some executives may look at the real bottom line on program effectiveness as being increased sales or increases in consumption of services; new customers or clients; or the success of a cause or issue.

More and more, clients and executives ask for accountability and want to know whether a campaign, program or project was cost-effective and contributed to the overall corporate mission and strategic plan. Using research is one way to provide the answer—and it must be budgeted as part of the overall program and decided before the campaign or project is ever launched. Dr. Walter K. Lindenmann, senior vice president and director of research at Ketchum Public Relations, says it not only is possible to measure public relations effectiveness, but doing so does not have to be either unbelievably expensive or laboriously time-consuming. He says there still are a "handful of cynics and skeptics in our business who are convinced it cannot be done. But, I feel their number is dwindling rapidly and—with the growing pressure throughout our field to be more accountable for what we do—I'm convinced that by the turn of the century those few skeptics should be all but gone from our profession (Lindenmann 1993)."

MEASURING MEDIA RESULTS

Companies including Bacon's, Burrelle's and Luce are press clipping services that read virtually everything in print, including daily and weekly newspapers, trade and consumer magazines and special interest and ethnic media. The cost is based on a monthly fee plus a charge for each clipping.

There are many firms that provide radio and television monitoring services, including Burrelle's and its affiliate, Video Monitoring Services of America. Results are provided on tape or in transcript forms. The company's Burrelle's Transcripts operation also regularly monitors and has available tapes and transcripts of a number of popular network television news and magazine programs and specials.

Detailed descriptions and addresses of these services appear in Chapter 4.

REPORTING THE RESULTS

There are many ways to report the data. One typical monthly or project report could include:

- Name of publication or broadcast outlet
- Date of publication and data and time of broadcast
- Column inches of space or length in minutes and seconds
- Circulation or listeners/viewers reached
- Comment regarding headline, product or type of mention
- Cost of the space or time if purchased as advertising

Some public relations firms have evaluated publicity programs on the basis that news coverage in print space and broadcast time has three times the credibility of advertising. Therefore, two minutes on ABC's "Good Morning America" would be three times worth the cost of the two minutes if it had appeared as advertising.

Software is even available to print out reports with dollar values attributed to the media exposure. Some practitioners go as far as to assign an index number to certain newspapers, magazines and television programs based on status and credibility. For example, Cartier International gives more points for a mention in an upscale magazine and fewer points for a mass-circulation magazine that does not pinpoint Cartier's elite audience. More points also are given for a Cartier mention in a headline or for a Cartier photograph (*PRJ* 1990).

Books of compiled clippings and edited highlights of important broadcast placements are important not only in letting others see the media results, but also to keep for archival purposes.

MEASURING EFFECTIVENESS

Ketchum's Lindenmann has developed what he calls a Public Relations

Effectiveness Yardstick that any professional can use to measure effectiveness of a campaign or program. He says the first step is to set objectives. He believes that in public relations, accomplishment expectations will fall into any one of four categories (Lindenmann 1994):

1. You, or your organization, are trying to get *certain messages, themes* or *ideas* out.
2. You would like these messages or ideas distributed to *certain key or target audience groups.*
3. You envision distributing these messages to your target audiences by *certain pre-selected or specific communications channels*—perhaps through the media, by word-of-mouth or by a direct-mail approach.
4. Ultimately, for what you say, for how you say it, and to whom, there are *certain short-term or long-term "ends"* or objectives you are interested in accomplishing. Based on how and what you say and do, you would like those you reach to respond in a certain way.

After setting the objectives, Lindenmann says to then determine the level of measurement. He lists "basic" for measuring outputs, "intermediate" for measuring outgrowths and "advanced" for measuring outcomes.

Level 1: Basic. This level measures what was actually done in the way of media placements, impressions and targeted audiences. It can involve content analysis techniques to track or measure placements or a simple public opinion poll to see if targeted groups have been exposed to certain messages.

As an example, Lindenmann cites a pharmaceutical company that was promoting a product allergy sufferers could use to alleviate runny noses, itchy eyes, scratchy throats and dislocated dispositions. In a nine-month period the company had 300 newspaper, magazine, television and radio placements. Research determined how favorable or unfavorable toward the company and its product those press clippings ended up being. Content analysis of the clippings was the methodology used to measure the public relations outputs. The research took six weeks and cost less than $6,000.

Level 2: Intermediate. This level is more sophisticated and measures whether the target audience groups actually received the messages, whether they paid attention to those messages and whether they have retained those messages. Lindenmann says the intermediate level measures retention, comprehension, awareness and reception. To measure outgrowth he relies on a mix of qualitative and quantitative data involving focus groups, depth interviews with opinion-leader groups and extensive polling of key target audience groups by telephone, by mail or face-to-face.

For years a health group had been distributing messages throughout the media about the benefits of a particular medical product. The organization needed to assess the effectiveness of its publicity efforts. More important than just counting the newspaper and magazine clippings, or adding up the total audience reached, was to know if the people received, understood and retained crucial aspects of the message. Interviews were conducted with 300 adults at six different malls using unaided and aided-recall questions. The project was completed in five weeks for a cost of less than $20,000.

Level 3: Advanced. This level is the most detailed measurement on Lindenmann's yardstick and involves change in behavior, attitude or opinion. To measure outcomes, the researcher relies on techniques such as before-and-after polls; development and use of experimental and quasi-experimental research designs; use of unobtrusive data collection methods such as observation, participation and role playing; use of advanced data analysis involving perceptual mapping, psychographic analysis, factor and cluster analysis and conjoint analysis; or the conducting of comprehensive, multifaceted communications audits.

Enrollment was dropping at a medical university that trained health and medical care practitioners. Its management wanted to know what impact, if any, its marketing communications efforts were having on prospective students. A five-stage project was designed that included a secondary analysis of opinion data; a review and critique of previous surveys and questionnaires internally by the school; tabulation and analysis of data from a university-conducted survey of non-applicants; conducting six focus groups with existing and prospective students; and conducting a series of in-depth interviews by telephone with 90 key "influentials," including selected high school and college teachers, high school guidance counselors and area health care employees.

The project cost $35,000 and was completed in four months. The result was a clear-cut understanding of target audience awareness levels, comprehension levels, opinion and attitudes, and behavior patterns, which led to the development of a new and expanded marketing-based communications program for the medical school.

EVALUATING CORPORATE SPONSORSHIP OF EVENTS

According to Don Smith of Don Smith Consultants, with companies paying high sponsorship fees there has emerged an increased need to justify costs and evaluate the success of corporate sponsorship of an event.

Measuring the effectiveness of sponsorship requires different approaches because one company may sponsor primarily for client entertainment; another to impact the trade; a third to change consumer attitudes toward a product; a fourth to gain straight-out publicity and media exposure; and a fifth to introduce a new product or service.

Smith believes you cannot compare event sponsorship to straight advertising and use a cost-per-thousand scale. Here is what he believes can be measured (Smith 1994):

Changes in Awareness or Image. By conducting pre- and post-event surveys, a company can determine if the event helped produce a shift in awareness and perception.

Spending Equivalencies. A sponsor can place a monetary value on media exposure generated by measuring the comparable advertising cost in newspapers and magazines and on radio and television.

This type of measurement cannot be simplistic because, for example, television exposure for a tobacco company that cannot buy advertising on this medium would be significantly greater than for a soft drink producer.

Sales Impact. There are two ways to make sales analysis easier: (1) use short-term or localized sponsorships, which provide more control for measuring results, and (2) design a tie-in, such as couponing or label redemption.

Tips for Measuring Event Impact

Smith (1994) lists the following conditions and tips for measuring impact of sponsoring a special event:

1. Have narrowly defined objectives. Know what you want the sponsorship to provide *before* getting involved. Target a specific audience and look for an event that is compatible to that consumer group. Estimate budgets and time of the sponsorship.
2. Set a measurable goal. Create a sponsorship program that enables you to measure the results—that is, local or regional events that impact a smaller audience, but which permit more accurate measurement of results. It is more difficult to measure national or international, multimillion-dollar sponsorships.
3. Measure against existing standards. If you are trying to increase trade accounts, know exactly where you stand in this area before starting the sponsorship. If you are attempting to increase the sale of a particular product to a special audience, be certain you know in advance your share of market before the campaign is launched.
4. Do not change other marketing variables during the sponsorship. This clouds the measurement process.
5. Do not interpret negative results to mean the sponsorship was wrong. Don't place too much emphasis on sheer numbers or statistics.
6. Incorporate evaluation into the overall corporate sponsorship and marketing program. If short-term results are not what they should be, perhaps the long-term prognosis is better.

7. Put aside 1 percent to 5 percent of the sponsorship budget to pay for the evaluation process.

REFERENCES

Lindenmann, Walter K. 1993. “An Effectiveness Yardstick to Measure Public Relations Success. *Public Relations Quarterly* 3, no 1(spring).

———. 1994. Correspondence with the author. Ketchum Public Relations. April.

Public Relations Journal. 1990. “Evaluating the Impact of Public Relations. November.

Smith, Don. 1994. Interview and correspondence with author. New York: Don Smith Consultants. April-May.

19

HOW TO PLAN AND BUDGET

All too often the most overlooked part of any marketing public relations campaign or project is the planning and budgeting process. If the campaign is not executed precisely when it should be, chances are it will fail. The person directing the campaign fails if costs exceed the budget or funds are depleted well before the program has been completed.

Strategic plans, campaign plans and budgets are a manager's best friends. They are invaluable management tools. The campaign or program is being undertaken for a reason, and the creative plan for the marketing public relations effort should be in synch with the overall objectives of the company or organization.

STRATEGIC PLANNING

A director responsible for creating and executing a marketing public relations campaign or project will not normally be called on to produce a strategic plan. However, it is important to understand strategic planning because most organizations, regardless of how large or small, will have a strategic plan.

Strategic planning is a process that has been used over the ages by most successful armies and commercial organizations. Only in recent years did it bear the catchy title of strategic planning or was grist for the mills of a large consulting industry.

Something is not strategic simply because it is going to happen in the distant future. It is strategic because it can have a major impact on an organization's success, even next week, or during a campaign. How to go about deciding what those important things are and how to address them is what strategic planning is all about. The process is quite personal to an individual organization.

THE MISSION STATEMENT

Strategic planning starts with a mission statement, a concise statement of the reasons for an organization's existence. It is philosophical in nature and constitutes the primal policy statement of the organization. All else flows from it—what is legitimate or unacceptable for subordinate organizations and employees.

The mission statement should never be complex, but the higher in the hierarchy it is created, the more general it must be. Clearly, the mission statement for a major corporation looks nothing like the mission statement for one of its smaller subsidiary divisions. The mission of a division will be compatible with and contribute to achievement of the parent's mission.

At every organizational level, the next step is to define the long-run strategic goals that will lead to mission accomplishment. The statement first must define what is right and important for the organization before addressing timing or resources needed. The next step is to anticipate the major environmental forces that might constrain or empower an organization in its pursuit of its goals.

Action alternatives and strategies that could be successful are designed. Resource and timing implications are analyzed. A small set of realistic strategies is agreed upon—one primary, and the others for fallback. These are translated into near-term objectives and priorities. At this point, the organization is almost ready to look at budgets. First, however, there must be effective communication and agreement all the way back to the chief executive officer. It is critical to have commitment for the plan from the CEO, who will energize the commitment to the lowest levels.

As any project or campaign plan is designed, it is important to be aware of the immediate strategic plans of the parent company and the subsidiary or division. If you are in the agency business, it also is important to be aware of and sensitive to the agency's strategic plan. There could be constraints in the way in which a project can be approached.

Almost all organizations update their strategic plans annually. Mission statements and long-run goals are usually rather stable in the short run, unless a major downsizing is suddenly ordered. The same cannot be said for favored strategies, priorities and timing at the division or project level. Any practitioner should stay close to his or her client to avoid surprises (Dempster 1994).

THE CAMPAIGN PLAN

The marketing public relations campaign or project plan should incorporate the objectives of the strategic plans of both the public relations department and the overall organization. Research will help focus on what must be done and techniques that can be used to reach target audiences.

Once the public relations plan is written, then a basic budget must be prepared and a time line or production schedule prepared.

THE BASIC BUDGET

The budget is prepared from the public relations plan. Once all needs have been defined, costs are put to the plan (Table 19.1). Personnel services can be determined based on people, or an agency will estimate the hours needed to accomplish a program and then build that into its retainer or project fee for services.

Estimate what needs to be done and then put a cost figure to the project. The director will be a hero if she or he comes in under budget, but being over

Table 19.1. Basic budget

Line Item	Budget ($)
1.0 Press releases	
1.1 Production and mailing	3,500.00
1.2 Distribution service	8,500.00
1.3 VNRs	12,000.00
2.0 Photography/graphics	
2.1 Photography	4,000.00
2.2 Graphics/logos design	7,500.00
2.3 Quantity prints	2,500.00
3.0 Postage, messenger and delivery services	3,000.00
4.0 Telephone and fax	5,000.00
5.0 Press conferences (2 cities)	10,000.00
6.0 Special events (TBA)	10,000.00
7.0 Travel and per diem	15,000.00
8.0 Results measurement	
8.1 Clipping service	4,000.00
8.2 Audio/video monitoring	3,000.00
Subtotal	88,000.00
9.0 10% contingency	8,800.00
Total	96,800.00

Table 19.2. Campaign production schedule

Project	Jan	Feb	Mar	Apr	May	Jun	Jul	Aug	Sep	Oct	Nov	Dec	Jan	Feb
1. Design letterhead, logo, materials	/———	———/												
2. Interview and select spokesperson		/———	———/											
3. Prepare press kit materials				/———	———/									
4. Press conferences														
Advance, finalize arrangements					/-/									
New York						/-/								
Atlanta						/-/								
Dallas							/-/							
Los Angeles							/-/							
5. Special events														
Advance, finalize arrangements								/-/						
Concert								/-/						
10K bicycle event										/-/				
6. Distribute news releases, as appropriate		/———	———	———	———	———	———	———	———	———	———	———/		
7. Prepare, distribute video news releases						/-/		/-/		/-/		/-/		
8. Report on media results					/———	———	———	———	———	———	———	———	———/	
9. Research														
Precampaign		/———	———/											
Campaign evaluation													/———	———/

budget creates problems. It is always wise to build in a contingency if other opportunities arise as the program unfolds.

THE PROGRAM SCHEDULE

This becomes the road map and calendar for the program. List the projects that need to be undertaken and then determine in what month or months the work actually will take place (Table 19.2). Some efforts will be ongoing, with activities in each month. In other cases, major events such as a press conference or a special event will only be in a particular month.

Some calendars can be even more specific and detailed and set up on a computer program with boxes for each week of the month. Determine what works best for you and your people and establish that as your format.

OTHER BUDGETS

In order to keep on top of expenses, have the accounting department set up a budget balance for each program or campaign. This will show the original budget, the amount spent to date and the balance (Table 19.3). In some cases, another column can be added, such as "Committed," so you know that funds from the budget already have been obligated or committed and will be spent, even though they have not been spent to date. This is important because

Table 19.3. Budget balance

Line Item	Budget ($)	Spent ($)	Balance ($)
1.0 Press releases			
1.1 Production and mailing	3,500.00	1,542.36	1,957.64
1.2 Distribution service	8,500.00	5,355.75	3,144.25
1.3 VNRs	12,000.00	6,126.17	5,873.83
2.0 Photography/graphics			
2.1 Photography	4,000.00	3,228.94	771.06
2.2 Graphics/logos design	7,500.00	8,755.44	(1,255.44)
2.3 Quantity prints	2,500.00	1,685.25	814.75
3.0 Postage, messenger and delivery services	3,000.00	1,942.63	1,057.37
4.0 Telephone and fax	5,000.00	3,112.37	1,887.63
5.0 Press conferences (2 cities)	10,000.00	9,847.81	152.19
6.0 Special events (TBA)	10,000.00	4,789.34	5,210.66
7.0 Travel and per diem	15,000.00	9,891.47	5,108.53
8.0 Results measurement			
8.1 Clipping service	4,000.00	2,341.96	1,658.04
8.2 Audio/video monitoring	3,000.00	2,246.87	753.13
Sub-total	88,000.00	60,866.36	27,133.64
9.0 10% contingency	8,800.00	—0—	8,800.00
Total	96,800.00	60,866.36	35,933.64

some budget balance figures can be deceiving if the manager is not aware of all expenses being made.

Add two columns to the budget balance and you can have a comparison with the same program or a similar program for the previous year or previous years (Table 19.4). This can be further defined with a cash flow analysis showing in what month expenses were incurred in the event some programs become seasonal with expenses for certain line items higher in certain months. This is especially important for a budget in the first half of the year because campaign expenses and some line items run twice as much in the second half. The cash flow can be set up on a monthly or quarterly basis or however it best works for the manager in charge.

OTHER MANAGEMENT CONTROLS

To ensure that staff members do not overcommit a budget, have some type of purchase order for expenses over a certain amount of money. In this way the accounting department will have purchase orders for goods or services being purchased that might not yet have been billed. It is a flag that expenses have been incurred and a bill will be coming in against the budget. The purchase order can be added to the "committed" column on a budget balance. Purchase orders also offer another degree of control over expenses.

Time sheets are important. They tell how much time is being spent on

Table 19.4. Budget balance and comparison

Line Item	Budget	Spent	Balance	Budget Last Year	Balance Last Year
	($)	($)	($)	($)	($)
1.0 Press releases					
1.1 Production and mailing	3,500.00	1,542.36	1,957.64	3,500.00	1,843.47
1.2 Distribution service	8,500.00	5,355.75	3,144.25	7,500.00	1,862.57
1.3 VNRs	12,000.00	6,126.17	5,873.83	10,000.00	3,376.83
2.0 Photography/graphics					
2.1 Photography	4,000.00	3,228.94	771.06	4,000.00	1,182.32
2.2 Graphics/logos design	7,500.00	8,755.44	(1,255.44)	1,500.00	(336.97)
2.3 Quantity prints	2,500.00	1,685.25	814.75	2,500.00	1,192.46
3.0 Postage, messenger and delivery services	3,000.00	1,942.63	1,057.37	3,000.00	1,255.23
4.0 Telephone and fax	5,000.00	3,112.37	1,887.63	5,000.00	1,754.88
5.0 Press conferences (2 cities)	10,000.00	9,847.81	152.19	5,000.00	(1,008.78)
6.0 Special events (TBA)	10,000.00	4,789.34	5,210.66	8,000.00	(1,438.34)
7.0 Travel and per diem	15,000.00	9,891.47	5,108.53	12,500.00	4,987.29
8.0 Results measurement					
8.1 Clipping service	4,000.00	2,341.96	1,658.04	4,000.00	1,774.56
8.2 Audio/video monitoring	3,000.00	2,246.87	753.13	3,000.00	1,422.18
Sub-total	88,000.00	60,866.36	27,133.64	64,500.00	17,867.70
9.0 10% contingency	8,800.00	—0—	8,800.00	6,450.00	6,450.00
Total	96,800.00	60,866.36	35,933.64	70,950.00	24,317.70

one project or another, or even a phase of a project or campaign. A review of time sheets may find that some projects are not cost-effective or that the results achieved by a special event did not warrant the hours spent on the project. If personnel time and expenses are being rebilled, it is essential to have time sheets.

Time sheets can be turned in weekly, twice a month or in whatever period of time best works for the organization. Individuals should be asked to keep time to the nearest quarter-hour. This should not be difficult as most accountants and attorneys keep time to the nearest one-tenth of an hour.

Almost any program can be computerized so data are immediately available to a manager. If the budget balance and purchase order commitment program is computerized, there can be a daily look at costs and available funds. This can be critical for success in the case of megadollar campaigns or where a great deal of money may be spent in a short period of time.

A MANAGER'S CHECKLIST

Develop a strategic plan.

Be sure the department or campaign plan fulfills the objectives of the organization's strategic plan.

Create a campaign or project plan that will help accomplish the objectives of the strategic plan.

Prepare a basic budget based on the campaign or project plan.

Prepare a time line or schedule when elements of the plan will be undertaken.

Stay on top of the budget so it is not exceeded.

REFERENCE

Dempster, Anthony G., executive director of strategic planning. 1994. Interview. Texas A&M University. May.

AFTERWORD

The results of the best planned and executed marketing public relations campaign or project can be affected by events or circumstances well beyond anyone's control.

This author was responsible for the public relations effort opening the Ronald McDonald House in Los Angeles. The initial media response to the event being held at Children's Hospital was beyond all expectations. But when the time came for the announcement to be made, no television cameras or radio microphones were hooked up to the mult box. Representatives from McDonald's and its national public relations agency thought that the ICPR public relations firm had completely failed them.

As it turned out, while the camera crews were enroute to the Hollywood-located hospital, the police radios announced that another victim of the "Hillside Strangler" serial murderer had been found. All crews in the area had been diverted to that location. As a result of a quick response by our broadcast relations director, we were able to get several of the crews to visit the hospital and meet with the McDonald's executives and hospital physicians before returning to their home base. An important event was almost lost because of something that could not have been anticipated.

The reverse was true just before the movie *The China Syndrome* was released to theaters nationwide: the now-famous Three-Mile Island nuclear incident happened, almost making the theme of the feature film become a reality.

Sometimes good things that could never be orchestrated happen to nice people. Entertainment executive Marsha Robertson, a former vice president of MGM responsible for national publicity campaigns, was consulting for the producers of *Jurassic Park* on their overall marketing public relations campaign. "This was a multidimensional campaign, and no single department can receive credit for such an enormous undertaking," she says in an interview.

But like *The China Syndrome,* it benefited tremendously from great serendipity in the world of current events. For several months prior to and during the production of the movie, there were several major archaeological discoveries about dinosaurs and also about DNA research that proved to be a terrific foundation from which to launch a campaign. Robertson adds,

> It seemed that every other week we would find another story in The New York Times about an astounding dinosaur dig in Montana, or a DNA discovery in a piece of amber. The media coverage off the entertainment pages successfully fueled the engine for a campaign in the entertainment media. At the same time there had been a growing interest from the children's market in dinosaurs, as witnessed in toy, book and game sales. There's no question that the film delivered the goods—a stunning visual effects achievement that made us believe that dinosaurs were real. But one can never underestimate the power of good timing.

INDEX